Mistral 2

LIVRE DU PROFESSEUR

ANNE O'REILLY
ET ANN SWARBRICK

D.C. Shepherd.

OXFORD UNIVERSITY PRESS 1993

Oxford University Press, Walton Street, Oxford OX2 6DP

Oxford New York Toronto
Delhi Bombay Calcutta Madras Karachi
Kuala Lumpur Singapore Hong Kong Tokyo
Nairobi Dar es Salaam Cape Town
Melbourne Auckland Madrid

and associated companies in
Berlin Ibadan

Oxford is a trade mark of Oxford University Press

First published 1993

ISBN 0 19 912134 6

Acknowledgements

The authors and publishers would like to thank Roger Blamire (NCET), John Lemon, Kathy MacFarlane, Iain Mitchell, Carole Shepherd, and John Thorogood for their help.

The publishers would like to thank the following for permission to reproduce copyright material: National Curriculum Council, reproduced with the permission of the Controller of Her Majesty's Stationery Office (pp.xiv–xv); The Concept Keyboard Company Ltd. (concept keyboard template).

Illustrations are by Oxford Illustrators.

The photograph on page E8 was taken by David Simson.

All acknowledgements for the Students' Book pages are to be found on p.2 of the Students' Book.

Every effort has been made to contact copyright holders of material reproduced in this book. Any omissions will be rectified in subsequent printings if notice is given to the publisher.

The song, *L'écocide*, was sung by Danièle Bourdais, with lyrics by Roderick O'Reilly, and music by Paddy Kingsland.

The cassettes were recorded at Post Sound Ltd, London, and were produced by Marie-Thérèse Bougard and Peter Waygood.

Designed and typeset by OXPRINT, Oxford.
Printed in Hong Kong.

Contents

The symbols used in this book are as follows:

(symbol)	listening
(symbol)	speaking
(symbol)	reading
(symbol)	writing
(symbol)	pair work
(symbol)	group work
(symbol)	dictionary work
(symbol)	IT suggestions
TN 1	detailed teaching notes
CK 1	concept keyboard overlays
R 1	repromasters
T 1	transcripts
E 1	listening sheets

Introduction

Mistral has been written specifically for lower-attaining students in Years 10–11. It is suitable for Basic Level candidates at GCSE or students following short courses for whom sitting a public examination is inappropriate. **Mistral 2** is the second part of this two-part course. The course covers the National Curriculum programmes of study and all the areas of experience. It is also broadly compatible with modular GCSE examination requirements and the Scottish Examination Board's topic areas and language purposes.

More than any other group, these students need and deserve a sympathetic approach, a challenge and, above all, the opportunity to experience success. These factors underlie every aspect of **Mistral**.

Its aims are:

- to encourage success
- to develop student autonomy
- to build student self-esteem
- to promote a positive attitude to the learning of French
- to present the French language in its global context
- to develop a co-operative, non-judgemental atmosphere within the group

How?

- with short units and uncluttered pages
- with emphasis on independent listening and active learning
- with the requirement to write only selectively, albeit purposefully
- with a broad angle on GCSE topics and covering all the National Curriculum areas of experience
- with built-in assessment and profiling
- with IT suggestions

We acknowledge that the capacity of such students to acquire, retain and use language is limited and that this often results in frustration and lack of motivation. For these reasons, we have carefully selected unusual angles on often familiar themes. Though the language is simple, the content of **Mistral** is aimed at young adult learners and often demands a creative, imaginative response.

Mistral is all about encouraging students to experiment with language to try and express themselves without being dependent on the teacher. Learning and using a language successfully means taking risks. That means having the confidence not to give up when you don't understand every word of what is said or written. **Mistral** is structured to promote student autonomy.

Mistral does not seek to teach formal grammar, but it does seek to develop the learners' awareness of language structures. They learn to recognize recurring patterns and to use them as models.

Active learning is the backbone of **Mistral**. All the tasks depend on an active and creative response. Students need to work in pairs and small groups: this builds confidence and offers a natural context for practising language within the classroom. This involves discussion, project work and surveys.

Some of the tasks, students will do on their own, regulating and controlling the pace at which they work. The listening activities in particular are designed for individual use. We have used a number of teaching ideas which originate from curriculum areas other than from Modern Languages.

The components

Each part of the course consists of a Students' Book (**Livre de l'étudiant**), a Workbook (**Cahier d'activités**), a set of two cassettes, and a Teacher's Resource Book (**Livre du professeur**).

Livre de l'étudiant

Each of the five modules of work consists of six units in double spreads. A double-page collage of realia and key vocabulary introduces each module. See page vii for ideas on how to exploit these. The last unit of each module is an assessment unit (*Contrôle*). The work in each unit is designed to last at least two hours. This will vary according to teaching style and the needs of the group. There is a glossary of all the instructions used at the back of the book.

Cahier d'activités

This is an integral part of the course. It is designed to be filled in by the student. All the activities relate directly to units in the **Livre de l'étudiant**. Also included are pages to record answers to the *Contrôle* units, and pages called *Page dictionnaire,* where students can build up a personal aide-mémoire.

Cassettes

These are intended for either group or individual listening and will fit well into an autonomous learning environment. The tape should be played back by the listener as many times as he/she needs in order to complete the activities. Reading and listening tasks are often interdependent.

Livre du professeur

Detailed teaching notes for each unit are interleaved with the pages from the **Livre de l'étudiant.** Appropriate pages from the **Cahier d'activités** are reproduced in miniature in these teaching notes.

For each unit, the notes include:

- details of areas of experience covered
- a description of the context
- a language focus
- a way in
- a suggested route
- answers
- follow-up ideas
- IT suggestions

There are also reference grids, and a section on assessment, with a teacher's record of progress. Additional notes on IT, with a number of suggestions for concept keyboard overlays are also supplied. A full tape transcript, repromasters for vocabulary presentation and supplementary activities, and a photocopiable *Page dictionnaire* and glossary are to be found at the back of the book.

Using Mistral in the classroom

Each module involves the presentation and investigation of one particular theme. The detailed teaching notes provide ideas for the teacher to introduce each language item, in the section 'a way in'. Students investigate the theme in the activities that follow in the *Livre de l'étudiant* and the *Cahier d'activités*. The 'suggested route' in each unit of teaching notes gives an indication of the order in which the students might do this. You will find extension activities under the heading 'follow-up ideas'.

Using French in the classroom

Teachers who successfully use French in the classroom find that they persistently use the same selected language and that students of all abilities do respond positively to the challenge. Does the whole lesson have to be in French? It certainly can be, particularly if your students have been used to this practice in earlier years. Otherwise gradually build up the amount of French that you use, explaining to students what you are doing and keeping note of the amount of time spent in the lesson where French is the only means of communication. This will increase both teacher and student confidence. Understanding even the most simple instructions or statements in French is a rewarding experience.

Here are some useful strategies:

- ask a student to interpret
- use non-verbal communication
- use cognates (words which in both English and French have the same root)
- habitually use the same classroom language
- echo the language used by the student
- rephrase when necessary
- use clear visuals
- use familiar props
- talk in French beyond the normal confines of work (for example, praising students, talking to a visitor or the Assistant/Assistante)
- encourage students to ask the meaning of words in French
- ask a student to check on who is not conducting an activity in French and to report back
- display relevant classroom language around the room
- encourage a student to ask others in the class for help
- accept half phrases and inaccuracies that do not impede communication
- refuse to accept English

Where appropriate, the detailed teaching notes for each unit provide examples of questions and phrases for the purposes of recapping and presentation. This has the non-specialist teacher in mind.

Here are some of the most useful classroom phrases:

Are you ready?	*Tu es prêt(e)?/Vous êtes prêts?*
Be quiet!	*Tais-toi!/Taisez-vous!*
Can I help you?	*Je peux t'aider?/Je peux vous aider?*
Check in the glossary	*Vérifie(z) cela dans le lexique*
Choose	*Choisis(sez)*
Come here	*Viens (venez) ici*
Come to the overhead projector	*Viens (venez) au rétroprojecteur*
Could you speak a bit louder?	*Parle(z) un peu plus fort*
Decide	*Décide(z)*
Do you need ..?	*Tu as besoin de ..?* *Vous avez besoin de ..?*
Do you understand?	*Tu as compris?* *Vous avez compris?*
Get into groups (of three/four)	*Formez des groupes (de trois/quatre)*
Give out the books	*Distribue(z) les livres de l'étudiant*
Go and get ...	Va (allez) chercher ...
... the tape	*... la cassette*
... the tape recorder	*... le magnétophone*
... the headphones	*... les écouteurs*
... the computer	*... l'ordinateur*
... the disc	*... la disquette*
... the dictionary	*... le dictionnaire*
Is everybody here?	*Tout le monde est là?*
Is there a problem?	*Il y a un problème?*
How do you spell ..?	*Comment ça s'écrit ..?*
Just a minute	*Un moment*
Listen again	*Ecoute(z) encore une fois*
Look at the screen	*Regarde(z) l'écran*
Look it up in a dictionary	*Cherche(z)-le dans le dictionnaire*
OK?	*Ça va?/D'accord?*
Pack up	*Range(z) tes (vos) affaires*
Pardon?	*Comment?*
Take a card	*Prends (prenez) une carte*
Try again	*Essaie (essayez) encore une fois*
Wait!	*Attends!/Attendez!*
What does ... mean?	*Qu'est-ce que ça veut dire ..?*
What's the French/English for..?	*C'est quoi en français/anglais ..?*
Work with a partner	*Travaille(z) avec un ou une partenaire*
You may go now	*Tu peux (Vous pouvez) sortir maintenant*

Vocabulary building

Learners need to be made aware that there are many strategies for finding out the meanings of unknown words. For example: recognizing cognates, breaking down a word into components, guessing from the context, using another person as a reference.

Ultimately, a language learner may need to refer to a dictionary. Knowing how to use a bi-lingual dictionary gives him/her the freedom to check and expand his/her existing vocabulary. Students need to be encouraged to use a dictionary. For the low attainer, this is not an easy task, and using a dictionary is a skill which needs to be taught systematically and reinforced regularly. A number of tasks to encourage the use of dictionaries have been incorporated into the **Mistral** activities, but for some students an introduction to this skill will be needed.

Here are some ideas for developing dictionary skills:

- It is best to start by establishing that students are aware of alphabetical sequence.
- Ask students to get into alphabetical order, by their first names. This may be a team game.
- Give students several words on individual cards or papers and ask them to put them into alphabetical order. If you include more than one word beginning with the same letter, the activity will be more difficult. So the game can have differentiated versions to be used as their skills become more sophisticated.
- With a dictionary, students should find the first word beginning with a letter or a combination of letters, of your choice. (For example: *Trouvez le premier mot dans le dictionnaire qui commence avec Ch ...*)
- Give two words which follow each other in the dictionary and ask students to find the next word in the sequence.
- Give the students several words with pictures to represent each one. Among these, there should be some which are unfamiliar. Students, with the help of the dictionary, find out what these words mean. If they choose to use the picture clue they will obviously need to refer to the English-French side of the dictionary. Alternatively, they may look up the French word.
- Students read a sentence, in which one word is partly obliterated. They think about the context and look up the missing word, using the letters which do appear. (For example: *Un instit... travaille dans une école primaire*)
- Give three definitions of a word - only one of them is correct. (For example: *imperméable: c'est une sorte de fruit; ça veut dire calme; on porte un imperméable quand il pleut.*)
- See who can most quickly look up a list of given words and provide definitions for them.

The dictionary definitions used throughout the course have been taken from **The Oxford French Minidictionary.**

At the back of the *Cahier d'activités* there are pages called *Page dictionnaire*. These are intended to encourage students to record any language which they have found out for themselves and which they consider important. In order to keep a full vocabulary record, students need to consider how they discover the meanings of the new words. **Mistral** does not seek to decide which language any one student may or may not know or want to record. For this reason, its glossary is limited to covering only the language of the instructions used in the *Livre de l'étudiant* and the *Cahier d'activités*. A photocopiable *Page dictionnaire* has been provided, in case you need to make extra copies for some students. These could then be attached to the back of the *Cahier d'activités*.

Presenting new language

This section is primarily aimed to help non-specialist teachers and is therefore not an exhaustive list of ideas. Ways of practising and reinforcing language are suggested in every unit of the detailed teaching notes, under the heading 'a way in'.

Flashcards, OHT (overhead projector transparency) cues, and props are commonly used for presenting new language, and the ideas below may refer to any of these. Present the items one by one, starting with the easy ones and being sure not to clutter the OHP screen or board.

- Ask students to guess which single item is missing from the whole sequence.
- Play picture Loto.
- Point to one of the cues, saying a word which might or might not be the right word for the item in question. If what you say is true, students need to repeat the word, if it is not true, they must keep silent.
- Reveal the cue gradually, students calling out the word that belongs to it as soon as they can guess what it is.
- Give a flashcard or item to one of the students, who must pass it to the next person, saying the word for the item. This student, in turn, does the same. Once a rhythm is established, introduce a second card into the chain, giving it to a student in a different part of the room or circle. Work in as many flashcards or items as you think the group is able to cope with.
- Play noughts and crosses with the cards or OHT cues.
- One student chooses one of the items and simply keeps it in mind, while the rest of the group try to guess what it is.
- Put all the cards/cues/props in a row. One student has to point at each item that is called out. This is done at great speed.
- Show the cue/card/item so that one of a pair of students is unable to see it. The other student needs to mime anything to allow the 'blind' partner to guess the word.
- Using a soft ball, start the game rolling by throwing it to a student, saying an appropriate word. The student must catch the ball and give a response within a time limit, for example: *la géographie . . . j'aime ça.*

Mistral 2

The skills and processes introduced throughout **Mistral 1** are further developed in **Mistral 2**. Students' vocabulary is broadened and students are carefully introduced to more complex structures, even if not always for active use. Organizational and interactive skills continue to be developed. We have included more text on some pages; these will be accessible to students who have developed appropriate research and reading skills.

Module 4, *Paris: Le Guide Mistral*, is designed to be fitted into your Year 11 scheme of work where you feel it is most appropriate. The focus is on transactional and survival language, with opportunities to explore this in a creative way. The module is intended to be flexible; you may decide that these units are to be teacher-led, though students may use the materials independently.

The final module, *Feuilleton*, recycles much of the language featured in both **Mistral 1** and **Mistral 2**. Work on the structure and characteristics of soap operas offers the students the opportunity to revise key language and topic areas, and to create their own soap operas. This is a project-based module dependent on collaborative work.

How to use the double-page realia spreads

As for **Mistral 1**, there is a double page of realia at the beginning of each module. You may want to look at this with students as a general introduction to the topic, or use it as extension material. Here are some ideas.

TOUS LES JOURS Ask students to:

- use the dictionary definitions to work out what these headlines from French newspapers mean: *La princesse se met en ménage avec un professeur!; Un monstre habite chez moi; Une journée fantastique à Eurodisney; Les footballeurs se disputent; L'agenda d'un prince*
- look at the receipt and work out where these missing parts of abbreviations go: *-OLAT; -ISE; -E; -ES*
- design a wedding invitation for two unlikely characters
- invent more *objets introuvables*, for example: *un couteau pour les petits pois; un objet pour aider la lecture dans le bain.* Invent captions for any new inventions
- play a memory game with a partner with the prices on the receipt
- write captions for the photos, starting with the word *pour*, for example: *pour la cuisine, pour maman,* etc.
- choose five things they would buy and five things they wouldn't buy. Then try to predict what their partner would do. Compare what is chosen.
- make a tape of supermarket promotions for objects in the photos. For example: *six bols - cinquante francs!*
- complete the diary pages for themselves, someone else in the class, or a fictional character.

L'ECOLO Ask students to:

- look at the wanted poster and put the crimes in order starting with the most serious
- look at the wanted poster and invent one for someone who cares for the environment. This could be entitled *Héro-écolo*
- look at the photos and invent slogans that start with *Non*, for example, *Non aux paquets en plastique!*
- look at the posters and slogans and decide on a suitable place for them in their town/village
- make a list of the words that are similar to English
- copy out the dictionary words, starting with those most like English. Then put the nearest connected word they can think of in English.

LES MEDIAS Ask students to:

- list all the American and French famous people they can see on the pages. Compare the two lists
- make a grid – down one side copy all the titles of the publications, across the top, devise a list of different types of people: *un garçon de 12 ans; une femme de 30 ans; mon professeur; ma correspondante française; moi*, etc. Tick in the correct boxes who would read what
- write short explanatory sentences for each publication, for example: *OK, c'est pour les filles de 11 à 16 ans*
- look in local newsagent's and decide which British title looks closest to each of the French ones
- look through French magazines at school and sort them into groups nearest to those in the book
- choose which publications the following titles would be most likely to appear in: *Ce garçon, il est beau, il est fantastique!; Les problèmes pour le gouvernement; Le look cool pour le collège*
- sort as many words as possible under the headings: *journaux; télévision; cinéma.*

PARIS: LE GUIDE MISTRAL Ask students to:

- work out where all the photos were taken, using a map
- name the places in the photos, using guides and brochures on Paris. Find out as many facts as possible
- look at the photos, copy down all the French words they can see, and add the English
- play a game, using the captions from repromaster 16. Captions are dealt. In turn students read them out and place them on an appropriate photo
- use the same captions and rules as above to play noughts and crosses
- play a game with dice to advance around the board of photos. When a student lands on a photo, they must say something about it in French
- arrange the captions (see above) under these different headings: *Transport à Paris; les monuments de Paris; Manger à Paris; Les musées de Paris; Paris pour les enfants; Les magasins de Paris*
- make acetate overlays with some of the above headings. When placed over the pictures the overlay will cover up most of the photos leaving only those connected with that particular category visible.

(For further ideas, see page TN 44.)

FEUILLETON Ask students to:

- Choose their favourite soap. Explain the relationships between all the characters, with diagrams and French labels, but no English!
- create slogans for different soap characters
- describe a soap opera using the dictionary words
- invent silly captions for the photos, for example: *Je fais votre portrait. Ne bougez pas!; Ah! voilà mon serpent!; Où est mon chapeau?*

Summary of contents

MISTRAL 1

Habitation

UNIT	AREAS OF EXPERIENCE	CONTEXT	LANGUAGE FOCUS
Chez Madeleine	C F	Describing rooms, homes, where people have lived, and life in the future.	**Part I:** une maison, un appartement, la cuisine, la salle de séjour, la salle de bains, la salle à manger, la chambre, le garage, le jardin, la porte d'entrée, à gauche, à droite, à côté, au rez-de-chaussée, au premier étage. **Part II:** à l'âge de . . . ans, je serai célibataire, marié(e), j'habiterai en Grande-Bretagne, à l'étranger, j'aurai . . . enfants.
Là où j'habite	A B C	Talking about your home town, saying what you can do there, assessing the relative importance of facilities, asking the way, understanding and giving directions.	**Part I:** un musée, un complexe sportif, une poste, un marché, un parking, un collège, un centre commercial, un cinéma, une gare, une discothèque, une piscine. C'est très important/assez important/pas du tout important. **Part II:** pour la gare, l'hôtel, le café, l'église, l'office de tourisme s'il vous plaît? Tournez à gauche/à droite. Allez tout droit **Part III:** ici on peut faire du sport, regarder des films, prendre le train, danser, regarder des sculptures, acheter des fruits et des légumes, nager.
Autour de chez moi	C F G	Describing your local area.	C'est joli, moche, industriel, résidentiel, propre, sale, intéressant, commercial, chic, calme, vert, moderne, vivant.
Tu es architecte	C G	Town planning. Explaining where places are situated.	Il y a, au nord, au sud, à l'est, à l'ouest, ici, là, près de, à droite, à gauche, à côté. (Revision of places, adding): l'église, les maisons, les bungalows, l'épicerie, la boulangerie.
Où ça?	C D	Working for a pizza delivery service. Taking orders on the telephone. Reading addresses and locating customers' homes on a map. Giving and understanding directions.	**Part I:** Vous désirez? Quel nom? Et l'adresse? On arrive dans . . . minutes, à côté, en face, à gauche, à droite. (Revision of numbers.) **Part II:** Allez tout droit, tournez à gauche, tournez à droite.

Personnellement

UNIT	AREAS OF EXPERIENCE	CONTEXT	LANGUAGE FOCUS
Fascination fatale	B	Talking about an ideal partner. Matching couples by looking at photographs and considering stereotyping.	**Part I:** riche, beau/belle, sportif/sportive, intelligent(e), qui travaille, comme moi, de mon âge, qui aime danser, qui aime les enfants. **Part II:** Ils sont tous les deux petits/grands, ils ont tous les deux les cheveux longs, l'air intelligent, le même âge, ils portent des vêtements modernes/démodés, ils se ressemblent, ils ne se ressemblent pas.
Histoire vraie	B G	The story of a mixed-race relationship.	Il/elle préfère, il/elle a les cheveux blonds/noirs, les yeux bleus/marron, il/elle veut sortir avec . . .
La rencontre	B E G	Suggesting going out, accepting and declining invitations.	Tu veux aller, sortir, venir (+ place)?
SOS cœur brisé	B E	Describing people. Teenage problems, problem-page letters.	Gentil(le), méchant(e), sympa, désagréable, sévère, cool, moche, beau/belle, timide, sociable, cheveux gras/secs, il/elle aime beaucoup, déteste, adore, a horreur de.
Liberté et responsabilité	B F G	Questionnaire about teenage independence. Looking at the rights of the child (UNICEF), and of teenagers.	**Part I:** avoir la permission de sortir, fumer, partir en vacances, inviter des amis, boire de l'alcool, avoir un job, te coiffer et t'habiller comme tu veux. **Part II:** avoir le droit à un nom, une nationalité, un niveau de vie adéquat, l'éducation, la protection, avoir le droit d'exprimer son opinion, béneficier de services médicaux.

UNIT	AREAS OF EXPERIENCE	CONTEXT	LANGUAGE FOCUS
Des progrès	A B D F	Subjects studied at school. Strengths and weaknesses at school. School reports.	**Part I:** anglais, sciences, maths, français, géographie, histoire, technologie, art dramatique, instruction religieuse, sport, éducation manuelle et technique, cuisine, dessin, musique, informatique. **Part II:** Es-tu fort(e) en (+ subject)?, très fort(e), fort(e), assez fort(e), faible, nul(le).
Une journée à l'école	A B F G	Comparing normal school routines in different countries.	On fait, commence, finit à (+ times).
Du bavardage	B E	Sending and reading messages about other people.	(Present tense using): rencontrer, aimer, jouer, parler, connaître, casser, attendre, sortir.
Image de la classe	B	Thinking about the characteristics of the class, using a questionnaire. Making excuses.	**Part I:** (present tense using): adorer, détester, passer le temps, fumer, lire. **Part II:** (questions): tu aimes, tu fais, tu as, tu manges, tu fumes, tu es? **Part III:** Ce n'était pas moi, je ne comprends pas, pardon, j'ai oublié mon cahier, je n'ai pas fait mes devoirs.
Image de l'école	A G	School rules and school uniform.	**Part I:** Il est défendu de porter, sortir, jurer, manger. **Part II:** chemise, jupe, chaussures, chaussettes, pantalon, veste, pull-over, confortable, pratique, moderne, pas cher, pas colorié.
Temps libre	A G	Free time, with particular reference to music.	Je m'intéresse, j'aime, je fais, je joue, je sais, je n'aime pas, j'écoute, je lis, je collectionne, je préfère. (The same verbs with il and elle.) Sportif/sportive, le jogging, le basket, la moto, la musique classique, la musique pop, le reggae, une chanson folklorique, le hard rock, le punk, les disques, les compacts, les livres, la science-fiction, la mode, les animaux, l'informatique, un ordinateur, le désordre, l'injustice.
La forme	A B E	The relative nutritional value of common foods, and focussing on diets. Taking a look at how much exercise you do and how fit you are.	**Part I:** le petit déjeuner, le déjeuner, le goûter, le dîner. On mange mal, on mange assez bien, on mange bien. Mange plus de/moins de . . . Les hamburgers, les frites, le coca, le chocolat, les saucisses, le gâteau, les bonbons, les chips, les biscuits, la confiture, le sucre, les œufs, la crème fraîche, la mayonnaise, le jambon, le beurre, les pâtes, le riz, le poulet, la salade, le poisson, les frites, les légumes, le pain, la margarine, le lait, le yaourt, les jus de fruits. **Part II:** semaine, lundi, mardi, mercredi, jeudi, vendredi, samedi, dimanche, kilomètre, la promenade, le footing, le sport, la natation, le cyclisme, la danse, le badminton. L'exercice, très énergique, (peu) fatigant, modéré, facile. Note, multiplie, divise, le pouls, superbe, excellent, bien, assez bien, faible, très faible.
Handisports	A B G	Sport and investigation into how disabled sportsmen and women meet the challenge of practising a sport.	**Part I:** le sport, le tennis, le football, le golf, le ski, le squash, le basket, le badminton, la natation, le cyclisme, la planche à voile, la voile, l'escrime, l'haltérophilie, le tir, le tir à l'arc, le disque, le javelot, le poids, le marathon. **Part II:** le problème d'argent, d'équipements, de transport, d'égalité de chances, d'image. Très grave, grave, peu grave.
Parc Vacances	A C E G	Leisure and sports activities in a holiday centre. Preparing publicity material and planning a new holiday centre.	**Part I:** un restaurant, une piscine, un sauna, des promenades en fôret, le tennis, le cyclisme, le gymnase, le tir à l'arc, la voile, la planche à voile, l'équitation. **Part II:** près de, autoroute, route principale, route secondaire, halle, hangar, serre, église, chapelle, tombe, statue religieuse, verger, plantation, surfaces bâties, terrain de sport.
Bien chic!	B G	Fashion: different styles and preferences. Describing the clothes you like.	Une veste, une (mini) jupe, une robe, un t-shirt, une boucle d'oreille, des chaussures, un pantalon, des bottes, une ceinture, des bracelets, un pull-over, un sweat-shirt, les joggings, les baskets, une chemise, un jean, un blouson. Acheté, emprunté, un cadeau, cheveux, coiffés, décontracté, larges, amples, long/longues, courts/courtes, rayés/rayées, étroits/étroites, fleuris/fleuries, en denim, en cuir, en laine, en coton, géants/géantes. C'est chic, c'est moche. J'adore ça, j'aime ça, ce n'est pas mal ça, je n'aime pas ça, j'ai horreur de ça.

Classe de Mistral ◊ Relaxez-vous!

Le boulot

UNIT	AREAS OF EXPERIENCE	CONTEXT	LANGUAGE FOCUS
Au travail	A D	Looking forward to work experience. Comparing daily routine at school and on work experience.	**Part I:** ça va être chouette, fatigant, difficile, facile, tranquille, plein de bruit, intéressant, sympa, amusant, énervant, dur, mieux/pire que le collège. **Part II:** je me lève, je quitte la maison, j'arrive chez . . ., je commence mon travail, je mange . . ., je finis mon travail, j'arrive à la maison, je me couche (+ times).
A mon retour	C D	Looking back on work experience placements.	J'ai travaillé . . ., avec les enfants, dans un bureau, dans un magasin, à l'intérieur, à l'extérieur, dans une usine, comme réceptionniste, dans une école, avec les handicapés, tout(e) seul(e), dans une cantine, dans un garage, avec le public, en ville, à la campagne.
La personne et l'emploi	B D	Matching personal qualities to jobs. Looking at CVs and suitability for jobs.	**Part I:** j'aime les enfants, je suis ponctuel(le), j'aime les machines, je parle le français, j'aime les animaux, j'ai beaucoup de patience, j'aime travailler avec les autres, j'aime la responsabilité, j'aime la solitude, j'ai une bonne mémoire. **Part II:** cuisinier/cuisinière, électricien/électricienne, maçon, vendeur/vendeuse, plongeur/plongeuse, opérateur/opératrice, ouvrier/ouvrière, coiffeur/coiffeuse, agent de police, serveur/serveuse, assistant(e) de laboratoire, ouvrier/ouvrière agricole, barman/barmaid, ingénieur/femme ingénieur, mécanicien/mécanicienne, secrétaire.
L'entreprise	D	The hierarchical structure of a company.	Le président, les directeurs, les chefs de service, les secrétaires, les représentants, les ouvriers/ouvrières, les employés de cantine, les employés de surface, les employés du service médical, les employés d'entretien, les employés du service de sécurité, les chauffeurs. (Revision of numbers.)
Super Mac au travail	B D G	Talking to French-speaking visitors to this country.	Comment t'appelles-tu? Où habites-tu? Qu'est-ce que tu aimes faire? Tu es marié(e)? Tu fais du sport? Tu veux sortir avec moi? Tu veux aller au cinéma? Tu travailles où? Tu aimes ton travail? (A review of language about yourself and questions to others.)

MISTRAL **2**

Tous les jours

UNIT	AREAS OF EXPERIENCE	CONTEXT	LANGUAGE FOCUS
Tout le confort moderne	A B G	Wedding presents. Considering household items and their uses; expressing an opinion about them. Inventing time-saving devices for an easier life.	**Part I:** un téléviseur, des serviettes de bain, une couette, des taies d'oreiller, une nappe, une horloge, une cafetière, un saladier, un service, des tasses, des soucoupes, des verres, un sucrier, un pot à lait, un plateau. Je voudrais ... C'est pour (+ infinitive). C'est ridicule, super, moche, pratique. **Part II:** si on tire/pousse... x arrive/tombe/descend.
Le travail n'est jamais fini	A B	Looking at chores around the house and investigating the division of labour between the sexes.	**Part I:** On fait... le lit, le shopping, la vaisselle, la cuisine, le ménage, la lessive, le bricolage, le jardinage. **Part II:** Moi, je fais... Il/Elle fait. Mon père/Ma mère/Ma sœur/Mon frère fait.
Agendas	A B C D F	Talking about routines, weekend and holiday activities. Time management.	Manger, voyager, travailler, se relaxer. Qu'est-ce que tu as fait hier? J'ai (+ past participle).
Une journée de Jean-Denis	A B D G	Job shadowing. Revision of daily routine. Poetry and music.	Il/Elle se lève, il/elle part, il/elle va au travail (+ transport), il/elle commence son travail à..., il/elle travaille dans..., il/elle (+ activity), il/elle finit vers..., il/elle rentre à... Qu'est-ce que tu fais à (+ time).
La vie à deux	A B C	A further look into the division of domestic responsibilities. Predicting your attitudes when and if you leave home. Comparing different lifestyles.	Je vais... m'occuper des factures, faire la vaisselle, faire le ménage, m'occuper des enfants, faire le jardinage, changer un fusible, réparer la voiture, faire la cuisine, faire le repassage, faire la lessive, faire le shopping.

UNIT	AREAS OF EXPERIENCE	CONTEXT	LANGUAGE FOCUS
L'écolo			
Nous, les consommateurs	A C	A comparison of the 1930s with the 1990s in terms of what we consume.	**Part I:** (items in a kitchen, including): une chaise, une table, une fenêtre, une cuisinière, un placard, une poubelle, un frigo, une horloge, une machine à laver, des étagères, des paquets, un saladier, des bols, des casseroles, des verres, des assiettes, des cuillères, des fourchettes, des couteaux. En bois, en papier, en verre, en métal, en plastique. **Part II:** Plus de... Moins de...
Les ressources naturelles	C E G	A consideration of the number of natural resources we use, why we need each resource, which resources are essential and which are not.	**Part I:** on a besoin de ... (+ noun) pour ...(+ noun). L'eau, l'électricité, le papier, le métal, le verre. C'est essentiel, assez important, pas du tout important. **Part II**: nous plantons, nous exploitons, nous fabriquons, nous transportons, nous achetons, nous jetons, nous recyclons, nous buvons, nous lisons, nous coupons. Protégeons, sauvons, économisons, disons, aimons, défendons.
Le recyclage	A C	Recycling: what can and can't be recycled. The benefits of recycling.	La décharge publique. On peut recycler (+ noun). On ne peut pas recycler (+ noun). Le papier, les poubelles, le plastique, le verre, les journaux, le métal, les boîtes, les bouteilles, les vêtements, les sacs. Le recyclage économise/protège/réduit.
Les amis de la Terre	C G	Environmental fables: Bois-Tout, the oil-drinking creature, and Bouffe-Tout, the tree-eating machine, and a song on the environment. Stimuli for creative work.	(Revision of key language from the previous units. Present tense, in preparation for story writing/telling.)
Quiz éco	A B C	Ecological facts.	(Numbers, weights, volume and distance): kilos, litres, kilomètres. (Revision of key vocabulary from previous units.)
Les médias			
J'♥ lire	A E G	Investigating people's reading habits. Looking at French *bandes dessinées*. Drawing cartoons.	Je lis, je vais, je fais, je joue, j'écoute, je regarde. Tous les jours, x fois par semaine, x fois par mois, rarement. Des journaux, des magazines, des livres, des bandes dessinées. Tu as quel âge? Tu préfères lire...? Tu lis régulièrement? Tu passes combien de temps à lire? Dans le train, à la cantine, à la maison. (Revision of parts of the body.)
Reportages	E G	Investigating the different sections of a newspaper. Reading and writing short articles.	**Part I:** (newspaper headings.) **Part II:** (perfect tense.) Hier matin/après-midi/soir. (Revision of places and personal descriptions.)
Télémaniaques	A E	Television listings, watching habits and preferences. Arguments for and against watching television.	(Revision of time.) Une chaîne, une émission. C'est quel genre d'émission? Les comédies, les feuilletons, les jeux, les dessins animés, les films, les informations, les documentaires, les émissions de sciences naturelles, les émissions pour les enfants. Super, (très) bien, pas mal, lent, ennuyeux, affreux. Pour, contre. (Revision of expressions of opinion.)
Ciné-clips	E G	Looking at different types of films, making recommendations. Describing film stars.	Un film romantique, un film d'épouvante, un film de science-fiction, un film de guerre, un film d'aventure, un film à suspense, un film policier, un dessin animé, une comédie, un western. Il/elle a joué dans (+ film).
Idoles	B E G	Looking at people who are fanatical about their idols. Interviewing someone about famous people. Letter writing.	**Part I:** j'ai; j'adore; j'aime; je suis passionné(e) par...; je suis un/une fan de... **Part II:** quel est son nom/prénom/vrai nom/lieu de naissance/signe astrologique/poids/parfum? Quelle est sa date de naissance/situation de famille/taille? Qu'est-ce qu'il/elle préfère comme plat/boisson/musique/sport? Qu'est-ce qu'il/elle aime/déteste dans la vie? Où habite-t-il/elle? De quelle couleur sont ses yeux/cheveux?

UNIT	AREAS OF EXPERIENCE	CONTEXT	LANGUAGE FOCUS
Paris: Le Guide Mistral			
Bon voyage!	D F G	Getting to Paris. Buying a ticket at a railway station. Money equivalents, budgeting, changing money. Travelling within Paris.	**Part I:** en car, en voiture, par le train, en avion, par le ferry, en aéroglisseur. Un aller simple, un aller-retour, fumeur, non-fumeur, je voudrais réserver, une place, pour (+ destination), part (+ times), ça fait (+ prices). Je voudrais, un ticket, un carnet, une carte orange, un plan de métro, un plan des autobus. **Part II:** je voudrais changer (+ money), une pièce d'identité, un passeport.
Bienvenue!	D E F G	Choosing and checking in at suitable accommodation. Writing letters to book accommodation in advance. Using a tourist office.	**Part I:** je voudrais/avez-vous... Une chambre pour une/deux personne/s, avec douche. Une place, une nuit, un emplacement. C'est combien par nuit? Où est/sont ...? Une tente, une caravane. C'est à quel nom? C'est pour combien de nuits/ personnes? Comment ça s'écrit? Vous désirez? **Part II:** J'ai besoin de... Une liste des hôtels, campings, excursions, monuments importants, musées. Un horaire des autobus/trains. Un plan de la ville.
Bon appétit!	A F G	Food in Paris. Choosing an eating place. Reading a menu and ordering a meal. Shopping for food.	Je voudrais, je prends, pour moi, vous désirez? Et à boire? Et avec ça? C'est combien? Un kilo de; 500 grammes de. Une tranche de, une bouteille de, une boîte de (+ food).
Ville vivante!	A D F G	Shopping. Choosing souvenirs. What to do in Paris.	**Part I:** je voudrais, je prends. C'est combien? Je voudrais envoyer. Quelle taille? **Part II:** (revision of what you can do in Paris – vocabulary for main sights and places to visit, etc.)
Face à face	A B E F G	Introducing oneself. Taking the initiative in a conversation. Open and closed conversations. Inviting people out; suggesting where to go, what to do, etc.	**Part I:** (revision of personal details.) Comment tu t'appelles? Tu es en vacances ici? Tu voudrais boire quelque chose? Tu es britannique? C'est ta première visite en France? Tu habites à Paris? Je m'appelle... J'habite... **Part II:** si on allait ...? A quelle heure? Quand? On se retrouve où? Tu veux sortir? Je veux bien. Non, je ne peux pas. Je suis occupé/occupée.
Feuilleton			
Le voisinage	B C E G	Deciding on a setting for a soap opera. Typical settings, countries of origin, describing areas. different types of soap opera.	Les endroits principaux. Un café-tabac, un pub, une épicerie, une maison de la presse, des maisons, des appartements, un immeuble, un marché, une boulangerie, une église, un supermarché. Un quartier. Une rue moderne, une vieille rue, une grande ville, un village. Le sud des Etats-Unis, l'Australie, le nord de l'Angleterre, la France, la Grande-Bretagne. Rural, chic, calme, animé, riche, sympa.
Les personnages	A B G	The casting agency, types of characters found in typical soap operas. Choosing actors and actresses for suitable roles. Stereotypes.	Les personnes âgées, le couple BCBG, une famille solide et stable, le personnage malhonnête, le groupe de jeunes, la famille monoparentale, les gens de passage, la femme fatale. (Revision of personal descriptions.)
En scène	A C G	Soap opera sets and script. Stage props.	Des accessoires. Un miroir, des posters, des disques, une chaîne hi-fi, des vêtements, des coussins, des étagères, des fleurs, des plantes, un téléviseur, un calendrier, une addition, des sandwiches, un chapeau, un journal, des verres, une bouteille, un sac, un revolver. (Revision of prepositions): à droite, à gauche, entre, en face, à côté de, devant, derrière.
L'action	B E G	Story lines for a soap opera.	(Present tense using the idea of planning what is going to happen in a series of episodes.) X se marie, X va en vacances, X gagne de l'argent, X a un bébé, X meurt, X se dispute avec..., X rencontre Y, X part, X a un accident, X a une liaison avec Y, X divorce.
Moments à suspense	A B E G	Cliffhangers at the end of an episode of a soap opera. Looking at various possibilities.	(Personal preferences): aime, n'aime pas.

Assessment and recording of progress in Mistral

Mistral is intended to offer enjoyable and motivating language learning experiences to learners who might not in the past have continued with a modern language into Years 10 and 11 of a secondary course.

We want the assessment and recording of progress achieved during the course to enhance this motivation by providing suitable short-term goals for learners and rewarding their attainments.

Continuous assessment is of course required by the National Curriculum (NC), but it is in a sense missing the point of continuously assessing students' progress to regard it as nothing more than satisfying a legal requirement.

There are several features of assessment and recording which have in the last few years served to improve the experience of learning. These are: the use of positive levels of attainment, rather than negative marks out of x; the linking of levels to criteria which describe the nature of the attainments at those levels; the introduction of profiles of performance in which (a) these attainments can be recorded and (b) the communicative tasks performed can be described.

We have provided in this section:

- a quick reference chart of the statements of attainment (SoA) for Levels 1–5 of the National Curriculum for Modern Foreign Languages*
- a template teacher's record of progress

You can use the reference chart both to determine *how suitable an activity is* for assessing performance at a particular level, and to assess *the outcome of an activity* for any student.

For example, in *Contrôle 2A*, if a student successfully completes the task, he or she has achieved Attainment Target 1, Level 5(a) ('understand and respond to sequences of spoken language which include familiar words, phrases, and material from different contexts').

There are two types of assessment opportunities in the course: summative and continuous. The *Contrôle* section at the end of each module offers summative 'test' type material, for which precise marks can be awarded. These marks are not levels as such, but successful completion of the tasks can be converted into statements of attainment from NC levels. Details of these are to be found in the teaching notes for a given *Contrôle*.

The *Observations* space at the bottom of the *Contrôle* sheets in the *Cahier d'activités* can be used to record progress so far in NC levels as well as general comments of a less formal nature.

* though some students may progress beyond these Levels.

We have not attempted to relate tasks in the units to specific attainment levels, because in many instances the outcome of a given task may vary. But you, as teacher, can evaluate performance by referring to the statement of attainments chart on pages xiv–xv and then record attainment on the basis of *any* activity from the *Livre d'étudiant* or the *Cahier d'activités* which has features that relate to NC statements of attainment. For instance, satisfactory completion of the copy-writing task on page 11 of the *Cahier d'activités*, '*Une journée*', fulfils Attainment Target 4, Level 2(a) ('copy familiar short phrases correctly'). If, however, a student does not use the *Livre de l'étudiant* for reference, and writes his/her own sentences, then Attainment Target 4, Level 3 or 4 could be fulfilled.

Thus, although the *Contrôle* at the end of each module is provided as a revision assessment feature, *the recording of attainment should be possible at any time during the normal teaching process,* as is expected in the National Curriculum.

Such an attainment can be recorded by filling in the appropriate box beside a student's name (line 2, column (b) of Level 4), on the teacher's record of progress. The act of recording can be a tick, stroke or shading. It is up to individual teachers to decide whether to record the same SoA more than once for a given student. Sometimes you may find it helpful to do so.

Teacher's record of progress Group ____ Module ____________

Areas of experience covered in the module	A	B	C	D	E	F	G

Student's name	AT ↓	LEVEL 1 Statements of attainment satisfied			LEVEL 2 Statements of attainment satisfied			LEVEL 3 Statements of attainment satisfied			LEVEL 4 Statements of attainment satisfied			LEVEL 5 Statements of attainment satisfied			Highest level attained in this AT
		a	b	c	a	b	c	a	b	c	a	b	c	a	b	c	
	1																
	2																
	3																
	4																
	1																
	2																
	3																
	4																
	1																

Although to achieve a level in any of the four ATs, *all* SoA for that level must be satisfied, teachers should take comfort from knowing that the complete "set" of SoA for a particular AT can be collected from different activities at different times. The important thing is to record achievement when one sees it, using the recording chart as shown.

Perhaps the best advice on assessment for the National Curriculum is to *teach naturally and record achievement as it happens - don't forever be imposing NC targets on what you plan to do;* the SoA are a measure and a guideline, not a prescription, and this is what the authors have attempted to support in the course.

John Thorogood (assessment consultant)

Reference grid 2: Statements of attainment for Levels 1–5

ATTAINMENT TARGET 1	ATTAINMENT TARGET 2
Listening: the development of pupils' ability to understand and respond to spoken language. *STATEMENTS OF ATTAINMENT* Pupils should be able to:	Speaking: the development of pupils' ability to communicate in speech. *STATEMENTS OF ATTAINMENT* Pupils should be able to:
LEVEL 1 a) understand and respond to familiar utterances of up to four words. b) identify individual items in a list.	**LEVEL 1** a) respond very briefly to what is seen or heard. b) imitate with approximate pronunciation and intonation.
LEVEL 2 a) understand and respond to the gist of simple sentences. b) identify and understand specific details in familiar utterances.	**LEVEL 2** a) produce short simple responses to what is seen or heard. b) give and find out simple information. c) ask for help with comprehension.
LEVEL 3 a) understand and respond to short instructions, messages and dialogues made up of familiar language in simple sentences. b) identify and note main points and specific details in short instructions, messages and dialogues.	**LEVEL 3** a) initiate and respond with intelligible pronunciation using memorised language. b) adapt memorised words and phrases. c) express feelings, likes and dislikes in simple terms.
LEVEL 4 a) understand and respond to longer instructions, messages and dialogues made up of familiar language in simple sentences. b) identify and note specific and significant details in longer familiar messages or dialogues.	**LEVEL 4** a) initiate and respond in conversation or role play on familiar topics using appropriate forms of personal address. b) give a short presentation or prompted talk on everyday activities, interests or future plans. c) offer simple explanations in response to the question 'why?'
LEVEL 5 a) understand and respond to sequences of spoken language which include familiar words, phrases and material from different contexts. b) extract specific information or details from longer sequences of spoken language.	**LEVEL 5** a) maintain a short conversation, showing an ability to move between topics, and express feelings and opinions in simple terms. b) use simple descriptive language to make brief statements about people or places, and one's own recent experience and future events. c) speak confidently and intelligibly when using familiar language.

ATTAINMENT TARGET 3	ATTAINMENT TARGET 4
Reading: the development of pupils' ability to read, understand and respond to written language. ***STATEMENTS OF ATTAINMENT*** Pupils should be able to:	Writing: the development of pupils' ability to communicate in writing. ***STATEMENTS OF ATTAINMENT***
LEVEL 1 a) understand and respond to individual words presented in context.	**LEVEL 1** a) copy familiar words correctly.
LEVEL 2 a) understand and respond to familiar short phrases presented in context. b) find out the meanings of new words by referring to exercise books, text books or glossaries. c) identify individual consonants and vowels occurring in familiar words.	**LEVEL 2** a) copy familiar short phrases correctly. b) write individual words from memory.
LEVEL 3 a) understand and respond to texts consisting of short simple sentences in familiar contexts. b) recognise words and phrases encountered for the first time in the written form, using knowledge of script. c) choose from a pre-selected/limited range of short texts and begin to read independently.	**LEVEL 3** a) write short sentences to convey simple, factual information. b) write short phrases from memory.
LEVEL 4 a) understand and respond to short, factual and non-factual texts, both printed and handwritten, which include sentences containing short clauses and some unfamiliar language. b) deduce the meaning of unfamiliar words using knowledge of language and script.	**LEVEL 4** a) write a small number of related sentences from memory to find out and convey simple information or feelings. b) adapt a simple text by substituting individual words and set phrases.
LEVEL 5 a) understand and respond to texts, including short narratives, which include some complex sentences and some unfamiliar language, using appropriate reference materials, including a bilingual dictionary. b) predict the meanings of unfamiliar words and phrases from their context.	**LEVEL 5** a) produce a short piece of continuous writing, consisting of simple sentences, to seek and convey personal information, feelings and opinions. b) adapt a simple model text by substituting phrases and simple sentences of their own. c) apply basic elements of grammar to new contexts and generally adopt correct word order.

Teacher's record of progress

Group ______ Module ____________________

Areas of experience covered in the module	A	B	C	D	E	F	G

Student's name	AT	LEVEL 1 Statements of attainment satisfied			LEVEL 2 Statements of attainment satisfied			LEVEL 3 Statements of attainment satisfied			LEVEL 4 Statements of attainment satisfied			LEVEL* 5 Statements of attainment satisfied			Highest level attained in this AT
		a	b	c	a	b	c	a	b	c	a	b	c	a	b	c	
	1																
	2																
	3																
	4																
	1																
	2																
	3																
	4																
	1																
	2																
	3																
	4																
	1																
	2																
	3																
	4																
	1																
	2																
	3																
	4																
	1																
	2																
	3																
	4																
	1																
	2																
	3																
	4																
	1																
	2																
	3																
	4																
	1																
	2																
	3																
	4																
	1																
	2																
	3																
	4																
	1																
	2																
	3																
	4																

* Adapt Level numbers as appropriate.

Using IT with Mistral

Like the overhead projector, the cassette recorder and the video player, information technology has a role to play in language teaching; as with these other resources, it is not to be seen as an end in itself, but a means to an end – namely that of improving motivation, effective learning and consequently performance.

This is particularly true for the lower-attaining student for whom **Mistral** is designed. Such students are frequently overwhelmed by the complex of skills and demands placed on them in the whole-class environment. For them, the computer offers a supportive, non-threatening route into language learning. Working individually, or in groups of two or three, they have time to practise and consolidate basic skills using software with which, for the most part, they are already familiar. They therefore have greater control over the pace and level of learning, will attempt tasks that might otherwise seem too challenging, and can present their work at a standard that often compares favourably with that of the most able.

The National Curriculum Council's programmes of study further underline the value of IT to foreign language learners, and encourage its use in a number of recommendations. The chart on page xviii shows the main types of software (word-processing, DTP, etc.) and provides examples from **Mistral 2** to show how they might be used to develop IT as well as foreign language skills.

As with the content of the course, in putting together unit by unit suggestions for incorporating IT activities when using **Mistral**, we have tried to offer a range of possibilities to explore. Experience and experiment will certainly throw up a number of alternatives, and the authors would appreciate feedback of successful activities or types of programme which aren't mentioned in the notes (please send via OXED, Oxford University Press, Walton Street, Oxford, OX2 6DP).

In addition to suggestions, ten A4 concept keyboard overlay templates are included for use with *Touch Explorer Plus*, *Prompt Writer*, *Conform* or a similar programme. The art work can be readily enlarged for an A3 keyboard with a photocopier if required. There are also suggestions for other overlays that you can make by cut-and-pasting. Although a brief description of how these templates may be used is found on page xx, full explanations of programming keyboards and setting multi-level activities come with the software packages. After working through a few examples, the potential of the **Mistral** overlays should become apparent.

As a general point, it is important to stress that the level of difficulty for a given task must ultimately be determined by you, the teacher. 'Written' tasks, for example can be set in a number of ways, from unguided sentence production at one extreme to reassembling scrambled sentences or text blocks on the other. Gap-filling, in the form of a skeleton text with words supplied beneath, is a useful intermediate-level activity that can be designed to allow for a degree of personal response.

The IT suggestions come at the *end* of each unit of the teacher's notes. This is not because this is their place in the teaching sequence, but because they are optional. If you intend to use them, refer to this section *before* embarking on the unit in the classroom.

As with **Mistral 1**, the aim of this next section is to give a brief overview of software types and packages that are referred to in the notes for those teachers not familiar with what is on the market. This has been updated to take account of some recent software publications, but again makes no claim to be comprehensive. With so many packages on the market, we mention here some which have been found successful with less-able language learners.*

Some examples of IT-related tasks are included in the table on page xix. For a broader overview of this area, we suggest you consult the chart provided in the Modern Foreign Languages Non-Statutory Guidance document.

Abbreviations used in the teacher's notes:
WP = word-processing programme
DTP = desk-top publishing programme
CK = concept keyboard overlay
E-mail = electronic mail link

* For guidance here, and for information and support generally, we are indebted to NCET, Coventry.

An at-a-glance guide to suitable software

Type	Opportunities	Useful packages
Word-processing	This is the most versatile software tool you have. It is the basis of desk-top publishing and text manipulation and electronic communication, and provides the platform to launch concept keyboard activities. Word-processing enables learners to draft, create, or alter text and supports independent learning. It enables teachers to prepare text manipulation exercises and to vary the level of task and accessibility of text.	Archimedes: Folio, Pendown, Edit, Phases, Impression & Impression Junior, EasiWriter BBC B/Master: Prompt Writer, Folio, Advanced Folio, Sword RM Nimbus: Allwrite, Word for Windows, WriteOn, FlexiWrite Apple Mac: Claris Works
Desk-top publishing	One step further than word-processing, DTP allows you to manipulate the layout of text and graphics to produce professional-quality pages.	Archimedes: Folio, Pendown, Ovation, Acorn DTP, Impression & Impression Junior, EasiWriter BBC B/Master: Front Page Europe RM Nimbus: Publisher, Newspaper, PageMaker Apple Mac: Claris Works, Aldus PageMaker
Database	This is a collection of data which can be sorted and searched by a computer. Learners can create their own databases through response to simple questions, for example: Module 4 – what is there to see and do in Paris **1** for a weekend? **2** for a week? Once the data is gathered it can be presented graphically and the information can be used for reading or role-play activities.	Archimedes: Junior Database, DataSweet, Key Plus, Pin Point BBC B/Master: Grass, Find, Our Facts RM Nimbus: ML Find, Grass, Superbase, Excel, Key Plus, DataSweet Apple Mac: Claris Works
Art and graphics	Art and graphics packages allow you to create or edit images which you will be able to manipulate in other software such as DTP. There are many ready-made images for sale as clip art which are both versatile and useful.	Archimedes: Paint, Draw, Artisan, Roman II, Atelier, Revelation II BBC B/Master: Image RM Nimbus: Paint Spa Apple Mac: MacDraw, MacPaint, Superpaint
Electronic communications	Text can be sent and received through telephone lines uing a computer and a modem. Easy access is available to a number of French databases in England and in France. The information can be stored on disc and loaded into a word-processor or DTP for further exploitation. This major service is available through Campus 2000.	Archimedes: ArcComm 2 RM Nimbus: Contact Apple Mac: Claris Works
Concept (or **Overlay**) **keyboards**	A touch sensitive board which will initiate text or graphics on the computer by pressing a defined area of its surface. This system offers teachers and learners limitless possibilities for text exploitation through a word-processor. **Mistral** offers you printed overlays and ideas as to how to make the most of them.	Archimedes: Conform, Concept Designer, Touch Explorer Plus BBC B/Master: Touch Explorer, Prompt Writer, Folio RM Nimbus: Touch Explorer Plus, Concept, Windows Concept, Stylus Apple Mac: Mindstorm Overlay Designer
Text manipulation	Some software allows you to enter text which is then gapped or rearranged by the program. This allows learners to develop reading skills and vocabulary, and practise patterns and structures.	Archimedes: Fun With Texts, Gapkit, Discover, Clickword BBC B/Master: Fun With Texts, Gapkit RM Nimbus: Fun With Texts, Gapkit, Developing Tray, Minnie Apple Mac: Gapmaster, Storyboard, Matchmaster
Hypermedia	Learners can create 'folders' of their own work or create branching stories using multimedia packages to link text and graphics to any page in a document.	Archimedes: Magpie, Genesis, Highlighter, Optima RM Nimbus: Think Sheet, Guide, ToolBook Apple Mac: Hypercard, Hypertext

Further information, including addresses of suppliers and software prices, is found in the information sheets obtainable from:
Modern Languages Officer, National Council for Educational Technology (NCET), Science Park, Coventry CV4 7EZ; Tel: 0203-416994

Suggestions for IT activities in Mistral 2

Examples from units	Module/unit reference
Students produce a wedding invitation or wedding present list in alphabetical order Lists of useful phrases produced for wall-displays Real and imaginary diaries produced Students write simple environment fable for wall-display Short descriptions of favourite media stars produced for wall-display Students make personal cue-cards for French visit TV script produced by another group is edited/adapted	1.1 1.1, 1.2, etc. 1.2, 4.4 2.4 3.4, 3.5 4.1 5.4, 5.5
Data collection forms for surveys designed; results entered into database Students design posters for advertising/save the environment campaigns Students create police statement form Students produce a *Télé Sept Jours*-type information sheet Personal horoscopes, fan letters, etc. created for class magazine Students generate realia (tickets, timetables, menus, etc,) for Paris visit Posters of Paris produced for tourist office simulation	1.2, 1.5, 2.1, etc. 2.2, 2.5 3.2 3.4 3.5 4.1, 4.2 4.2
Data on who does which household chores collected and displayed as bar graph Students collect data on recycling of materials for graphic display Database on Paris built up by groups of students Information on stars fed in to set up dating agency	1.2 2.3, 2.5 4.2, 4.3 4.5
Students design and label their own whacky invention Students design and label a kitchen for wall display Students create simple cartoon story for younger pupils Students create wanted criminal poster Television studio set designed and labelled for soap opera	1.1 2.1 3.1 3.2 5.3
Students link with British or exchange schools to collect and compare information for surveys, etc. Using *Minitel*, students enquire about accommodation in Paris Using database, for example, *Chatter*, students set up dating agency	1.2, 2.2, 3.3, 5.2 4.2 4.5
Using CK1, students list rooms that objects are used in, who uses them. Using CK2, students explain who does what jobs; create job rota Using CKs 4&5, students explore evolution of modern kitchen Using CK6, students devise activities to revise personal description vocabulary Using CK7, students match well-known stars with personal descriptions Students use CK8 to discover information about Paris monuments, etc. CK9 used to revise soap opera place names and settings Using CK10, students decide which props are needed for various scenes	1.1 1.2 2.1 3.2 3.3 4.4 5.1 5.3
Using CK1, students list rooms that objects are used in, who uses them. Students edit and reconstitute poem *Métro boulot dodo* Students unscramble environment fable Students edit and rebuild stories, newspaper items, etc.	1.1 1.4 2.4 3.4, 3.5, 5.2
There are no examples of this in the "IT suggestions" as they stand, but several activities would lend themselves to this treatment, for example, the information on Paris in module 4.	

Working with the concept keyboard

In **Mistral 1** Teacher's Book (page xx), we provided step-by-step guidelines for using an overlay with *Touch Explorer Plus*. Here we offer some more general information for the first-time user, and give examples of possible activities on a sample overlay.

A concept keyboard (or overlay keyboard) is an A3 or A4 bed of 128 touch-sensitive squares which connect with a computer. When programmed, the board will initiate text or graphics within a variety of programs on the computer. Most commonly, text is sent to a word-processor by touching a symbol or cue printed on an overlay sheet placed on the keyboard. The word-processor will operate as normal which means that an overlay represents a further dimension of input, allowing the learner to concentrate on the language task rather than the mechanical task of typing. It is the ideal tool to aid basic word-processing, and it can be used to enter text into DTP applications or a database.

Entering text

Any pre-programmed text can be entered into a word-processor, re-ordered, edited, or expanded. One touch can produce single words, phrases, sentences or full paragraphs. A variety of programs exist for producing overlays. The process is to type the text into the program and link it to the appropriate section of keys on the keyboard. This is not difficult.

Preparing an overlay

There are three principal questions you need to ask:

- What language use will the overlay promote?
- What do you want the learner to see on screen when part of the overlay is touched?
- Which phase of learning do you intend to support – core, extension or revision?

Possible activities

Once you have decided on the purpose of the overlay, a variety of activities are possible:

- *Identifying* – By touching a picture, symbol or word an equivalent piece of text is displayed. This can be used to check vocabulary or prepare language for the learner to use.
- *Choosing* – The learner decides which of the overlay cues to select to fulfill a task, and appropriate text is displayed by the computer. Words or phrases can be entered into a partly completed text in a word-processor or the learner can select prompts or support.
- *Sequencing* – Sections of the overlay must be pressed in a particular order to complete a task. Learners can order a list of instructions or complete a task in a given sequence.
- *Discovering* – Learners explore the overlay by touching to find information. Information about a town can be displayed by touching parts of a town plan.

More amibitious overlay programming will allow you to mix these activities within one program and also call up graphics instead of text.

An example

Identifying
By touching a picture, students see the vocabulary for chores and members of the family.
For example:

→ "la vaisselle" OR "faire la vaisselle"

→ "le père" OR "papa" OR "Jacques"

All of these activities lead to students producing their own language on the word-processor.

Sequencing
Students decide on the order the jobs are to be done.
For example:

→ "la vaisselle"

→ "le bricolage"

Discovering
Students find out who did what chores. They press the pictures to find out.
Either:

→ "Lundi, maman a fait les courses. Samedi, Jacques est allé au supermarché"

Or:

→ "Sylvie a fait les lits et puis elle a fait la lessive."

This activity could be done in any tense; it could be who is going to do what chores, or who generally does what chores.

Choosing
Students decide who is going to do what.
They press different pictures to build up a list.
For example:

 + 

→ "Jean va faire la cuisine"

IT consultants:
John Lemon and Carole Shepherd

Tous les jours   Liste de mariage

CK 1

Align these edges precisely for photocopying

CK 2

Tous les jours *Le travail n'est jamais fini*

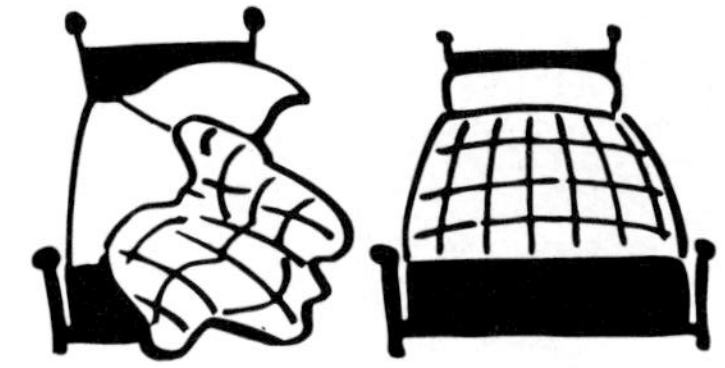

L'écolo Une cuisine des années 30

CK 3

L'écolo Une cuisine des années 90

Align these edges precisely for photocopying

L'écolo   Nos besoins essentiels

CK 5

Align these edges precisely for photocopying

CK6

Les médias   Crime ... Stop!

CK7

Les médias Télémaniaques

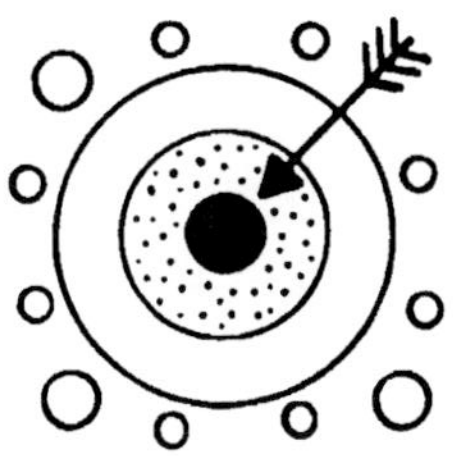

Align these edges precisely for photocopying

Paris: Le Guide Mistral

CK 8

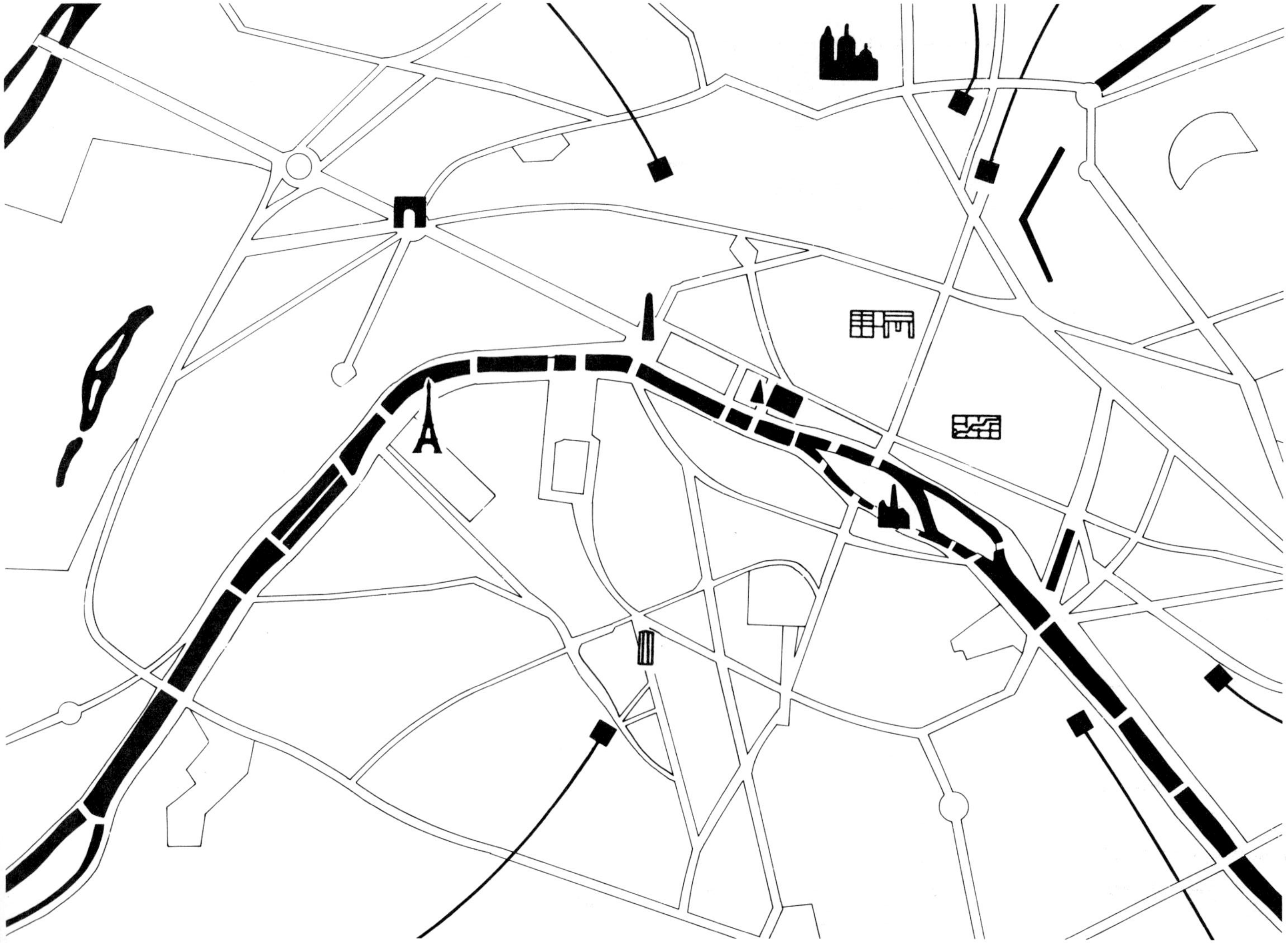

Monuments
cafés et restaurants
gares
transport
logement
distractions

Align these edges precisely for photocopying

CK9

Feuilleton *Des endroits principaux*

CK 10

Feuilleton *Des accessoires*

Mistral 2

DETAILED TEACHING NOTES

Welcome to Mistral!

Mistral 2 is like **Mistral 1** with its four parts; this Students' Book, a Workbook, cassettes and a Teacher's Book.

Just to remind you, they are all known by their French names:

Livre de l'étudiant

This is the Students' Book. As in **Mistral 1** there are five modules of work. Your teacher might suggest that you do them in a different order from the one we have chosen. Each module starts with a double page of pictures and photos. This gives you an idea of what the whole module is about.

Cahier d'activités

This is your Workbook. You don't need an exercise book or a file. You can do all of your written work in it. There are also pages for you to do rough work. You can tell which module you are on by the symbol at the top of each page.

Cassettes

You will probably know how you prefer to use these by now. You can do some of the listening activities in groups, with the whole class or on your own. If you're working in a small group or by yourself, feel free to rewind the tape and listen again, as often as you like.

Livre du professeur

This is the Teacher's Book. This includes extra ideas for lessons and any worksheets you might need. You will have to ask for this when you want to check your answers.

You will notice that the book is all in French again. You'll be familiar with many of the words in the instructions if you have used **Mistral 1**. There aren't too many new words here but remember you can have a guess at some of the words you don't know. If this doesn't work, use a dictionary. We've put a checklist, **Lexique**, at the back of the book in case you get stuck.

The **Page dictionnaire** is at the back of your **Cahier d'activités**. We hope you found it useful in **Mistral 1**. This is where you can keep a note of any new French words that you learn. We've put it in so that you'll have your own personal revision list or checklist.

If you have used **Mistral 1** you will know about the **Contrôle** at the end of every module. This is like a test for you and your teacher to see how much you've learnt. You can look things up, but make sure you do this on your own, not in a group or pair. There's a page in your **Cahier d'activités** where you write your answers and keep a record of your marks. We've also left a space for you and your teacher to write about your progress in each module.

The symbols are the same as in **Mistral 1**:

listen to the tape	reading
work with a partner	writing
work in groups	speaking

We really hope you enjoy using **Mistral**. We've used the talents of lots of people: designers, artists, photographers, art editors, picture researchers, teachers, computer experts, and editors. If you've got the time to write, we'd be interested to know how you get on and what you think of it.

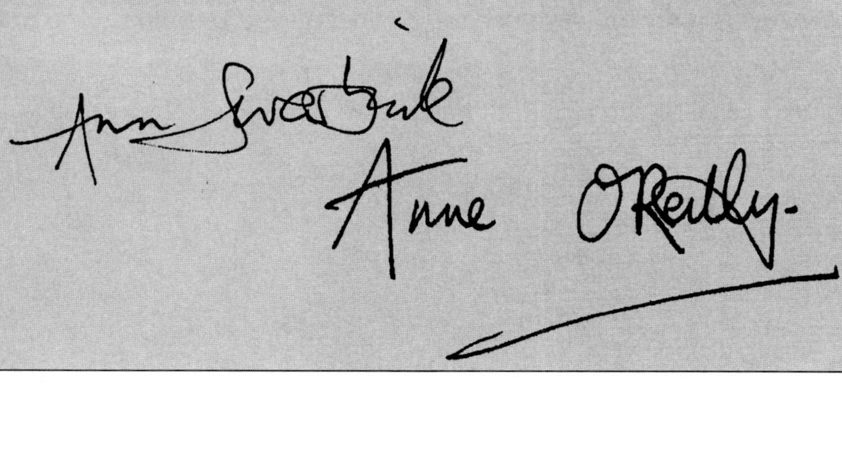

disputer /dispyte/ *v.t.* (*match*) play; (*course*) run in; (*prix*) fight for (**à qn.,** with s.o.); (*gronder*: *fam.*) tell off. **se ~** *v. pr.* quarrel;

trav|ail (*pl.* **~aux**) /travaj, -o/ *n.m.* work; (*emploi, poste*) job; **~aux ménagers,** housework.

journée /ʒurne/ *n.f.* day.

. RALLYE .
.S U P E R .
.PLOEMEUR.

L.LAIT	4.70
CREM CHOC N	7.90
CEREALES	12.95
CEREALES	12.95
CEREALES	12.95
3 X	7.10
YAOURT	21.30
L.LAIT	4.50
BARQUETTE F	4.50
BARQUETTE F	4.50
LAIT STERIL	3.90
MOUSELINE S	3.50
BIO	14.50
SUISSGERVA	15.85
COQUILLETTE	4.25
COQUILLETTE	4.25
SUCRE POUDR	6.80
COQUILLET R	6.95
RAPE	7.80
COQUILET LU	7.95
SPAGHETTIS	4.25
RAPE LOT 2	6.75
GERM SOJA S	5.60
GELEE MURES	8.85
OEUF FERMIE	9.95
SPAGHETTI	4.25
SPAGHETTI	4.25
CREMERIE	17.95
FRUIT/LEGUM	4.45
BAG.200G	2.50
FRUIT/LEGUM	4.20
BAZAR	3.80
TOTAL	238.80
TOTAL	238.80
CHEQUES	238.80
ARTICLES	33

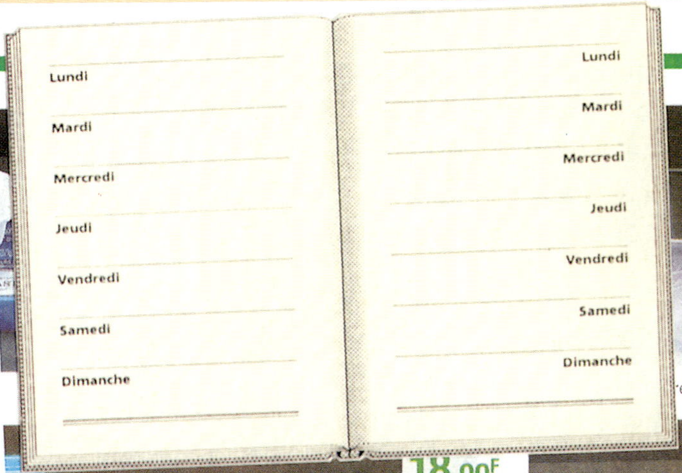

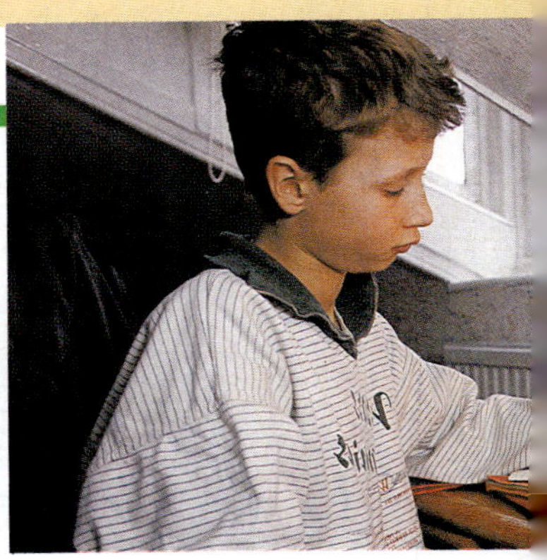

Lot 3 boîtes plastique, modèles assortis

Lot de 2 poêles émail 20 + 26 cm
Queue rouge

Bol faïence décor "Les Journaux"

Pack 3 verres à eau, à vin, ou flûtes NECTAR

Service 44 p. Océan blanc

chez /ʃe/ *prép.* at *ou* to the house of; (*parmi*) among;

ménage /menaʒ/ *n.m.* (married) couple; (*travail*) housework. **se mettre en ~**, set up house.

agenda /aʒɛ̃da/ *n.m.* diary; (*Amer.*) datebook.

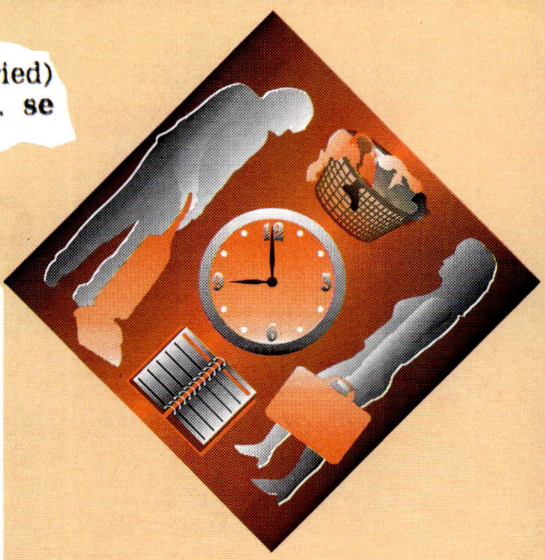

Tous les jours

Service 19 p. Menhir

Bol ou Jumbo faïence exotic

Série 5 casseroles émail MENASTYL

Pyrex 4, 2L

Cuit vapeur émail 24 cm

Hélène et Gilles
se marient le Samedi 22 Décembre à 11 h 30
à la mairie de Plœmeur.
Ils seraient heureux de vous retrouver
avec leurs parents et leurs amis
après la cérémonie de 12 h à 14 h 30
salle de l'Amicale Laïque
12, rue du Fort-Bloqué.

SAT 312009

cahier d'activités, pages 5–6

Tout le confort moderne

1 Lis la liste de mariage d'Alain et Elisabeth.
Trouve les objets.

Exemple: 1 téléviseur = **C**

fiançailles

Alain Belfort et Elisabeth Blanchard
sont heureux de vous annoncer leurs fiançailles

Alain Belfort	**Elisabeth Blanchard**
19 rue Fort Bloqué	2 bis rue Saint-Martin
Mistral-sur-Rhône	Mistral-sur-Rhône

Liste de mariage

1 téléviseur
2 serviettes de bain
1 cafetière
1 horloge de cuisine
1 housse de couette
2 taies d'oreiller
1 nappe et 8 serviettes
6 verres à vin
Service Fantaisie (4 tasses, 4 soucoupes; 1 sucrier; 1 pot à lait; 1 plateau)
1 saladier en verre

2 Ecoute la cassette.
Alain et Elisabeth ouvrent leurs cadeaux.
Quels cadeaux ont-ils reçu?

3 Imagine que tu prépares une liste de mariage.
Travaille avec un/une partenaire.

Exemple:

Unité 1 *Tout le confort moderne*

Areas of experience

A Everyday activities
B Personal and social life
G The world of imagination and creativity

Context

Wedding presents. Considering household items and their uses; expressing an opinion about them. Inventing time-saving devices for an easier life.

Language focus

Part I: *un téléviseur, des serviettes de bain, une couette, des taies d'oreiller, une nappe, une horloge, une cafetière, un saladier, un service, des tasses, des soucoupes, des verres, un sucrier, un pot à lait, un plateau. Je voudrais ... C'est pour* (+ infinitive). *C'est ridicule, super, moche, pratique.*

Part II: *si on tire/pousse... x arrive/tombe/descend.*

Materials

- *Livre de l'étudiant*, pages 8–9
- *Cahier d'activités*, pages 5–6
- *Cassette: La liste de mariage; Encore une invention!*
- Repromaster 1

PART I
A way in

- Produce a familiar object, a household object for instance, or a car accessory. Using the language structure: *C'est pour ...* (+ infinitive), state what the object is used for. For example: *Ici, j'ai un objet très utile dans la cuisine. C'est une théière. C'est pour faire du thé. C'est ça, une théière. C'est pour préparer du thé*. Try to duplicate some of the verbs which are to appear in the *Livre de l'étudiant*.

  Then, use the same familiar object in an unfamiliar or outlandish way, using mime and gestures. So, continuing the example, use the teapot as a pen: *Ici, j'ai un objet très utile. C'est une théière. C'est pour faire du thé, n'est-ce pas? Ben, non ... c'est pour écrire une lettre!*

  Here are some other verbs that would work in the same way: *C'est pour ouvrir, fermer, nettoyer, s'asseoir, se laver, se brosser, monter, descendre, indiquer.*
- Elicit suggestions from the class as to what your next object is used for. Then it is the turn of the students, in pairs, to prepare and present similar mimes. Their mimes may either use the same objects as you have used in your presentation, or others which students may have been asked to bring in. These other objects might be wrapped up so that before preparing their mime, the first task of each pair is to guess what the object is and what it is used for.

Suggested route

Livre de l'étudiant, page 8. Students are then ready to work through the activities on the page, recognizing the French names of the gifts.

Answers

1 téléviseur = C	2 taies d'oreiller = H
2 serviettes de bain = G	1 nappe et 8 serviettes = D
1 cafetière = A	6 verres de vin = E
1 horloge de cuisine = F	Service Fantaisie = J
1 housse de couette = I	1 saladier en verre = B

In the listening activity that follows, students should decide which of the gifts Alain and Elisabeth actually receive.

For transcript see page T1.

Answers

I, H, A, E, J

- Once students have chosen things for their imaginary wedding list and discussed their ideas in pairs, as outlined in the *Livre de l'étudiant*, they should write down their lists. Each person needs to write down the same number of presents. Students go round the class, read out the things on their lists and see if anybody has chosen exactly the same things for their list.
- *Livre de l'étudiant*, page 9. Students should look carefully at each of the gadgets photographed and decide what it is used for. This is a matching exercise, as the captions are provided on the page.

Answers

A = 6	B = 7	C = 5	D = 3
E = 4	F = 2	G = 1	H = 8

- Students may need dictionaries to research the meanings of one or two of the adjectives at the bottom of the page before they can give their opinions of each of the gadgets and some of the vocabulary in the definitions of the objects. Once they have jotted down both the captions and their opinions, in rough, students share their ideas in pairs.
- Using the opinion language acquired (*C'est ridicule, c'est pratique, c'est moche, c'est super*), students could also offer opinions on the wedding gifts on page 8 of the *Livre de l'étudiant.*
- Other activities to exploit these pages in the *Livre de l'étudiant*:
  – Mettez par ordre alphabétique la liste de mariage d'Alain et Elisabeth.
  – Mettez par ordre d'importance la liste de mariage.
  – Expliquez vos choix. Par exemple: les serviettes de bain, c'est le numéro 1, parce que c'est très joli et aussi pratique.

PART II
A way in

- Introduce the language needed for the *Cahier* **R 1** *d'activités*, page 5, by using an OHT of repromaster 1, the Heath Robinson invention for the dining room.

  Here are some ideas: *Voici une invention. C'est une invention bizarre. C'est pour la salle à manger. La salle à manger, c'est quoi en anglais? Que pensez-vous, c'est joli? C'est moche? C'est pratique? Voici le levier ... la chaîne ... la pédale ... le coussin pneumatique ... la corde ... l'assiette ... le trou. Et comment ça marche? Alors, si on tire la chaîne ici ... l'assiette tombe sur la table ...*

- Continue to work through the functions of the invention, using the language outlined in the *Cahier d'activités*, page 5. Ask students to participate in your presentation by, for instance:
  – imitating and repeating individual words
  – completing a sentence that you give
  – listening to you work through the presentation for a second time, more briskly than the first time, a pair of students may come up to the OHP and point out the parts of the invention as you mention them. The rest of the group may do the same, using their *Cahier d'activités*, page 5.

Suggested route
Cahier d'activités page 5

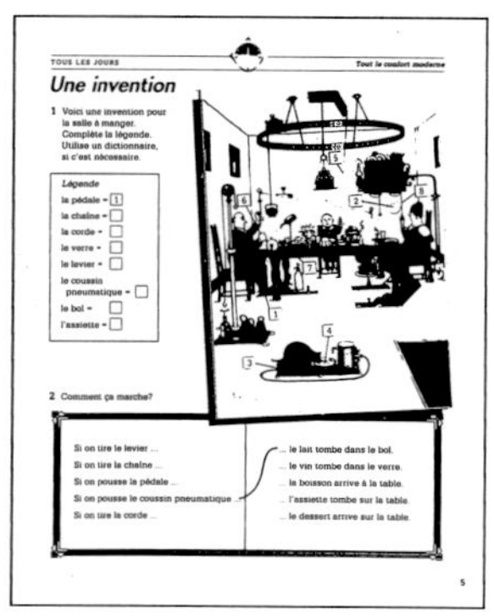

- Students will now be able to complete the key for the Heath Robinson invention and to match up the halves of the sentences telling you how the invention works.

Answers

la pédale = 1	le levier = 6
la chaîne = 8	le coussin pneumatique = 3
la corde = 5	le bol = 4
la verre = 7	l'assiette = 2

Si on tire le levier ... le vin tombe dans le verre.
Si on tire la chaîne ... l'assiette tombe sur la table.
Si on pousse la pédale ... la boisson arrive à la table.
Si on pousse le coussin pneumatique ...
le lait tombe dans le bol.
Si on tire la corde ... le dessert arrive sur la table.

Cahier d'activités page 6

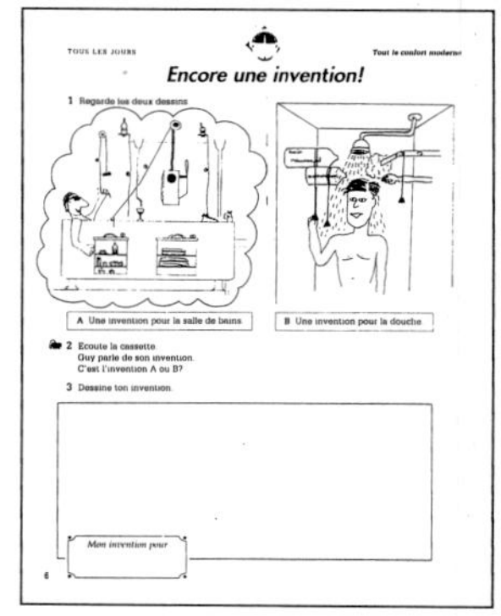

- The two further inventions have been designed by students, using the Heath Robinson one as inspiration. Before listening to the tape and deciding which of the two inventions is being described, students need to take a careful look at the pictures.

  For transcript, see page **T 1**.

Answer

A: Une invention pour la salle de bains

- There is space in the *Cahier d'activités* for students to design their own invention. This may be tackled at different levels. Students may simply give their invention a name and label its main parts or they may go on to write simple sentences about how it works, using those in the *Cahier d'activités*, page 5, as models.

Follow-up ideas

- Students make up announcements of their own engagements, using the example in *Livre de l'étudiant* as a model. Then, they make a collage of their own ideas for a wedding list and write them in French. Students working on this in male/female pairs might produce some interesting ideas!
- Some students may be able to present their inventions to either a small group or the whole class, as if trying to sell it at a convention. This would bring in opinion vocabulary, prices and so on.

IT suggestions

- **CK 1** Using CK1, devise reinforcement exercises to practise the vocabulary of the unit by including any words or phrases used in the *Livre de l'étudiant*. Use the overlay to enter the words into lists of which rooms the objects are used in, who uses them, when they are used, what they are used for, what jobs need to be done, etc., for example: *Je voudrais une cafetière. C'est pour faire du café. C'est utile.*
- Using WP or DTP combined with a graphics package or scanned images, students could produce a wedding invitation or wedding present list in alphabetical order.
- Using a graphics package, students could design and label their own invention.

1 Regarde ces gadgets.
Qu'est-ce que c'est?

Exemple: **E** = **4** C'est pour faire du café.

C'est pour ...
1 faire des calculs.
2 indiquer l'heure.
3 casser des noix.
4 faire du café.
5 indiquer la température.
6 boire de la limonade.
7 boucher une bouteille.
8 protéger les lunettes.

2 Travaille avec un/une partenaire. Que pensez-vous de ces gadgets?

Le travail n'est jamais fini

1 Regarde les dessins.
Notre artiste imagine la vie en 2050.

Lis les phrases.
Quelle est la bonne phrase pour chaque dessin?

Exemple: **1 = H**

A On fait la cuisine.
B On fait la lessive.
C On fait la vaisselle.
D On fait le bricolage.
E On fait le ménage.
F On fait le lit.
G On fait le shopping.
H On fait le jardinage.

Unité 2 *Le travail n'est jamais fini*

Areas of experience

A Everyday activities
B Personal and social life

Context

Looking at chores around the house and investigating the division of labour between the sexes.

Language focus

Part I: *On fait... le lit, le shopping, la vaisselle, la cuisine, le ménage, la lessive, le bricolage, le jardinage.*

Part II: *Moi, je fais... Il/Elle fait. Mon père/Ma mère/Ma sœur/Mon frère fait.*

Materials

- *Livre de l'étudiant*, pages 10–11
- *Cahier d'activités*, pages 7–8
- *Cassette: Dispute en famille; Monsieur Madame*
- Repromaster 2
- Repromaster 3
- Photos of your own family (optional)

PART I
A way in

- Introduce the chores vocabulary, with either flashcards or OHT cues using the pictures on repromaster 2. Numbering each chore makes it easier to introduce the new words.
- Give each pair of students a set of seven mini flashcards of the above chores from repromaster 2. These can be used to play recognition and memory games. For example, person A mimes a chore, and person B guesses what the chore is. They record the number of guesses they take to get all of the cards. The person with the least number of guesses wins.
- If the French is added to the reverse side of the flashcards, then spelling games can also be used.

Suggested route

- *Livre de l'étudiant*, page 10. The written form of all these chores appears here in a futuristic context. Once students have worked through the matching activity, invite opinions as to how likely each of these situations is: *Que pensez-vous... en 2050, on fera la vaisselle comme ça? C'est certain? C'est probable? C'est peu probable? C'est impossible?*

Answers

1 = H	2 = G	3 = D	4 = C
5 = F	6 = E	7 = A	8 = B

Cahier d'activités page 7

- Students listen to a parent arguing with his daughter, Marilyne, about the amount she does to help in the home. Students tick the pictures of the chores done by Marilyne.

For transcript see page T 1.

Answers

2, 3, 4, 6, 7

PART II
A way in

- Brainstorm French words for members of the family. Use your own family photos to reinforce these words. Repromaster 3 gives representational pictures of key family members if you prefer not to use your own photos.
- Present a family (yours or an imaginary one). Explain who does (or did) what around the house. You may be talking about a family context that mentions sons, daughters and partners or one that highlights parents, grandparents, brothers and sisters. Some new vocabulary might need to be included at this point: *mon grand-père, ma grand-mère, mon demi-frère, ma demi-sœur, mon beau-fils, ma belle-fille, mon beau-père, ma belle-mère,*

A presentation comparing how things were when you were younger and how things are now might be an interesting way in.

Suggested route

Cahier d'activités page 7

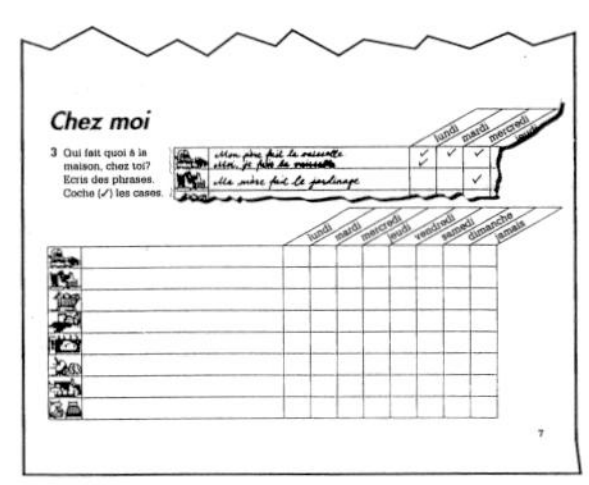

- Each student writes in who does what in their home and indicates how often. It may be necessary to pool on the board or OHT their ideas for sentences that follow the examples in the *Cahier d'activités*, so there is something for students to copy, if they need to do so.

  This activity should encourage students to think about whether in the class there is a division between the sexes as far as housework is concerned.

Cahier d'activités page 8

TOUS LES JOURS — *Le travail n'est jamais fini*

Qui fait quoi?

Travaille dans un groupe de six personnes. Pose des questions.

Exemple: Qui fait la vaisselle chez toi?

Ecoute la réponse.
Si c'est une femme, coche (✓) la case F.
Si c'est un homme, coche (✓) la case H.

Légende: le lit, la lessive, le ménage, la vaisselle, la cuisine, les courses, le bricolage, le jardinage

les travaux	F	H

8

- Once the students have done their own individual tick charts, build up a bar chart to show the division of labour in the students' households.This may be a group activity, as shown on the *Cahier d'activités*, page 8. Or, the responses of the whole class may be recorded on the board or OHT. Ask students: *Qui fait le ménage chez toi?* If the reply is "*mon père*", for instance, mark off one square of the bar chart on the left hand column, marked H(*homme*). If the reply is "*ma mère*", you mark off a square in the right hand column, F(*femme*). And so on ...

- Students should soon be able to take over asking the questions and recording the responses.

- *Livre de l'étudiant*, page 11: *Monsieur Madame*. This cartoon strip is based on the TV programme 'Mr and Mrs'. The object of this quiz show is to see how well one partner knows the other. Both husband and wife are asked individually and out of the other's hearing, questions about their partner. The same questions are then asked to the husband or wife themselves: do both sets of responses match?

  In this cartoon, if their answers tally, a point is scored. Students work out from the cartoon which prize is eventually won. Underneath the cartoon are pictures of the prizes with the number of points needed in order to win.

Answer

0 points – divorce!

For transcript see page T1.

Follow-up idea

- Once students have worked a similar scene, as indicated in the *Livre de l'étudiant*, they may perform it. They would decide on how many points would mean which prize. The rest of the group, watching, could keep a tally of the score as they listen and at the end, find out from the performing group what the prize is.

IT suggestions

CK 2

- Using CK2, devise reinforcement exercises to practise the vocabulary of the unit, explaining who does what and when they do it, for example: *Je fais la vaisselle. Il fait les courses. Elle fait le bricolage le week-end.* Using the family pictures, devise an activity for students to find out who does what.
- Using the CK overlay, students could also create a job rota, or draw up a list of jobs in order of priority.
- Using WP or DTP, students could devise data collection forms for a survey on the division of household chores.
- Using a simple database enter the data collected by overlay or keyboard and create bar graphs. Develop the data by comparing results with those of other classes or different year groups. This could lead to inter-class discussion about the evidence collected.
- Using E-mail, students could conduct a survey with another school on division of labour.

Monsieur Madame

1 Ecoute la cassette.
Lis la bande dessinée.

2 Monsieur et Madame Guiguin gagnent quel prix?

3 Travaille dans un groupe de trois personnes. Imaginez une scène semblable.

La personne A est l'animateur/l'animatrice.
La personne B est Monsieur X.
La personne C est Madame X.

Agendas

1 Lis cet agenda.
C'est un week-end avec le Président de la République française.

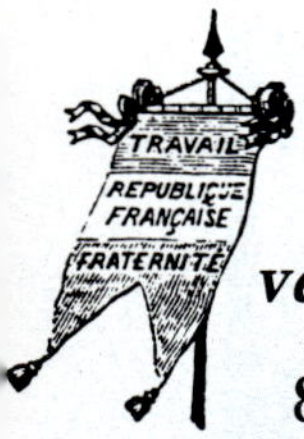

vendredi, 6 mai

8h	Petit déjeuner en famille. Lire les journaux.
9h	
10h	Réunion avec le secrétaire général de l'UNESCO.
11h	Lire les dossiers et préparer mon interview.
12h	Déjeuner avec des artistes.
13h	Essayage de mes nouveaux costumes.
14h	Départ pour Strasbourg en hélicoptère.
15h	Discours devant l'Assemblée européenne.
16h	
17h	Retour à Paris.
18h	Cocktails avec le ministre des affaires étrangères du Japon.
19h	
20h	
21h	Interview télévisée en direct sur Antenne 2.

samedi, 7 mai

8h	Petit déjeuner en famille
9h	
10h	Lire les journaux et les dossiers.
11h	
12h	
13h	Déjeuner avec des amis.
14h	Départ en voiture pour la campagne.
15h	
16h	
17h	
18h	
19h	
20h	Dîner en famille. L'anniversaire de Véronique.
21h	

dimanche, 8 mai

8h	Petit déjeuner en famille.
9h	
10h	Lire les journaux et les dossiers.
11h	
12h	Les enfants arrivent.
13h	Déjeuner en famille.
14h	
15h	Grande marche.
16h	Départ pour Paris.
17h	Envol pour New York en Concorde.
18h	
19h	
20h	
21h	

2 Ecoute la cassette.
Il y a trois scènes du week-end du Président.
Ça se passe à quelle heure?
Et quel jour?

Unité 3 *Agendas*

Areas of experience

A Everyday activities
B Personal and social life
C The world around us
D The world of education, training and work
F The international world

Context

Talking about routines, weekend and holiday activities. Time management.

Language focus

Manger, voyager, travailler, se relaxer. Qu'est-ce que tu as fait hier? J'ai (+ past participle).

Materials

- *Livre de l'étudiant*, pages 12–13
- *Cahier d'activités*, pages 9–10
- *Cassette: Un week-end avec le Président de la République française; Clémentine en Tunisie*
- Repromaster 4

A way in

- It may be necessary to revise numbers and times before starting this unit.
- Revise colours using coloured pens on OHT. Then refer to the colour code mentioned on page 9 of the *Cahier d'activités*: blue for eating, green for travelling, red for working, yellow for relaxing. In order to explain each type of activity, give lots of examples that refer to yourself. For example: *Bleu, ça signifie... manger. Les moments où je mange. Par exemple, mon petit déjeuner. Puis, à midi, je mange aussi... c'est l'heure du déjeuner. Le soir, je prends mon dîner vers sept heures...*
- Using repromaster 4, show on OHT the two clock faces, each one divided into 12 segments. Each segment represents one hour of the day. One clock face is labelled *minuit–11h* and the other, *midi–23h.*

  Go through the hours, saying what you do when, always referring to the vocabulary used in your presentation. *Dormir – je dors* is extra to the key vocabulary. As you speak, shade in the hours in the relevant colours, or get a student to do this. Try another example, with a student talking through their day and someone else shading in.

Suggested route

- Start with quickfire practice from the President's agenda on page 12 of the *Livre de l'étudiant.* For instance: you give a time/day and the students say which activity the President does then; then do the same activity but vice versa; you or a student mimes one of the activities and the rest of the group guesses which it is; you give a single word and someone gives the whole sentence that it comes from.
- There is a listening activity to go with this page. Students are to record the time and the day for each of the three scenes enacted on the tape.

  For transcript see page T1.

Answers

1 Samedi, 7 mai, 20h
2 Vendredi, 6 mai, 13h
3 Vendredi, 6 mai, 15h

Cahier d'activités page 9

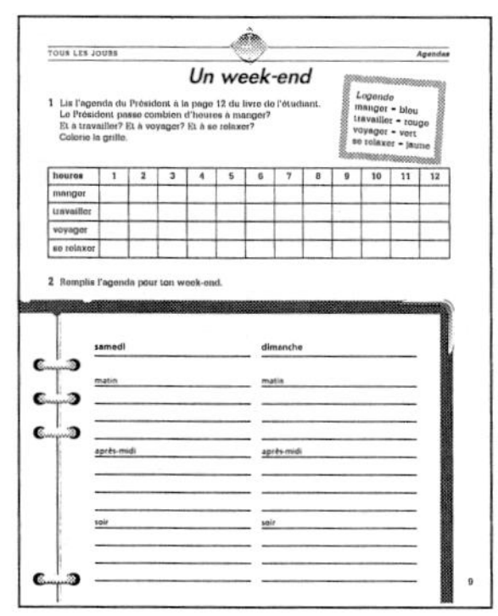

- The reading activity encourages students to read and re-read the President's diary pages in order to be able to fill in the time planner on this page.
- Before tackling their own weekends, students may need time to prepare and share ideas. Perhaps begin by getting them to draw out of the President's diary all the activities they can spot and writing them up on the board. Some whole-group work finding more relevant activites, using dictionaries, might follow this.
- Revision of the past tense (use of *j'ai* + past participles) may be necessary before tackling the rest of the unit. One possibility is to link the ideas in the weekend agendas that the students will have worked out for themselves in their *Cahier d'activités* with the reality of their last weekend. Going back to the initial coloured clock faces of your own and making a comparison between these and your own last weekend is a good way of providing a model.

Cahier d'activités page 10

Une soirée

- This activity asks students to record how they spent the previous evening. Once they have worked out their own colour code and key, they fill in their time line (*grille A*) for the particular evening. The other time lines are filled in as students interview each other about their evening.
- *Livre de l'étudiant,* page 13. This listening activity can be done independently by the students at any relevant stage as it provides simple use of past tense verbs in the interesting context of Clémentine's holiday in Tunisia.

For transcript see page **T 2**.

Answers

B, C, F, D, A, G, E

Follow-up ideas

- Students describe their own photos of a past holiday, using *c'est le moment où j'ai...* This could be done in the same way as Clémentine describes her photos: guessing which photo is being talked about. At a more simple level, just one photo may be described.
- Displaying holiday photos with captions alongside: students have to look at photos and find the correct caption for each one.
- Displaying students' holiday photos and inviting everyone to write a caption for each one, using the acquired language structure: *c'est le moment où....* Offer a prize for the most interesting and amusing idea.
- Discussion of time management with students in relation to preparing for an exam period or a coursework deadline. The aim of this would be to encourage students to plan their time in advance, taking perhaps just one evening and drawing up a time line that sensibly fits everything in. Follow this up with a comparison between the intended, pre-planned timetable and how the evening was actually spent.

IT suggestions

- Using WP or DTP and a graphics package or database, students could produce their own diary of daily routine activities, including times of day. Students could check and edit diary appointments and times of events.
- Using the package *Granville*, students could simulate a holiday abroad and print out their diaries in the perfect tense.
- Using WP or DTP, students could cut and paste captions for their own holiday photos. Scanned images could be used if the school has this facility.

1 Clémentine range ses photos des vacances en Tunisie. Regarde les photos.

A

B

C

D

E

F

G

2 Ecoute la cassette. Clémentine parle de ses photos. Dans quel ordre?

cahier d'activités, pages 11–12

Une journée de Jean-Denis

1 Regarde les photos de Jean-Denis Grancher.
Quelle légende va avec quelle photo?

Exemple: **A** va avec **2**

Ⓐ Il part au Centre de Kerpape.

Ⓑ La journée de Jean-Denis est finie.

Ⓒ Il travaille à la piscine. L'eau est très chaude : 37 degrés.

1
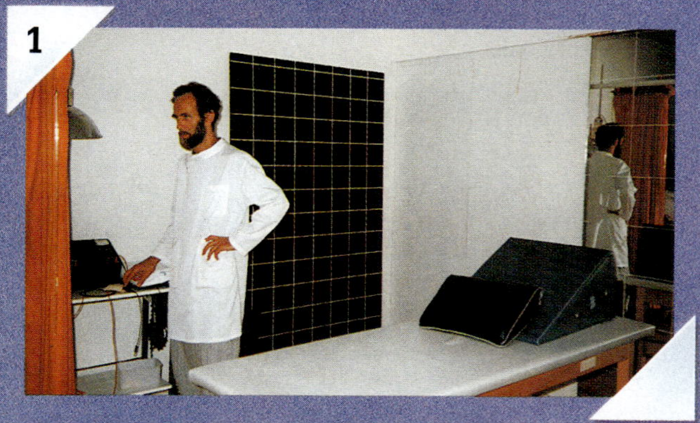

2

4
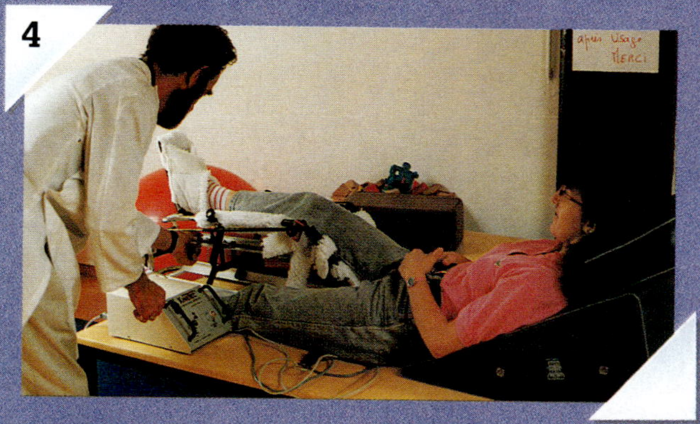

5

7
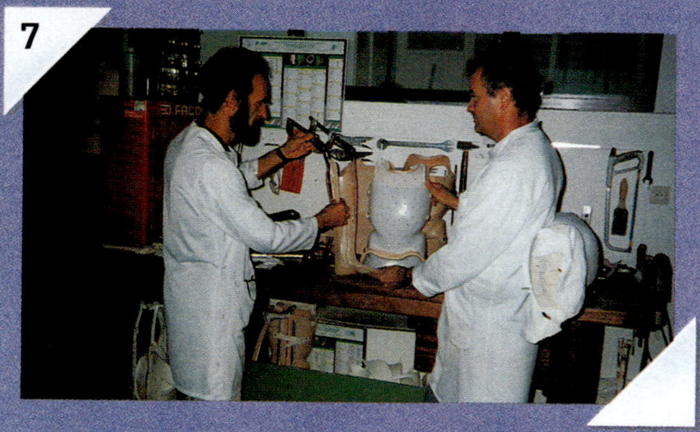

8

Unité 4 *Une Journée de Jean-Denis*

Areas of experience
A Everyday activities
B Personal and social life
D The world of education, training and work
G The world of imagination and creativity

Context
Job shadowing. Revision of daily routine. Poetry and music.

Language focus
Il/Elle se lève, il/elle part, il/elle va au travail (+ transport), *il/elle commence son travail à..., il/elle travaille dans ..., il/elle* (+ activity), *il/elle finit vers ..., il/elle rentre à ...*
Qu'est-ce que tu fais à (+ time).

Materials
- *Livre de l'étudiant*, pages 14–15
- *Cahier d'activités*, pages 11–12
- *Cassette: Métro boulot dodo; Je suis toujours pressée*
- Repromaster 5

A way in
- The above language is a skeleton for describing the day of someone that the students will know... say, the Headteacher. On OHT have the activities written up with blanks next to each phrase for the times. Get students to guess at what times this person does all of these things. Compare these predictions with the real account given to the teacher by the Headteacher.
- Students may then prepare to talk about someone else's routine – probably a partner's in the group. Then one of the pair comes to the OHP and explains their partner's routine in the same way as you presented that of the Headteacher. The class, once again, guesses the times and then compares with the true account.

Suggested route
- *Livre de l'étudiant*, pages 14–15. This double-page spread of photos of Jean-Denis Grancher (physiotherapist) at work illustrates the kinds of things his job entails and the timetable of his day. It is the work of a student whose school project is to shadow someone at work.

Cahier d'activités page 11

- Students first match the captions to the photos. There is space for students to write their answers on this page.

Answers

A = 2	B = 9	C = 8
D = 1	E = 4	F = 7
G = 5	H = 6	I = 3

- Students then complete the description of Jean-Denis Grancher's day at work. This can be a simple copy-writing task, or students could add their own ideas to the basics supplied in the *Livre de l'étudiant*. Students will also need to add suitable times.
- Students then need to prepare questions for their own research into someone's job. These may be in French (*Qu'est-ce que tu fais à ... heures?*) or in English but the write up will obviously be in French. The interview should then be written up, alongside Jean-Denis Grancher's day.

Cahier d'activités page 12

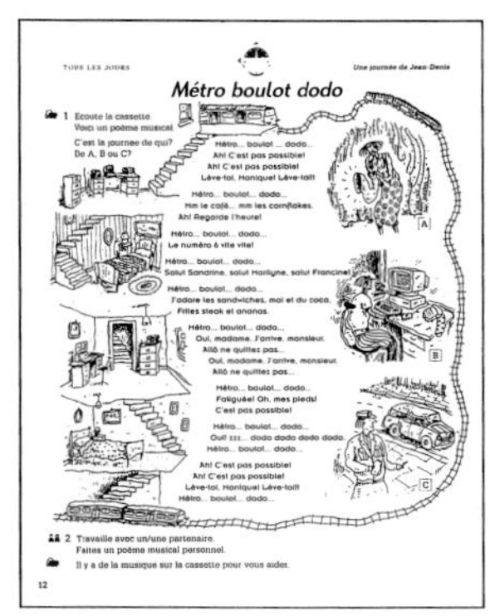

- This is a musical poem that tells the story of someone's day at work and their attitude towards it! Explain what the words of the title refer to, using the vocabulary form the previous unit: *voyager... travailler ... dormir.* Students first identify which of the three pictures depicts the person in the poem.

For transcript see **T 2**.

Answer
The office worker's day: B

- Students should be encouraged to listen to the poem as many times as they like, to perform it themselves, or to make up their own versions. The soundtrack on the tape which follows this musical poem is for the students to use as accompaniment to their own musical poems if they so wish.

Follow-up ideas

- Repromaster 5 is a French poem written by a British young person, entitled *Je suis toujours pressée*. The aim is to read the poem for pleasure and derive as much of its meaning as possible. By way of introducing the poem to your students, show them the English version on OHT first. Read this through first (either you or, better still, a student), then you read the French version. Give to each pair of students a version of the French poem which has been cut up (perhaps line by line, or else verse by verse to make it easier). Students then reconstitute the French poem with the English in front of them.

R 5

- There is a variety of sound effects on tape, to accompany the verses on the poem. Students listen to each of these, in turn and read out the line which the sound effect describes.

For transcript see page T 2.

- Copying this poem and then illustrating as many of its points as possible, or using it as a model to write their own are yet further possibilities!

IT suggestions

- You or the students could create a CK overlay based on the theme of daily routine to practise the vocabulary of the unit. This activity could be linked to the sound effects listening task in order that students learn to associate the correct spelling on screen with the sound. Sound effects can be recorded onto the computer to support the linking of words, sounds and pictures.
- Using an authoring package on which you have typed a version of the rhythmic poem, *Métro boulot dodo*, allow the students to edit and reconstitute the poem.
- Using WP or DTP, combined with a graphics package or a cut-and-paste activity, allow students to make up their own short poem or to copy and illustrate the one on repromaster 5.

R 5

Jean-Denis est kiné. Il travaille à Kerpape.

(G) Le petit Paul fait des exercices. Jean-Denis encourage beaucoup.

(E) Il commence avec Marie. Elle a eu un accident de moto.

(H) Le déjeuner: crabe, steak frites, fromage et tarte aux fruits.

…n on fabrique les attelles! On …rle de Chantal, qui est paralysée.

(I) Il arrive à Kerpape.

3

6

9

2 Lis l'article.

Une championne courageuse

A l'âge de quinze ans, Marie a un terrible accident de moto. Elle perd l'usage de ses jambes. Elle passe deux ans à Kerpape. Elle se partage entre le collège et le kiné. Un an au lit, huit mois en fauteuil. Enfin elle marche. Elle va en Angleterre avec les professeurs et six copains. La voilà maintenant championne de natation (200 mètres crawl). A dix-sept ans! Félicitations!

3 Tu connais des personnes courageuses comme Marie?
Fais une liste dans ton cahier d'activités.

cahier d'activités, page 13

La vie à deux

1 Regarde ces images.
Quatre versions de la réalité?
Quelle est ton opinion?

MAMAN, REPOSE-TOI POUR LA FETE DES MERES!

Unité 5 *La vie à deux*

Areas of experience

A Everyday activities
B Personal and social life
C The world of communications and technology

Context

A further look into the division of domestic responsibilities. Predicting your attitudes when and if you leave home. Comparing different lifestyles.

Language focus

Je vais... m'occuper des factures, faire la vaisselle, faire le ménage, m'occuper des enfants, faire le jardinage, changer un fusible, réparer la voiture, faire la cuisine, faire le repassage, faire la lessive, faire le shopping.

Materials

- *Livre de l'étudiant*, pages 16–17
- *Cahier d'activités*, page 13
- *Cassette*: *C'est quelle scène?*
- 6 Repromaster 6
- 7 Repromaster 7

A way in

- 6 Repromaster 6 shows two versions of the survey about the future on page 13 of the *Cahier d'activités*. These two versions are filled in – one is headed *Marie pense au futur*, the other *Marc pense au futur*. The headings make it obvious that one has been filled in by a boy and the other by the girl. NB: This is the only difference between the two grids and should not be revealed to the students. Cover up the headings when photocopying the repromasters for the students.

Students are in in pairs or threes. Each group should be all-girl or all-boy. The all-girl groups are given a copy of Marc's responses and the all-boy groups a copy of Marie's responses.

- The question under discussion is to be posed in French: *Tu t'imagines marié(e) avec cette personne*? *Discutez en anglais. Ecrivez vos raisons en anglais*. With Marie's or Marc's responses as their stimulus in the target language, the students will feedback in English. Your reactions to what they say will remain in French. It may be appropriate to write up students' opinions on the board, separating their opinions on Marc from those on Marie.

Cahier d'activités page 13

TOUS LES JOURS — La vie à deux

Sondage du futur

1 Pense au futur.
Remplis la grille.

Je vais...	oui bien sûr	non	à mon tour
m'occuper des factures			
faire la vaisselle			
faire le ménage			
m'occuper des enfants			
faire le jardinage			
changer un fusible			
réparer la voiture			
faire la cuisine			
faire le repassage			
faire la lessive			
faire les courses			

2 Compare tes résultats avec d'autres personnes dans la classe.
Pose des questions.
Exemple: Tu vas faire la cuisine? Oui, à mon tour. Non, absolument pas!

13

- Students will now be ready to fill in the questionnaire for themselves. Then, in groups of four, they record the proportion of girls to boys willing to do each of the things mentioned. Students may record group responses in their *Cahier d'activités*, alongside their individual answers.
- All the information may then be collated on the board. Draw up the three columns: *oui bien sûr, non, à mon tour*. Say one of the statements and each group says in turn how many boys and girls decided what. Two students (one calculating, the other writing up) could do this recording, as you call out the statements.

Suggested route

- *Livre de l'étudiant*, pages 16–17. Students are invited to look at the images of everyday life. Lead-in questions might be: *Quatre versions de la réalité? Quelle est ton opinion? Oui ... alors, pourquoi? Non ... alors, pourquoi? Tu peux t'imaginer dans une situation pareille ... dans une situation comme ça, par exemple? Ça te plaît, de t'imaginer dans cette situation ... tu aimerais ça? Il y a une situation que tu n'aimerais pas du tout?* Discussion may well be in English but try to investigate simple French structures, as a starter to the discussion: *C'est réaliste? Oui ... non, c'est trop romantique, sexiste, simple.*
- R 7 Alternatively, using repromaster 7 cut up onto cards, give students the phrases in French. Each of the phrases should go under one of two headings on the board/OHT: *SEXISTE; PAS SEXISTE*. Ask students to work in groups and put the cards under the one of the two headings. Alternatively, you could just read out the statements, or similar ones, and ask whether they are sexist or not, getting students to reply *oui* or *non*.

- Students are then ready to do the listening activity on page 17 of the *Livre de l'étudiant*. They should look at the pairs of cartoons and decide which one is enacted on the cassette.

For transcript, see page T 2

Answers

1A; 2B; 3B

- Students are then asked to say which of the characters on the pictures they would most like to be. They could then compare their answers with others in the group.

Follow-up ideas

- Students may look for an image of adult life which they agree might be a good model. They may compare two images, one less favourable, in their eyes, than the other and write a simple caption or opinion to go with each one.

- Students could enact the scenes on page 17 of the *Livre de l'étudiant*. They could put the three non-recorded scenes onto cassette.

CK 2

IT suggestions

- Using CK2, devise reinforcement exercises to practise the main phrases of the unit, for example: *Je vais faire de la lessive*.
- Using WP or DTP, students could devise data collection forms to collect students' opinions on Marc and Marie. Use two columns marked *SEXISTE* and *PAS SEXISTE*.
- Create a simple database to formulate the difference between male and female attitudes to the survey.

2 Regarde ces dessins.
Ecoute la cassette.
C'est quelle scène? A ou B?

1A

1B

2A

2B

3A

3B

3 Regarde les dessins.
Tu t'identifies avec quelles personnes?
Choisis trois phrases.

Je voudrais être la personne qui s'occupe de la voiture.
Je voudrais être la personne qui n'aime pas les voitures.

Je voudrais être la personne qui fait la cuisine.
Je voudrais être la personne qui se relaxe.

Je voudrais être la personne qui va au travail.
Je voudrais être la personne qui travaille à la maison.

Contrôle 1

Ecris tes réponses dans ton cahier d'activités, page 56

A

Ecoute la cassette.
Jean et sa mère sont dans la cuisine.
Jean passe quels objets à sa mère?
Donne cinq exemples.

Exemple: **C**

B

Marie-Thérèse va habiter dans un appartement avec Thierry.
Les caisses arrivent.
Choisis la bonne caisse pour chaque pièce.

Exemple: Le garage = **E**

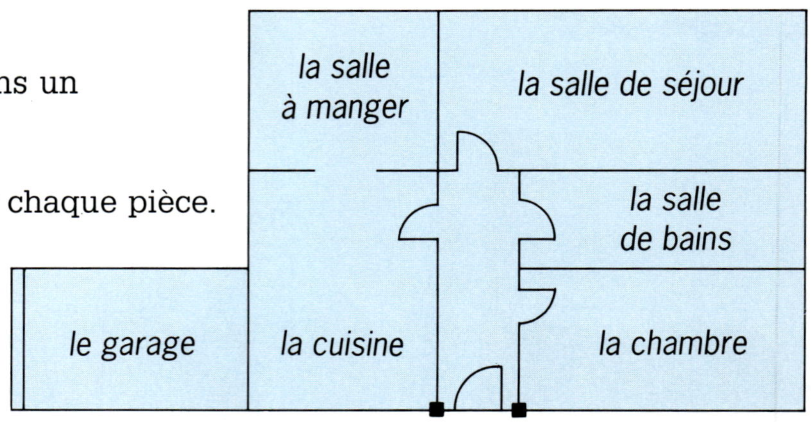

Contrôle I

	NOTE
A 1 · 2 · *See answers overleaf* · 5	**5**
B 1 La salle à manger = C 2 La salle de séjour = A 3 La salle de bains = F 4 La chambre = B 5 La cuisine = D	**5**
C 1 ..... 2 ..... 3 ..... 4 ..... 5 ..... *See guidelines overleaf*	**5**
D **Journal parlé** *See guidelines overleaf*	**5**
OBSERVATIONS	TOTAL
Date: Signature de l'étudiant: Signature du professeur:	**20**

CASSETTE 1 FACE 1

Contrôle 1
Livre de l'étudiant, page 18
Cahier d'activités, page 56

– Jean, tu peux m'aider à ranger les affaires, s'il te plaît?
– Ohh! Pitié... non!
– Allez, allez, pas de discussion. Tu m'aides. C'est tout! Donne-moi la cafetière, là... et puis, passe-moi les couteaux... là... et les cuillères. Non! Pas les fourchettes! J'ai dit les couteaux et les cuillères.
– Excuse-moi.
– Bon... Maintenant les verres... Merci! Et les bols là dans le coin. Et les tasses à café. D'abord les tasses... Attention là... Et les soucoupes... Attention!... Oh! Ce n'est pas vrai. Mes soucoupes! Jean, tu exagères. Fais attention! Maintenant, je n'ai plus de soucoupes. Tu es maladroit, vraiment. Quel maladroit!
– Pardon maman, je suis désolé. Je suis vraiment très désolé.

Answers to task A

Any five of the following:
J (couteaux)
H (cuillères)
B (verres)
K (bols)
E (tasses à café)
F (soucoupes)

Writing task guidelines (task C)

Each answer is worth one mark. The tasks are open-ended so that there are no 'right' answers. Answers should be marked positively. Students should have the opportunity to refer to their books and a dictionary, to check spellings. With this in mind, if a student successfully communicates a relevant message, a mark should be awarded. A mark should not be awarded if the spelling is so awry that a sympathetic native speaker would be unlikely to understand the message.

In certain instances, where a student has severe handwriting difficulties, he/she may be offered the option of dictating and spelling out answers for you to transcribe. Similarly, answers might be word-processed and then pasted into the answer pages of the *Cahier d'activités*.

Speaking task guidelines (task D)

Ideally, these contributions will be recorded onto a student's own individual tape which may also included other items from the course. Otherwise a class tape on which all students record their answers could be used.

A mark should be awarded for each relevant utterance understood by the listener. Here is some guidance as to what the speaker may be expected to say:

Le dimanche je joue au football.
Je rentre à une heure.
Je mange le déjeuner à deux heures.
Je fais la vaisselle.
Je regarde un film à la télé.

National Curriculum assessment

Task A	AT 1, level 3(b)
Task B	AT 3, level 2(a)
Task C	AT 4, level 3(a)
Task D	AT 2, level 4(b)

C

Dans ta famille, qui fait quoi le week-end?
Ecris cinq phrases en français.

Exemple: Mon père fait la lessive.
Ma mère fait les courses.

D

Journal parlé

Choisis un jour de la semaine.
Parle des moments importants.
Donne cinq exemples.

Exemple:

recycl|er /rəsikle/ v.t. (personne) retrain; (chose) recycle. se ~er v. pr. retrain. ~age n.m. retraining; recycling.
année /ane/ n.f. year.
consomma|teur, ~trice /kɔ̃sɔmatœr, -tris/ n.m., f. (comm.) consumer;
consomm|er /kɔ̃sɔme/ v.t. consume; (user) use, consume;
matière /matjɛr/ n.f. matter; (produit) material; (sujet) subject.
écolog|ie /ekɔlɔʒi/ n.f. ecology. ~ique a. ecological.
NOUS VOUS
Ille
LE M
ENVIRONMENTAL CHOICE
CHOIX ENVIRONNEMENTAL
YMPÄRISTÖMERKKI
MILJÖMÄRKT
ちきゅうにやさしい
Umweltzeichen
weil emissionsarm und abfallmindernd
Jury Umweltzeichen
Grande-Bretagne
Irlande
Belgique
Les Amis de la Terre
et le WWF France présentent
WWF
DOSSIER
SUR LA POLLUTION
ATMOSPHERIQUE
C'est ma planète
20 GESTES SIMPLES
POUR L'ENVIRONNEMENT
un guide est à votre disposition dans votre Mairie
LA POLLUTION EST FROIDE, AUJOURD'HUI !
CABRAL
LA BALEINE
N° 77 - 25 F • Juin 1989
France
RECYCLING-FL
Allemagne
GLASBA
Pays-Bas
DOSSIER :
VALORISER
L'ENVIRONNEM
N° 13 • JUIN 1991 • PRIX
PAPIER RECYCLÉ
CONSEIL GENERAL D'ILLE ET VILAINE

terre /tɛr/ *n.f.* (*planète, matière*) earth; (*étendue, pays*) land; (*sol*) ground; (*domaine*) estate. **à ~**, (*naut.*) ashore. **par ~**, (*tomber, jeter*) to the ground; (*s'asseoir*,

protég|er /prɔteʒe/ *v.t.* protect;

décharge /deʃarʒ/ *n.f.* (*salve*) volley of shots. **~ (électrique)**, electrical discharge. **~ (publique)**, rubbish tip.

L'écolo

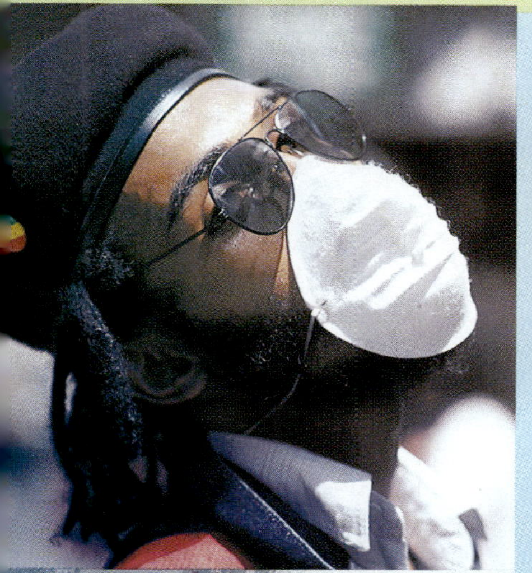

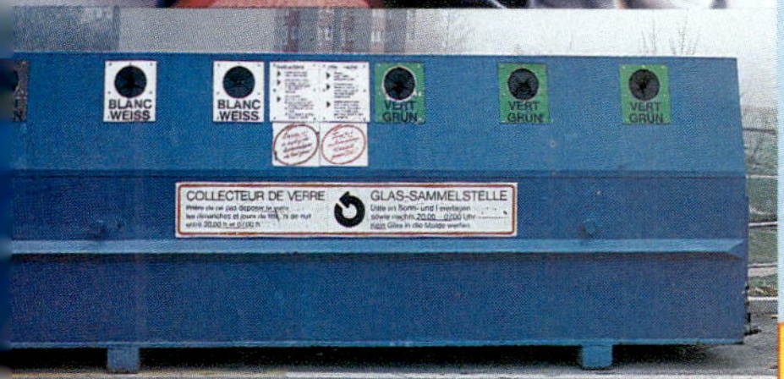

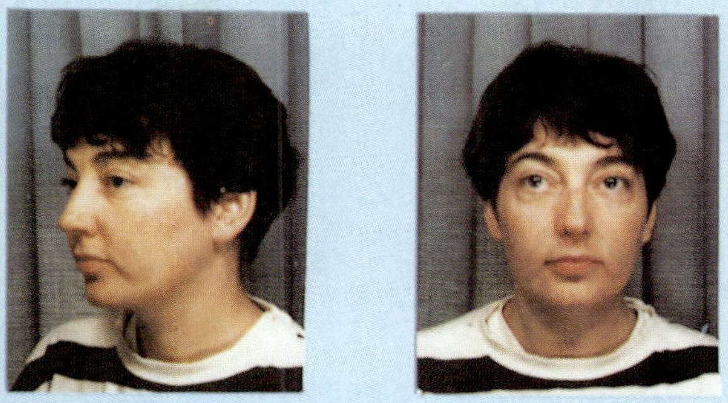

J'accuse!

Elle prend un bain tous les jours.
Elle utilise un déodorant en aérosol.
Elle a 20 sacs en plastique dans sa cuisine.
Elle mange le fast food dans des boîtes en polystyrène.
Elle a beaucoup de papier dans sa poubelle.
Elle a de vieux vêtements dans son armoire.
Elle a une voiture qui roule avec de l'essence super.

Elle est sympa!
Mais c'est une criminelle!

cahier d'activités, pages 15–17

Nous, les consommateurs

1 As-tu une bonne mémoire?
Travaille avec un/une partenaire.
Vous avez trois minutes.

La personne A regarde la photo A.
La personne B regarde la photo B.

A Une cuisine des années 30

Unité 1 *Nous, les consommateurs*

Areas of experience

A Everyday activities
C The world around us

Context

A comparison of the1930s and 1990s in terms of what we consume.

Language focus

Part I: Items in a kitchen, including: *une chaise, une table, une fenêtre, une cuisinière, un placard, une poubelle, un frigo, une horloge, une machine à laver, des étagères, des paquets, un saladier, des bols, des casseroles, des verres, des assiettes, des cuillères, des fourchettes, des couteaux. En bois, en papier, en verre, en métal, en plastique.*

Part II: *Plus de... Moins de...*

Materials

- *Livre de l'étudiant*, pages 22–23
- *Cahier d'activités*, pages 16–18
- *Cassette: Les années 30 et les années 90*
- Ten or more kitchen objects with a price tag for each.

PART I
A way in

- In the first instance you want the group to name as many things from a kitchen as they are able. Access to dictionaries will be useful for this activity. These headings should be written at the top of four columns on the board or OHT: *vaisselle, ustensiles, meubles, autres.* The group should first discover the meanings of the headings using the dictionaries. Then give them ten minutes to look back over module one and/or use the dictionaries to find and list the French for anything they might find in a kitchen: *Vous avez dix minutes pour remplir les colonnes. Vous avez le module 1 comme référence et aussi les dictionnaires.*
- The group now pools their ideas, filling in the columns on the board or OHT and ticking off their own lists. As a continuation, you might try a game like 'town, river, country' where one person calls a letter and pairs have a limited amount of time to jot down the name of a town, river and country beginning with that letter.

Change the headings to *en bois, en papier, en verre, en métal, en plastique* to fit the context of the kitchen. You will need to demonstrate the meaning of *en bois* and *en verre* by showing them objects made from each material. It will probably be a more successful activity if there is a time limit to each round and if students only have to fill in three of the headings per letter. Not all letters will be useful. You might prefer to select the letters, write them on scraps of paper, put them in a hat and ask different students to pick from the hat.

Suggested route

- *Livre de l'étudiant*, pages 22–23. This is a memory test to be done in pairs. Students take three minutes to study one of the kitchen photos each. They then take turns to cover the photo and tell their partner as much as they can about it, listing the things they can remember. The partner looks at the picture in question in order to check that what is said is correct.
- This could also lead into a dictionary activity, where students in pairs or groups list as many items as possible in one of the photos.

Cahier d'activités page 15

Les années 30 et les années 90

- The first activity is a listening activity and will be best done if students listen as many times as they need. They are asked to decide whether the person speaking would be found in a kitchen in the 1930s or 1990s.

For transcript see page **T 3**.

Answers

1 les années 90
2 les années 90
3 les années 30
4 les années 30
5 les années 90
6 les années 90

- In the next activity students look at the kitchen photos again, and record the number of objects they can see made from different materials. They then compare their findings with a partner.

Cahier d'activités page 16

- This is a writing activity to consolidate the work on the different kitchens. It should become clear that plastic was not used in the 1930s and that we now use more of some materials than others.

PART II
A way in

- This is a short section to introduce *plus* and *moins*. Bring in a selection of at least ten kitchen objects which they are likely, by now, to know the French for. Once they have named all of the objects put a different price tag on each one. Hold up two of the objects with the price showing. Make a series of comparisons using *plus* and *moins*, for example, (holding up the plate and bowl: *l'assiette coûte plus*, holding up the knife and fork: *la fourchette coûte moins*.)
- Once students are clear about the meaning of *plus* and *moins* you could try a variation on the noughts and crosses game using your kitchen objects. Draw a grid on the board filled with the numbers 1–9. Write on bits of paper pairs of objects and give each scrap a number 1–9. The group is divided into two teams. The team which starts says a number from the grid. A member of the other team chooses the scrap of paper marked with that number and reads it out. The opposing team has to say which of the two objects is more or less expensive, for example: *Le bol coûte plus* or *l'assiette coûte moins*. If they are correct the number on the grid is replaced by a nought or cross.

Cahier d'activités page 17

- This page completes the work of the unit asking students to think again about the materials we use now and used to use in the 1930s in the kitchen, with this colouring activity. Students finally decide what materials we use more of and less of now than in the 1930s.

Follow-up ideas

- Students could set up similar memory games with other pairs of pictures of rooms.
- Other colour-coding activities could be devised, using a number of different drawings.

CK 3
CK 4

IT suggestions

- Using CK3 and CK4, students could explore kitchen evolution from the 1930s to the 1990s. For example: *il y a un frigo/il n'y a pas de frigo*. You could also devise activities where students press items for basic vocabulary, or press items to discover who in a family does what and when.
- Using a package such as *Quelle Tête* and *Jeu des Ménages*, students could practise arranging furniture in a house and revise household vocabulary.
- Using WP or DTP, students could devise data collection forms entitled *LA CUISINE*, in order to check which gadgets people have in their homes. They could also interview older relatives and neighbours to ask what gadgets were available in the 1930s.
- Using a graphics package, scanned images or cut and paste, students could design and label a 1990s or 1930s kitchen for wall display.

Après trois minutes ...

2 Couvre ta photo.
Parle avec ton/ta partenaire.
Qu'est-ce qu'il y a sur ta photo?

Exemple:

B Une cuisine des années 90

cahier d'activités, pages 18–19

Les ressources naturelles

1 Regarde le cycle.
C'est la vie d'une boîte de Coca.
Quel est le bon ordre des phrases?

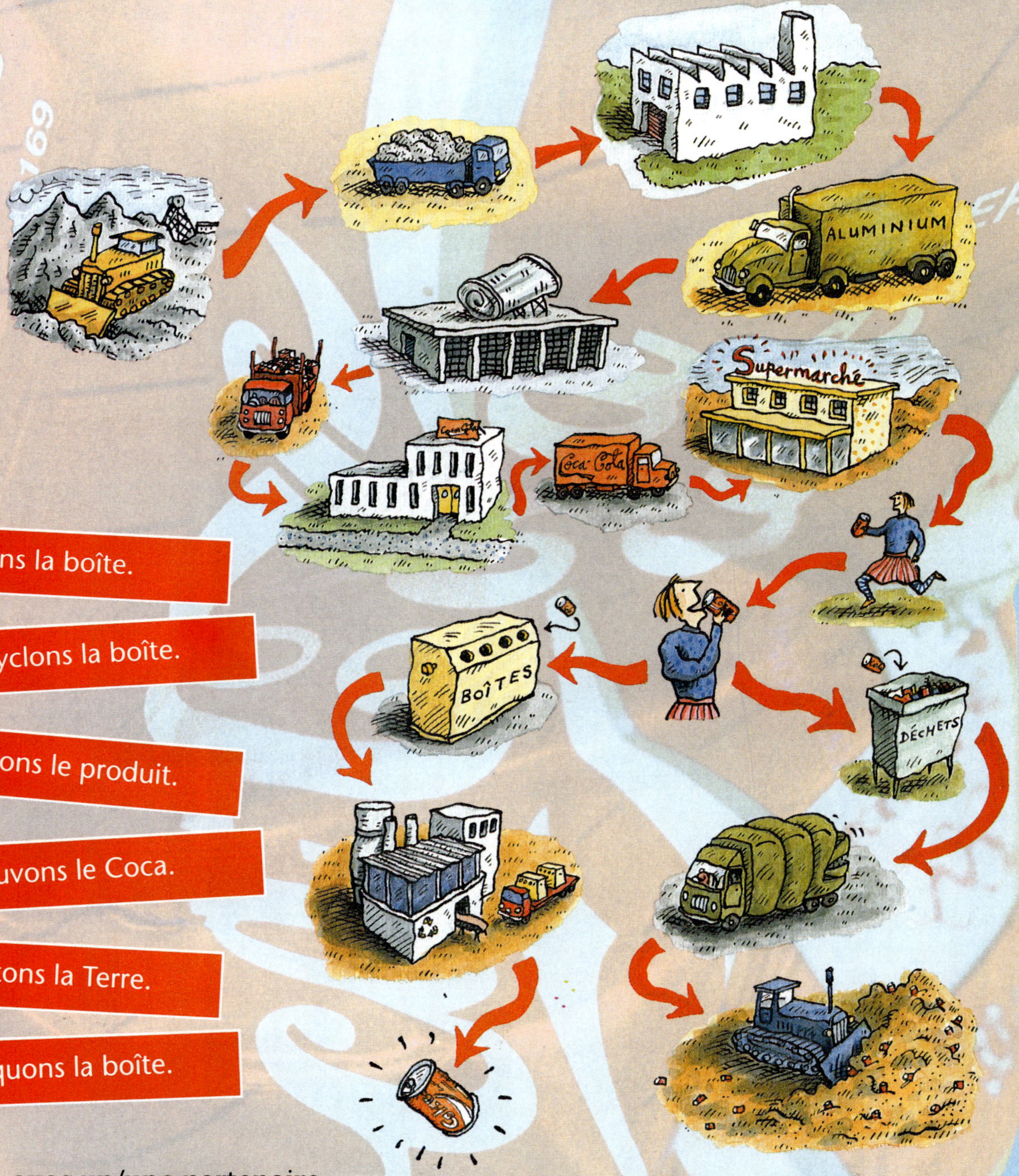

Nous jetons la boîte.

Nous recyclons la boîte.

Nous achetons le produit.

Nous buvons le Coca.

Nous exploitons la Terre.

Nous fabriquons la boîte.

2 Travaille avec un/une partenaire.
Comparez vos idées.

3 Ecoute la cassette.
Tu as choisi le bon ordre?

Unité 2 *Les ressources naturelles*

Areas of experience

C The world around us
E The world of communications and technology
G The world of imagination and creativity

Context

A consideration of the number of natural resources we use, why we need each resource, which resources are essential and which are not.

Language focus

Part I: *on a besoin de ...* (+ noun)*pour ...* (+ noun). *L'eau, l'électricité, le papier, le métal, le verre. C'est essentiel, assez important, pas du tout important.*

Part II: *nous plantons, nous exploitons, nous fabriquons, nous transportons, nous achetons, nous jetons, nous recyclons, nous buvons, nous lisons, nous coupons. Protégeons, sauvons, économisons, disons, aimons, défendons.*

Materials

- *Livre de l'étudiant*, pages 24–25
- *Cahier d'activités*, pages 18–19
- *Cassette: La vie d'une boîte de Coca; La vie d'un journal; Des jeunes dans la rue*
- Cooking ingredients (or pictures of the same): eggs, sugar, flour, butter, salt, pepper and milk.
- 8 Repromaster 8

PART I
A way in

- Use recipes to present the structure *on a besoin de* (+ noun). Present the group with a set of ingredients. They must guess what dish the ingredients are for. The ingredients for a cake are useful to begin with since you can use different combinations of the same ingredients to make many other things, for example:

– *On a besoin de deux œufs, de sucre, de farine et de beure pour quoi faire?* (answer: *un gâteau*).
– *On a besoin de farine, de sel, d'un œuf, de lait et de beurre pour quoi faire*? (answer: *des crêpes*).
– *On a besoin de deux œufs, de sel, de poivre, de beurre et de lait pour quoi faire*? (answer: *une omelette*).
– *On a besoin de farine, de sel, d'un œuf, de lait et de beurre pour quoi faire*? (answer: *le Yorkshire pudding*).

- Get the students to feed back the language by giving them the name of the dish and they say the ingredients. If this is a team game a mistake means no point is gained. You will also need more than these four lists of ingredients.

Suggested route

- R 8 Widen the idea of need with the illustrated examples on repromaster 8. Use some of the following language: *un poisson a besoin d'eau, un oiseau a besoin de vers, une fleur a besoin de lumière, une voiture a besoin d'essence, un moteur a besoin d'huile, un bébé a besoin de lait. Et le reste de la race humaine? On a besoin de quoi?*

- Ask students to think of things that we need to conduct our lives the way we do, encouaging them to ask for French words which they do not know or to use a dictionary. You might use the world of advertising to start them off tongue-in-cheek: *On a besoin de Lucozade pour avoir de l'énergie, on a besoin de cornflakes pour les vitamines, on a besoin de Mentadent P pour avoir de belles dents.*

Cahier d'activités page 18

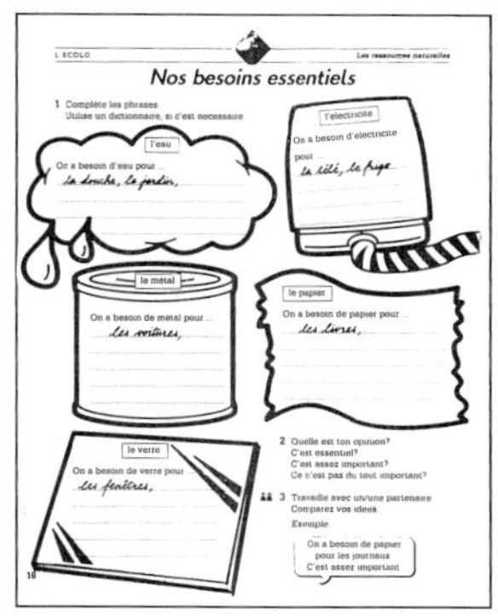

- This page develops the theme of our needs in a written exercise, which asks students to consider whether some resources are more essential than others.

PART II
A way in

- Introduce a variety of verbs through work on all of the things we do which exploit the earth compared with the things we do which benefit it. Draw two columns on board, with the headings: *BENEFICES* and *EXPLOITATION*.

Give students a statement and ask them to say whether it's something that exploits or benefits the earth: *Je vais vous donner une phrase. Décidez si c'est bon ou mauvais pour la Terre.* Here are some statements you could use; they include language that will be needed in subsequent exercises:

nous plantons des arbres
nous recyclons le papier
nous cultivons la terre
nous coupons les arbres
nous polluons l'eau
nous polluons l'air
nous jetons les ordures
nous recyclons le métal
nous recyclons le verre

Write the statements up as you go or have them ready prepared for the OHT.

- *Livre de l'étudiant*, page 24. As students look at the life cycle of the Coke can and decide on the correct order for the sentences, they should be encouraged to use a dictionary to look up unknown verbs. You could point out to them, as in **Mistral 1**, that they are unlikely to find the verb exactly as it is spelt on this page. They must find the first half of the word in the dictionary and then make assumptions about its meaning depending on the context of the word. *'Nous buvons'* is given in the *Lexique* as it is so irregular.

The correct sequence of the cycle is on cassette, so that students can listen and check their answers.

For transcript see page **T 3**.

Answers

Nous exploitons la Terre.
Nous fabriquons la boîte.
Nous achetons le produit.
Nous buvons le Coca.
Nous jetons la boîte.
Nous recyclons la boîte.

- With some groups, you might like to talk through the cycle in more detail, following the art work on the page, and pointing out the two possible versions: recycling or landfill.

Cahier d'activités page 19

- This page asks students to work out another consumer cycle, this time the life cycle of a newspaper. Students should work out the order of the cycle – they can cut out the phrases and place them on the page. The answers are on cassette, so that answers can be checked before the cycle is stuck down.

For transcript see page **T 3**.

Answers

Nous plantons les arbres.
Nous coupons les arbres.
Nous transportons les arbres au moulin.
Nous fabriquons du papier.
Nous transportons le papier chez l'imprimeur.
Nous achetons le journal.
Nous lisons le journal.
Nous jetons le journal.
Nous recyclons le journal.

- *Livre de l'étudiant*, page 25. This looks at environmental protection posters. First, students match the captions to the the posters.

Answers

A: Défendons la Terre!
B: Aimons les animaux!
C: Disons NON à la pollution!
D: Economisons l'eau!
E: Protégeons la forêt!
F: Sauvons la couche d'ozone!

- Students then listen to the cassette and work out what the demonstrators are shouting. Answers could be given in French or English.

For transcript see page **T 3**.

Answers

1 Non aux armes!
2 Défendons les animaux!
3 Sauvons nos rivières!
4 Non à la pollution!
5 Protégeons notre ville!

- Students are then asked to design their own environmental protection posters:
  – They could provide new designs for the captions on *Livre de l'étudiant*, page 25.
  – They could provide posters for the demonstrators on the cassette.
  – There are also further ideas for posters on the double-page spread at the beginning of the module; pages 20–21.

Students might like to pool ideas before starting this activity and they should be encouraged to keep slogans very simple. They will probably want to use you as a language resource.

Follow-up ideas

- Students design their own art work and text for the work on our needs, using repromaster 8 for inspiration. **R 8**
- A display of environmental protection posters designed by the group. You might like to leave this until the end of the module.
- Students research and work out a life cycle of a different product that we consume and take for granted.

IT suggestions

CK 5

- Using CK5, devise a reinforcement exercise to practise: *On a besoin de... pour...*
- Using WP or DTP, students could devise an advertising campaign by choosing a popular product and using the expression: *On a besoin de... pour...*
- Using WP, DTP and graphics or scanned images, students could design posters with slogans explaining how we are destroying the earth and/or what we can do to save the environment.
- Students could also use a WP or DTP, combined with graphics to illustrate the life cycle of a product.

1 Regarde les posters.
Quel slogan va avec quel poster?

Protégeons la forêt!

Economisons l'eau!

Sauvons la couche d'ozone!

Disons NON à la pollution!

Défendons la Terre!

Aimons les animaux!

2 Ecoute la cassette.
Il y a des jeunes dans la rue.
Qu'est-ce qu'ils crient?

3 Ecris un slogan et dessine un poster.
Regarde les pages 20–21 pour d'autres idées.

cahier d'activités, pages 20–21

Le recyclage

1 Regarde cette décharge publique.
Qu'est-ce qu'on peut recycler?
Qu'est-ce qu'on ne peut pas recycler?

2 Ecoute la cassette.
Des étudiants parlent de ce qu'on peut recycler.
Tu es d'accord avec les étudiants?

Unité 3 *Le recyclage*

Areas of experience

A Everyday activities
C The world around us

Context

Recycling: what can and can't be recycled. The benefits of recycling.

Language focus

La décharge publique. On peut recycler (+ noun). *On ne peut pas recycler* (+ noun). *Le papier, les poubelles, le plastique, le verre, les journaux, le métal, les boîtes, les bouteilles, les vêtements, les sacs. Le recyclage économise/protège/réduit.*

Materials

- *Livre de l'étudiant*, pages 26–27
- *Cahier d'activités*, pages 20–21
- *Cassette: La décharge publique*
- Examples of household rubbish (bottles, cans, newspapers, yoghurt pots, jars, clothes, rags, tea leaves, aerosols, stamps, coins, foil, tights)

A way in

- To introduce the idea of recycling, show students the British recycling sign:

Ask students to explain what they think it is: *Qu'est-ce que c'est?* They are likely to reply in English but give them the French once they have recognized it: *Oui, c'est le symbole de recyclage.*

- Show alternatives for different kinds of recycling and ask what is to be recycled under each sign: *C'est le symbole de recyclage de quoi?* You might also at this stage point out the six glass recycling symbols on the double-page spread at the beginning of the module. (See also the follow-up ideas.)
- From a bag, tip out a selection of rubbish (for example, bottles, cans, newspapers, yoghurt pots, jars, clothes, rags, tea leaves, aerosols, stamps, coins, foil, tights). Ask if each of the items can be easily recycled: *On peut recycler les bouteilles?* Expect monosyllabic answers. As a revision point from the last unit you might point out that plastic is difficult to recycle. Ask what recyclable material might be used instead for different household objects, for example wood, glass, paper.

Suggested route

- *Livre de l'étudiant*, page 26. Students are asked to look at the refuse tip and decide which things can be recycled and which cannot. They should then work with a partner and compare notes.
- Students then listen to the class discussion about recycling, and should check that they agree that the same things can be recycled.

For transcript see page T3.

Answers

Les boîtes, les journaux, le plastique, les vêtements, les bouteilles, le métal.

- *Livre de l'étudiant*, page 27. As a preparation for the activity on Luc's homework, put the following trigger phrases on the board or OHT. This should focus students' attention on the meaning of what he has written. They should read the passage and complete the sentences:

Recycling saves...
Recycling protects...
Recycling saves...
Recycling reduces...
Recycling reduces...

Cahier d'activités page 20

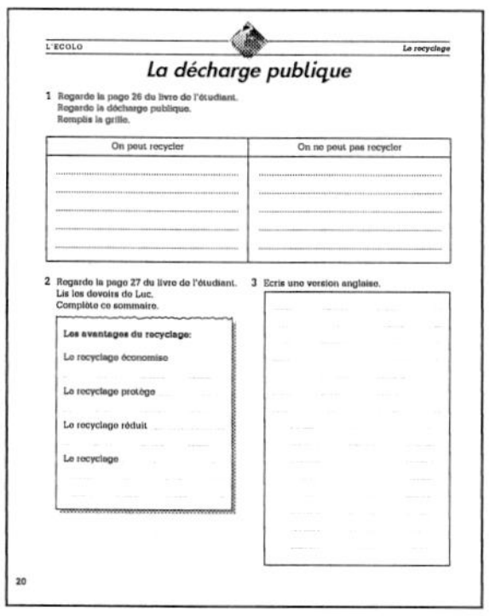
L'ECOLO   *Le recyclage*

La décharge publique

1 Regarde la page 26 du livre de l'étudiant.
Regarde la décharge publique.
Remplis la grille.

On peut recycler	On ne peut pas recycler

2 Regarde la page 27 du livre de l'étudiant.
Lis les devoirs de Luc.
Complète ce sommaire.

Les avantages du recyclage:
Le recyclage économise
Le recyclage protège
Le recyclage réduit
Le recyclage

3 Ecris une version anglaise.

20

- This page is designed to reinforce language already met in this unit, and to encourage the use of the dictionary. Students complete the lists on what you can and can't recycle, and then complete the French and English summaries of Luc's homework on recycling.

Answers

On peut recycler les boîtes, les journaux, le plastique, les vêtements, les bouteilles, le métal.
On ne peut pas recycler les machines à laver, les frigos, etc.

Les avantages du recyclage.
Le recyclage économise des ressources naturelles.
Le recyclage protège l'environnement.
Le recyclage réduit la pollution.
Le recyclage économise l'énergie. Le recyclage réduit les ordures. Le recyclage a beaucoup d'avantages!

Cahier d'activités page 21

L'ECOLO — Nous, les consommateurs

Sondage du recyclage

Qui recycle quoi dans ta classe?
Fais un sondage.
Pose des questions et note les réponses.

Exemple:
Vous recyclez les bouteilles à lait?

Vous recyclez ...?	oui (✓)/non (✗)	total ✓	total ✗
les bouteilles à lait			
les pots à confitures			
les bouteilles à vin			
les journaux ou les magazines			
les boîtes de conserve			
les bouteilles en plastique			
les sacs en plastique			
les vêtements			
les timbres			
les pièces de monnaie			
le papier d'aluminium			

Nombre de personnes interviewées: ....

21

- This is a survey to investigate who in the group recycles what. The trigger question will probably need some choral repetition before students begin their interviews.

Follow-up ideas

- To go with the different glass recycling symbols which feature in the double-page spread you might use the idea of symbol design bearing in mind the variety of places that the symbol might appear. Lots of detail is probably inappropriate. Symbols are usually bold, simple and memorable: *Voici les symboles des dépots de verre usagé de différents pays: la Grande-Bretagne, l'Irlande, la Belgique, la France, l'Allemagne, les Pays-Bas. Dessine un symbole européen pour le recyclage de matériaux différents.*

You might point out that plastics recycling is fairly a recent development. Can they therefore invent a symbol for it? Or even invent symbols for the different plastics which might be recycled – bottles, bags, pots etc. (There are fifty different types of plastic!)

- Follow up the survey on recycling. Work out which item is recycled most. Put the items in order of popularity for recycling. Work out the percentage of people that recycle each item and make a graph of the results.

IT suggestions

- Using WP or DTP and graphics or cut and paste, students could create a short article on items which are recyclable.
- Students could design data collection forms for a recycling survey in their neighbourhood or for their twin school to complete and return.
- Create a database with simple field names of objects which are recyclable (for example: *bouteilles, boîtes*, etc.) and enter data as appropriate. Findings (on who recycles what) could then be divided into neighbourhood provision or differences in provision in this country and abroad.
- Students could use a graphics package to design European recycling symbols.

3 Luc a fait du travail sur le recyclage. Lis ses devoirs.

Le recyclage et moi

Le recyclage

On sait que le recyclage est important. Mais pourquoi?

Le recyclage économise des ressources naturelles: le pétrole, les arbres, les minéraux. Chez nous, nous recyclons le papier et les boîtes.

Le recyclage protège l'environnement.

Le recyclage économise l'énergie. Chez nous, nous avons des produits recyclés: le papier hygiénique, les sacs en plastique...

Le recyclage réduit la pollution. Si on utilise moins d'énergie, on fait moins de pollution.

Le recyclage réduit les ordures. Chez nous, nous recyclons le verre, le métal, le papier et les ordures végétales.

Le recyclage a beaucoup d'avantages!

Les amis de la Terre

1 Ecoute la cassette.
Lis la fable de Bouffe-Tout.

La dernière aventure de Bouffe-Tout

Unité 4 *Les amis de la Terre*

Areas of experience
C The world around us
G The world of imagination and creativity

Context
Environmental fables: Bois-Tout, the oil-drinking creature, and Bouffe-Tout, the tree-eating machine, and a song on the environment. Stimuli for creative work.

Language focus
Revision of key language from the previous units. Present tense, in preparation for story telling/writing.

Materials
- *Livre de l'étudiant*, pages 28–29
- *Cahier d'activités*, page 22
- *Cassette: Bois-Tout; La dernière aventure de Bouffe-Tout; L'écocide*
- Repromaster 9

A way in
- Photocopy *Cahier d'activités* page 22 onto OHT and cut out each picture. Using the OHP and mime, where appropriate, tell the story of Bois-Tout, the greedy oil-drinking creature, gradually building up the story with the pictures. It is important that you tell rather than read the story aloud since telling involves the listener much more. A version of the story is recorded onto the cassette to help non-specialist teachers, and could also be used with small groups for reinforcement work. (See page T3). Tell this story, or a similar one:

– Voici Bois-Tout, le personnage principale de l'histoire. Il s'appelle Bois-Tout parce qu'il boit beaucoup. Sa boisson préférée n'est pas le Coca, non, ni le whisky, ni la bière, ni le thé. Non! Sa boisson préférée, c'est le pétrole. Mm... Il adore ça! Il boit le pétrole de la Terre. Il y a des gisements de pétrole partout. Voilà un puits. Il y entre et il boit le pétrole. Il murmure, "J'ai soif... Mmmmiam, mmmiam, slurp, slurp. Comme c'est délicieux!"

De loin il voit un autre puits. Il s'approche. Il entre dans le puits et il boit le pétrole. Il boit des millions de litres de pétrole. Il pousse et il pousse. Il devient gros... Très très gros. Il devient énorme, archi-énorme.

Le temps passe. Un jour il s'approche d'un puits mais le gisement de pétrole est très petit. Il s'approche d'un autre puits, et le gisement de pétrole est minuscule. Il a soif. Il n'y a plus de pétrole. Bois-Tout devient de plus en plus faible. Il n'y a plus de pétrole à boire. Le pauvre Bois-Tout! Maintenant il est mort.

- After every three pictures students should recap the events so far trying to remember any of the language you used to tell the story. They might contribute one word, one phrase or a whole sentence. The idea is that they work together as a group to reconstruct the story. You may decide to write key words on the board but you should avoid writing whole sentences at this stage. As you tell the story you may decide to elaborate so that the students are receiving much more language than they actually need to tell the basic story.
- Once you have told the whole story, split the class into groups. These groups may write any notes they like. They have to think back over the story and remember how you told it in as much detail as possible.

  After a set amount of preparation time you start the feedback game. Each group in turn can give a word, a phrase or a whole sentence from the story which must follow on from the previous group. A correct response wins one Smartie (!) (or your preferred reward) for the group. Any group may challenge by adding a detail which has been missed and a correct challenge, une correction, is worth one Smartie. Groups should be encouraged to control the collection of their Smarties to deter greedy members!
- It is at this stage that you might decide to give them access to some of the written phrases. Ask groups to choose a picture and the rest of the class must recall any words or phrases from that picture. You write up the language they contribute.

  Depending on the ability of the group you may decide to write up whole sentences so that the writing activity in the *Cahier d'activités* is a sorting and copy-writing activity. Some groups will be able to manage the caption writing with just a selection of phrases on the board. This will obviously give more freedom for interpretation.

Suggested route

Cahier d'activités page 22

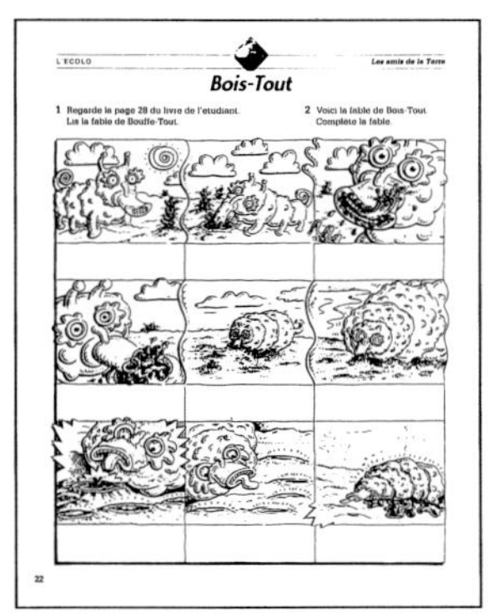

- Following on from the above sequence students write the story of Bois-Tout. You may like to discuss with them, probably in English, the moral of the story.
- *Livre de l'étudiant*, pages 28–29. This is another environmental story with a moral (*La nature prend toujours sa revanche*). The story of Bouffe-Tout, the greedy tree-eating machine, is also on cassette. You may prefer to begin the unit with this and follow it with the above sequence.

  For transcript see page T4.
- *Livre de l'étudiant*, page 29. This song can be found on cassette and is intended as listening for pleasure. Students should be encouraged to listen as many times as they wish.

R9 The words and a translation can be found on repromaster 9. You may prefer to use this as a reading comprehension activity by cutting up the different lines or verses of the song. The students then listen and put the lines or the verses in order. They then match the French lines or verses with the English.

Follow-up ideas

- If the group takes to the idea of story writing students might like to work on some stories of their own for presentation to younger pupils. This means that they must use very simple language, short sentences and illustrations. They could use the story board idea on *Cahier d'activités*, page 22 of **Mistral 1**. Show any successful stories to your younger learners.
- Students could tell the story of Bouffe-Tout, using the cassette for inspiration! They could record their own versions onto cassette. They could also do the same for Bois-Tout.

IT suggestions

- Using an authoring package such as *Fun with Texts*, you could write part of one of the environmental fables, and students could unjumble the story.
- Using WP or DTP, students could write out one of the fables for wall display or try making up their own simple moral story, poem, or song on the dangers of pollution, for younger pupils.
- Using E-mail, students could exchange and edit stories, and/or devise different endings.

2 Ecoute la cassette.
C'est une chanson sur l'environnement.

L'écocide

On dit que la forêt partout disparaît,
On dit que la Terre perd ses poumons,
On dit que la mer devient une poubelle,
Et qu'on tue les dauphins en tuant les thons.

On dit qu'il existe un trou dans l'ozone,
On dit quand il pleut, il pleut de l'acide,
On dit que le monde est tombé malade,
Et voilà comment on fait l'écocide.

Tant pis! N'oublie pas:
Nous sommes riches,
Nous sommes riches,
Et je m'en fiche,
Car nous sommes riches!

On dit qu'on fabrique trop de voitures,
On dit que les puits de pétrole s'épuisent,
On dit qu'on a faim dans un pays lointain,
On dit que la Ville des Anges est en crise.

Tant pis! N'oublie pas:
Nous sommes riches,
Nous sommes riches,
Et je m'en fiche,
Car nous sommes riches!

Nous sommes riches,
Nous sommes riches,
Et je m'en fiche,
Car nous sommes riches!

cahier d'activités, pages 23–24

Quiz éco

Travaille dans un groupe de quatre personnes.
La personne A est l'arbitre.
(Va à la page 76).
Les personnes B, C et D sont les joueurs.

Il faut quinze trombones par personne.

Voici comment jouer:

1. L'arbitre pose les questions.
2. Choisis une réponse.
3. Mets **un** trombone, si tu n'es pas très sûr/sûre.
4. Mets **deux** trombones, si tu es sûr/sûre.
5. Mets **trois** trombones, si tu es absolument sûr/sûre.
6. L'arbitre donne la réponse.
7. Tu gagnes? Prends tous les trombones.

1. Quel est le total des ordures produites par un bébé en un an?
2. Quel est le total des ordures produites par un Européen en une vie?
3. Quel est le pourcentage de l'eau par rapport à la Terre?
4. Quel est le nombre de poubelles remplies par un Britannique en un an?
5. Quel est le nombre d'arbres consommés pour le papier par un Français en un an?
6. Quel est le total des boîtes de conserve jetées en un an, par personne?
7. Quel est le total des bouteilles jetées en un an par personne?
8. Quel est le nombre de kilos de plastique jetés en un an par personne?
9. La couche d'ozone est à combien de kilomètres de la Terre?
10. Quelle est la date de la découverte du trou dans la couche d'ozone?
11. Il y a combien d'arbres affectés par la pluie acide en Grande-Bretagne par an?
12. Combien d'espèces de fleurs ont disparu entre 1900 et 1992?
13. Une chasse d'eau consomme combien de litres d'eau?
14. Un bain consomme combien de litres d'eau?
15. Une douche consomme combien de litres d'eau?

Unité 5 *Quiz éco*

Areas of experience

A Everyday activities
B Personal and social life
C The world around us

Context

Ecological facts.

Language focus

Numbers, weights, volume and distance (*kilos, litres, kilomètres*). Revision of key vocabulary from previous units.

Materials

- *Livre de l'étudiant*, pages 30–31
- *Cahier d'activités*, pages 23–24
- *Cassette: Quiz éco*
- A box of paper clips for use as counters
- Tape measures, metre rules, trundle wheel and calculators from the Maths department
- 10 Repromaster 10

A way in

- 10 The following activity enables students to use some mathematics as well as their language skills. It is an environmental observation activity to find out what percentage of the school site is green ie given over to flower beds, garden tubs, playing fields etc. You will obviously choose not to do this if your school has no green area whatsoever. Repromaster 10 is available for this task.

First discuss the boundaries of the site with the group. Either sketch the shape of the site on the board or OHT:

Le collège a (quatre) côtés A, B, C, D. On va calculer le pourcentage de la surface qui est verte (le terrain de sport, la pelouse, les jardins, les grands pots de fleurs, le bassin etc.) Copiez le plan et marquez les différentes parties. Par exemple, voici les bâtiments et ça c'est le jardin, et voilà les courts de tennis.

You should begin to mark in the areas on your plan on OHT; students then carry on for themselves, using rough paper, or repromaster 10.

If possible the group should now go and measure the different green areas. Divide the class into groups and give each group a different area to measure. Make sure they have paper and pens and discuss how they are going to record the information, what equipment they are going to use (tape measure, metre rule or trundle wheel): *Vous avez besoin de stylos et de papier. Prenez un mètre à ruban, un mètre ou une roue à lanterne* (trundle wheel). *On va le mesurer en millimètres, centimètres, mètres ou kilomètres?* When they return they must work out the area of their section using a calculator.

To find the area of a rectangle multiply the length by the width. To find the area of a circle 3 x radius x radius (beware of students doubling the radius and multiplying by three). Once they are back in the classroom with all of the information, they should find the total of all the green areas, and the percentage of green on the school site.

If there are unusual shapes involved ask the Maths department for advice to find out what you can expect these students to cope with. It is also worth checking if they have already done this sort of activity with these students and if they therefore already have the data.

- As a follow-up you might get students to write up their experience, probably in English, for display in or near the Maths department.

Suggested route

Cahier d'activités page 23

L'ECOLO — Quiz éco

Eau Mistral

1 Tu utilises combien de litres d'eau?

Une douche consomme 50 litres d'eau.	Un bain consomme 200 litres d'eau.	Une chasse d'eau consomme 11 litres d'eau.

2 Prends une calculatrice.
Calcule combien de litres tu consommes par semaine.

Nombre de bains par semaine = ... x 200 litres = ... litres
Nombre de douches par semaine = ... x 50 litres = ... litres
Nombre de chasses d'eau par semaine = ... x 11 litres = ... litres
Total d'eau utilisée par semaine = ... litres

3 Es-tu extravagant/extravagante si tu compares avec le reste de la classe?
Rassemble les résultats de la classe.

bains	douches	chasses d'eau

Total d'eau = ... ÷ Nombre dans le groupe = ... Moyenne = ...

Tu utilises plus que la moyenne pour les bains? oui/non
Tu utilises plus que la moyenne pour les douches? oui/non
Tu utilises plus que la moyenne pour les chasses d'eau? oui/non

Et ta famille?
Vous utilisez combien de litres d'eau par semaine? ....

23

- You may decide not to do the above activity, in which case go straight into this activity which asks students to calculate the amount of water they use in a week. This also requires using mathematical skills; use the Maths department for advice if you are unsure.
- *Livre de l'étudiant*, pages 30–31. This is a game to test or extend students' general knowledge about environmental matters. They should be encouraged to look carefully at the statements in the game before they start, using dictionaries where necessary but also taking into account words they have already met and the picture cue beside each statement.
- The game is a betting game which students play in groups of four. One of the group acts as the referee and holds the questions and the answers. There are four possible answers to each question. The idea is for students to bet on the answer they think is most likely, using paper clips as counters. After each bet is laid the referee gives the answer and the person who has placed his/her counters on the correct square wins all of the counters placed in that round. If two students bet on the right answer they halve the winnings. If more than two people bet on the right answer the winnings are held over until the next round.

The instructions as to how to play the game, as well as the questions with all the possible answers have been recorded onto cassette, to provide support if needed.

For transcript see page T 4.

Cahier d'activités page 24

- This is a French style cross-word in which all of the clues are environmental.

Answers

	1	2	3	4	5	6	7	8	9	10	11	12	13	14	15
1						D	E	C	H	A	R	G	E		
2							A				E				
3							V				C	O	C	A	
4	T	E	R	R	E						Y				P
5		C							E		C		M		L
6		O				P			N		L		E		A
7	E	N	V	I	R	O	N	N	E	M	E	N	T		S
8		O				L			R		R		A		T
9		M				L			G				L		I
10		I				U			I						Q
11		S				T			E			V			U
12		E		B	O	I	T	E				E			E
13		R		O		O				F	O	R	E	T	
14				I		N						R			
15				S				P	O	U	B	E	L	L	E

IT suggestions

- Using WP or DTP, students could make up a simple quiz for younger pupils, perhaps in the form of a WP or DTP quiz sheet which could be sold and small prizes offered.
- Using a simple database, results of the survey could be set up and bar graphs produced.
- All results could be produced using IT and displayed around the school to promote environmental awareness issues.

I Z E C O Q U I Z E C O	A	B	C	D
	20 kg	200 kg	250 kg	500 kg
	300 tonnes	450 tonnes	650 tonnes	655 tonnes
	40%	50%	71%	70%
	50	100	75	85
	1	2	3	4
	90	30	200	10
	50	plus de 100	40	30
	6	25	45	15
	18–48 kilomètres	12–15 kilomètres	5–10 kilomètres	2–4 kilomètres
	1922	1968	1985	1840
	200 millions	450 millions	2 millions	2,000
	20	5	17	19
	12 litres	20 litres	11 litres	15 litres
	200 litres	40 litres	50 litres	100 litres
	200 litres	40 litres	50 litres	100 litres

Q U I Z E C O Q U I Z E C O Q U I Z E C O Q U I Z E C O Q U I Z E C O Q U I Z E C O Q U I

Contrôle 2

Ecris tes réponses dans ton cahier d'activités, page 57

A

Ecoute la cassette.
Denise et Patricia parlent de Jacques.
Jacques n'est pas écolo. Pourquoi?
Donne cinq raisons en anglais.

Exemple: He doesn't go to Friends of the Earth meetings.

B

Lis les slogans.
Choisis le bon symbole.

Exemple: **6 = A**

A B C D E F G H

Contrôle 2

NOTE

A

1 ....

2 ....

3 ....

4 ....

5 ....

See answers overleaf

5

B

1 C	2 D	3 B	4 E	5 G

5

C

Journal parlé

See guidelines overleaf

5

D

1 Pour les journaux: ....

2 Pour la douche: ....

3 Pour les bouteilles: ....

4 Pour les voitures: ....

5 Pour les lampes: ....

See guidelines overleaf

5

OBSERVATIONS

TOTAL

Date:

Signature de l'étudiant:

Signature du professeur:

20

CASSETTE 1 FACE 2

Contrôle 2
Livre de l'étudiant, page 32
Cahier d'activités, page 57

- Tu es copine avec Jacques, toi?
- Oui, moi je le trouve sympa! Pas toi?
- Ben... non... Je ne l'aime pas beaucoup! Il n'est pas écolo du tout, tu sais. Pas comme toi, ou moi.
- Ah bon? Jacques n'est pas écolo? Ça alors! Jacques n'est pas écolo! Pourquoi tu dis ça?
- Ecoute, d'abord, il jette ses papiers de chewing-gum par terre! Ce n'est pas très bien...
- Oui, d'accord. Tiens, c'est vrai, il ne vient pas à la réunion des Amis de la Terre aujourd'hui.
- Exactement! Il préfère regarder le foot à la télé! Et puis... Il va au Fast Food et il achète des frites dans des boîtes en plastique! Et il jette la boîte par terre!
- Il jette la boîte par terre!?
- Oui! Il jette la boîte par terre. Et il jette sa boîte de Coca par terre aussi!
- Hé ben!
- Il achète des aérosols aussi. Il ne pense pas à la couche d'ozone!
- Il achète des aérosols!
- En plus, il ne recycle pas ses journaux!

Answers to task A

Any five of the following:

He throws his chewing-gum wrappers on the ground.
He buys chips in plastic cartons.
He throws the cartons on the ground.
He throws Coca-Cola tins on the ground.
He buys aerosols.
He doesn't think of the ozone layer.
He doesn't collect his newspapers for recycling.

Speaking task guidelines (task C)

Ideally, these contributions will be recorded onto a student's own individual tape which may also included other items from the course. Otherwise a class tape on which all students record their answers could be used.

A mark should be awarded for each relevant utterance understood by the listener. Here is some guidance as to what the speaker may be expected to say:

Tu recycles le papier?
Tu recycles le métal?
Tu as combien de poubelles à la maison?
Tu recycles les bouteilles?
Tu recycles le plastique?
Tu achètes du papier recyclé?

Writing task guidelines (task D)

Each answer is worth one mark. The tasks are open ended so that there are no 'right' answers. Answers should be marked positively. Students should have the opportunity to refer to their books and a dictionary, to check spellings. With this in mind, if a student successfully communicates a relevant message, a mark should be awarded. A mark should not be awarded if the spelling is so awry that a sympathetic native speaker would be unlikely to understand the message.

In certain instances, where a student has severe handwriting difficulties, he/she may be offered the option of dictating and spelling out answers for you to transcribe. Similarly, answers might be word-processed and then pasted into the answer pages of the *Cahier d'activités.*

Answers to task D

Here are some possibilities:

1 le papier
2 l'eau/le métal/le plastique
3 le verre/le plastique
4 le métal/le verre
5 l'électricité/le métal/le verre

National Curriculum assessment

Task A	AT 1, level 3(b)
Task B	AT 3, level 2(a)
Task C	AT 2, level 3(a)
Task D	AT 4, level 2(b)

C

Journal parlé

Tu fais un sondage écolo.
Pose cinq questions à ton/ta partenaire.

Exemple:

D

On est tous consommateurs.
On consomme quoi?
Complète les phrases.

Exemple: Pour le papier: *le bois*

1 Pour les journaux:...
2 Pour la douche:...
3 Pour les bouteilles:...
4 Pour les voitures:...
5 Pour les lampes:...

journ|al (*pl.* **~aux**) /ʒurnal, -o/ *n.m.* (news)paper; (*spécialisé*) journal; (*intime*) diary; (*radio*) news.

bande¹ /bɑ̃d/ *n.f.* (*de papier etc.*) strip; (*rayure*) stripe; (*de film*) reel; (*radio*) band; (*pansement*) bandage. **~ (magnétique)**, tape. **~ dessinée**, comic strip.

chaîn|e /ʃɛn/ *n.f.* chain; (*de télévision*) channel. **~e de montage/fabrication**, assembly/production line. **~e hi-fi**, hi-fi system. **en ~e**, (*accidents*)

	TF1	ANTENNE 2	FR3
LUNDI	20.45 FILM TV **FAUX FRÈRE** de Vincent Martorana 22.30 MAGAZINE **SANTÉ À LA UNE LES TRAUMATISMES DE LA SEXUALITÉ**	20.45 FILM **RÉVOLUTION** de Hugh Hudson avec Al Palcino Nastassia Kinski 22.45 THÉÂTRE **BUNNY'S BAR**	20.45 FILM **LE BON ROI DAGOBERT** de Dino Risi avec Coluche 23.00 MAGAZINE **OCÉANIQUES**
MARDI	20.45 FILM **TROP BELLE POUR TOI** de Bertrand Blier avec Josiane Balasko 22.20 FILM **LA BRUTE**	20.45 FILM **L'EMPIRE DU SOLEIL** de Steven Spielberg avec John Malkovich 23.25 FILM TV **RUBY ET OSWALD**	20.45 FILM TV **LES GRENADINES** de Patrick Jamain avec Elizabeth Vitali Didier Kaminka 22.30 MAGAZINE **MARDI EN FRANCE**

8 h 10 Météo
8 h 15 Télé shopping
8 h 50 Club Dorothée vacances
11 h 30 Jeopardy
11 h 55 Tournez... manège
12 h 25 Le juste prix
12 h 55 Météo des plages
13 h Journal
13 h 20 Météo
13 h 25 Faisons la route ensemble
13 h 30 La Bourse
13 h 35 Les feux de l'amour
14 h 25 Tribunal
14 h 55 Club Dorothée vacances
16 h 55 Tiercé Quinté +
17 h Chips
17 h 50 Hawaii police d'État
18 h 35 Une famille en or
19 h 5 Santa Barbara
19 h 30 La roue de la fortune
20 h Journal

Les médias

émission /emisjɔ̃/ *n.f.* emission; (*de message*) transmission; (*de timbre*) issue; (*programme*) broadcast.

genre /ʒɑ̃r/ *n.m.* sort, kind; (*attitude*) manner; (*gram.*) gender.

vedette[1] /vədɛt/ *n.f.* (*artiste*) star. **en ~**, (*objet*) in a prominent position; (*personne*) in the limelight.

Vous vous demandez peut-être qui se cache sous ce drôle de nom : « Benny B » ? Et bien, ils sont trois, Ben, Alain et Serge et ils sont les rois du rap en France. Et vos enfants ou vos petits-enfants les connaissent bien et même, les adorent.

TÉLÉ, RADIO, JOURNAUX

QU'EN PENSEZ-VOUS?

Le petit écran a bouleversé la vie des Français

Attractive avec ses programmes variés, elle a aujourd'hui cinq chaînes. En 1950, elle en avait une. À cette époque, 297 privilégiés la possédaient. Aujourd'hui, 48 millions et demi de personnes la regardent!

C FRANKIE ET JOHNNY (Frankie and Johnny) – Amér., coul. (91). Comédie sentimentale, de Garry Marshall : A sa sortie de prison, Johnny se fait engager comme cuistot dans un snack de New York et tombe amoureux de Frankie, une serveuse qui n'entend pas devenir la femme de sa vie.

F TORTUES NINJA N° 2 (LES) (Les héros sont de retour – Teenage mutant ninja turtles II: the secret of the ooze) – Amér., coul. (90). Comédie fantastique, de Michael Pressman : Les tortues ninja n'auront pas trop de leurs profondes connaissances des arts martiaux pour venir à bout de leur vieil adversaire, Shredder, les sommant d'affronter de monstrueux mutants.

P DIVA – Franc., coul. (80). Policier, de Jean-Jacques Beineix: Les aventures d'un postier en possession de deux enregistrements pirates d'une célèbre cantatrice et d'un couple étrange formé par une jeune fille et un quadragénaire.

cahier d'activités, pages 26–27

J'♥ lire

1 Les bandes dessinées (BD) ont beaucoup de succès.

Regarde ces exemples:

A

B

2 Voici les titres des BD. Quel est le titre de A, de B et de C?

3 Ecoute la cassette. Identifie les BD.

4 Voici comment dessiner un personnage de BD.

Unité I J'♥ lire

Areas of experience
A Everyday activities
E The world of communications
G The world of imagination and creativity

Context
Investigating people's reading habits. Looking at French *bandes dessinées*. Drawing cartoons.

Language focus
Je lis, je vais, je fais, je joue, j'écoute, je regarde. Tous les jours, x fois par semaine, x fois par mois, rarement. Des journaux, des magazines, des livres, des bandes dessinées. Tu as quel âge? Tu préfères lire...? Tu lis régulièrement? Tu passes combien de temps à lire? Dans le train, à la cantine, à la maison. Revision of parts of the body.

Materials
- *Livre de l'étudiant*, pages 36–37
- *Cahier d'activités*, pages 26–27
- Cassette: *La Presse: les préférences; Les bandes dessinées*
- Small pieces of card, eight per pair of students
- 11 Repromaster 11

A way in
- Introduce the following words and phrases: *régulièrement, tous les jours, x fois par semaine, x fois par mois, rarement.* Taking the page of a calendar, showing one month, cross off on individual dates to indicate how often you do certain things, for example: *je fais des exercices, je regarde la télé, je joue au tennis, je vais au cinéma.* Differentiate between the activities, by using different colours on the calendar or by writing a key word from the statement.
- 11 Have similar statements visible on the board or on the OHT (repromaster 11): *je regarde la télé, je vais à la disco, je lis des magazines, je lis des livres, je fais mes devoirs, je fais la vaisselle, je fais mon lit, je fais du sport, je vais au cinéma, je lis des journaux, j'écoute de la musique, je fais le shopping.*

These statements might be best displayed on the wall, poster size. Each pair of students has each of the frequency words or phrases written on a card. As you say each of the activities on the list, each student chooses and holds up the card appropriate to their own experience. Repeat the activity in a number of ways: you say the number of each statement, not the whole sentence so that students have to read it for themselves; do the same at double the usual speed; ask one of the class to read out the statements as they are relevant to her/him.

- On the board, write up the infinitives of the verbs which have been used in the statements. Students look these up in dictionaries and tell you what they mean. Practise switching from the infinitives to the *je* forms of the verbs. Provide the *tu* form of each and record all this in three columns on the board: *version dans le dictionnaire/je .../tu ...*

Suggested route

Cahier d'activités page 26

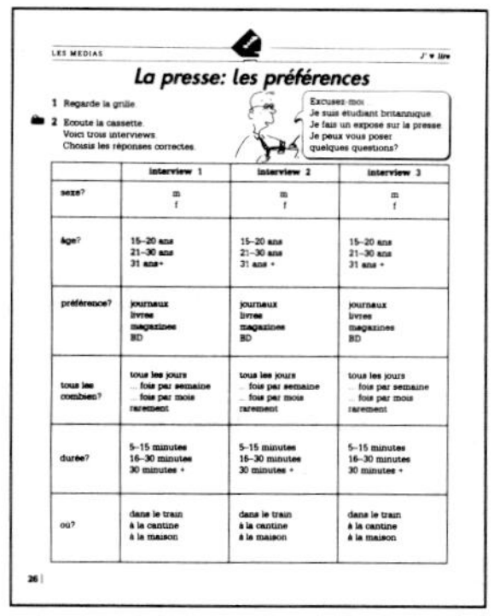
LES MEDIAS J'♥ lire

La presse: les préférences

1 Regarde la grille.
2 Ecoute la cassette. Voici trois interviews. Choisis les réponses correctes.

	interview 1	interview 2	interview 3
sexe?	m f	m f	m f
âge?	15–20 ans 21–30 ans 31 ans+	15–20 ans 21–30 ans 31 ans +	15–20 ans 21–30 ans 31 ans +
préférence?	journaux livres magazines BD	journaux livres magazines BD	journaux livres magazines BD
tous les combien?	tous les jours ... fois par semaine ... fois par mois rarement	tous les jours ... fois par semaine ... fois par mois rarement	tous les jours ... fois par semaine ... fois par mois rarement
durée?	5–15 minutes 16–30 minutes 30 minutes +	5–15 minutes 16–30 minutes 30 minutes +	5–15 minutes 16–30 minutes 30 minutes +
où?	dans le train à la cantine à la maison	dans le train à la cantine à la maison	dans le train à la cantine à la maison

26

- Students are now ready to listen to the interviews which question three people about their reading habits. Students should circle or underline the correct answers.

For transcript see page T5.

Answers
Interview 1: m; 21–30 ans; magazines; 16–30; dans le train.

Interview 2: f; 31 ans+; livres; tous les jours; 30 minutes+; à la maison.

Interview 3: f; 15–20 ans; magazines; une fois par mois; 5–15 minutes; à la maison.

Cahier d'activités page 27

LES MEDIAS J'♥ lire

Tu es journaliste

1 Tu es journaliste. Interviewe quatre personnes dans la classe.
2 Ecris les resultats dans la grille.

Voici des questions:

		Nom	Nom	Nom	Nom
	sexe?				
1	age?				
2	preference?				
3	tous les combien?				
4	duree?				
5	ou?				

27

- Students may follow up the listening activity with their own interviews of classmates, teachers, people of different ages. You may need to do a quick check of their understanding of these questions, before they begin their interviews: *Tu as quel âge? Tu préfères lire des magazines...? Tu lis régulièrement? Tu passes combien de temps à lire? Tu lis où?* Encourage students to listen to the interviewer on the cassette again, if they need more help.
- *Livre de l'étudiant*, pages 36–37. These pages provide the students' first look at some authentic French reading matter in this unit. Having looked carefully at each one, they choose the correct title for each of the cartoons.

Answers

A: Histoires de Schtroumpfs
B: Les Aventures de Tintin
C: Les Motards

The text of the cartoons, including the actions and sounds, is also on tape: listening to the transcript at any stage will help their comprehension. Students are asked to match the recordings to the correct cartoon.

Answers

1 Les Aventures de Tintin
2 Les Motards
3 Histoires de Schtroumpfs

For transcript see page **T 5**.

- Students then have the opportuinity to draw the cartoon character at the bottom of the pages, following the step-by-step instructions.

Follow-up ideas

- If they have access to any simple cartoon extracts, students could record a transcript for them.
- Make a display of the characters drawn from the instructions in the *Livre de l'étudiant.*
- Using the example in the book as a model, students may be able to provide a set of similar instructions for the drawing of one of their favourite cartoon characters. These could be produced for other classes in the school.

IT suggestions

- Using WP or DTP, students could produce data collection forms for a reading habits survey.
- They could also produce a diary page, where each day includes a certain activity, for example: *Je vais à la disco.*
- By adding graphics or using a cut-and-paste activity, students could create their own cartoon characters and story for younger pupils.

C

LES MOTARDS

ES AVENTURES DE TINTIN

Histoires de Schtroumpfs

Reportages

1 Lis les trois articles.
Quel titre correspond à quel article?

Un poulet en vol!

Un petit chien enfermé dans la machine à laver!

La drogue ou la prison? Une mère a choisi pour son fils.

Hebdo Est

Roanne, le 17 avril

Hier matin, vers dix heures, Mme Molins est entrée dans le supermarché du coin pour faire du shopping. Rien d'extra-ordinaire.

A 10h 20, Mme Molins a fait la queue à la caisse. Soudain, elle s'est sentie très malade et elle est tombée par terre.

La propriétaire du supermarché, Mme Floriot, a téléphoné au médecin. Le docteur Roissy est arrivé immédiatement et il a examiné Mme Molins. “Mme Molins avait de la difficulté à respirer et à parler. En examinant la malade, j'ai trouvé la cause principale de ses difficultés. Mme Molins tenait tout près de son cœur... un poulet congelé.”

En effet, le docteur Roissy a trouvé le poulet dans le soutien-gorge de Mme Molins. C'était un poulet congelé, première classe, qui valait 65 francs.

Vénissieux, le 18 avril

Hier matin, vers neuf heures, Aurélie Foncier a trouvé un adorable petit chien dans la rue. Aurélie a neuf ans. Le chien s'appelle Maxi.

A ce moment-là, Mme Pasteur préparait le petit déjeuner de son chien, Maxi. Mme Pasteur a bientôt découvert que son chien avait disparu!

Affolée, Mme Pasteur est descendue et elle a cherché Maxi devant l'immeuble. Mais il n'était pas là. Elle a couru dans le café du coin, mais malheureusement il n'était pas là.

Finalement, désespérée, Mme Pasteur est entrée dans la laverie automatique. Soudain, elle a entendu des jappements qui venaient... de l'intérieur de l'une des machines! C'était son Maxi! Comment cela s'est passé?

Apparemment, vers neuf heures du matin, la petite Aurélie Foncier a “kidnappé” le chien. Ensuite, elle a enfermé Maxi dans la machine à laver pour “jouer à la capsule spatiale”.

Lyon, le 18 avril

Hier après-midi, Philippe Renier, 19 ans et trafiquant de drogue, a été condamné à trois ans de prison. Ainsi s'est terminée une longue et triste histoire.

Le 11 avril, Liliane Renier, la mère de Philippe, a dénoncé son fils à la police comme revendeur de héroïne. Elle a dit: “J'ai fait ça... parce que j'adore Philippe. Voir mon fils se transformer peu à peu en zombie, c'était insupportable.”

Pour l'instant, Philippe refuse toute discussion, tout contact avec sa mère. Mais, Liliane attend le moment où elle dira à son fils: “Philippe, je t'aime.”

2 Ecoute la cassette.
Voici un bulletin à la radio.
Relis les articles.
Quel article correspond au bulletin?

Unité 2 *Reportages*

Areas of experience

E The world of communications
G The world of the imagination and creativity

Context

Investigating different sections of a newspaper, reading and writing short articles.

Language focus

Part I: Newspaper headings.
Part II: Perfect tense. Hier matin/après-midi/soir. Revision of places and personal descriptions.

Materials

- *Livre de l'étudiant*, pages 38–39
- *Cahier d'activités*, pages 28–29
- *Cassette: Bulletin à la radio; Crime ... stop!*
- Repromaster 12
- Repromaster 13
- Copies of newspapers, both in French and in English

PART I
Suggested route

Cahier d'activités page 28

- This provides students with guidance for looking at newspapers, both in English and in French. First of all, with a British paper in front of them, students pool all the possible sections that they can find, in English. For instance: weather, news in brief, international news, home news, editorials, cinema listings, TV/radio information, sport, financial news, small ads, personal ads., letters to the editor. They should write up their ideas on OHT, as they come up.
- Then, referring to a French paper, ideally one each or between two or three of them, students try to work out as many of the French equivalents as possible.

If newspapers are not available, students will need to be given the equivalent categories in French so that students can match these with the English. Once the French sections have been discovered, they should be written up alongside the equivalent English ones.

As they find any of the relevant sections, in either a French language or an English language paper, they write down the names of the categories in both languages and shade off one of the appropriate mini newspapers on the *Cahier d'activités* page.

PART II
A way in

- *Livre de l'étudiant*, page 38. Put onto OHT a blown-up version of the first article, *Roanne, le 17 avril*. Ask students for the gist of the story. Together, find the verbs and list them or highlight them on the OHT.
- Students then try to find the gist of the story in the other two articles on the page. Help them, if necessary, by putting onto board/OHT the English versions of the verbs.
- Select a sentence from one of the articles which includes an example of the perfect tense and ask students to change it as much as they can, seeing which group can change most words in the sentence and leave the sentence still making sense. Try this again if the first example is successful.

Suggested route

- Students should first match the titles to the articles.

Answers

Roanne, le 17 avril: Un poulet en vol!

Vénissieux, le 18 avril: Un petit chien enfermé dans la machine à laver!

Lyon, le 18 avril: La drogue ou la prison? Une mère a choisi pour son fils.

- Having worked through the articles in the way suggested above, students are now ready to do the listening activity.

For transcript see page T5.

Answer

Lyon, le 18 avril: La drogue ou la prison? Une mère a choisi pour son fils.

Cahier d'activités page 29

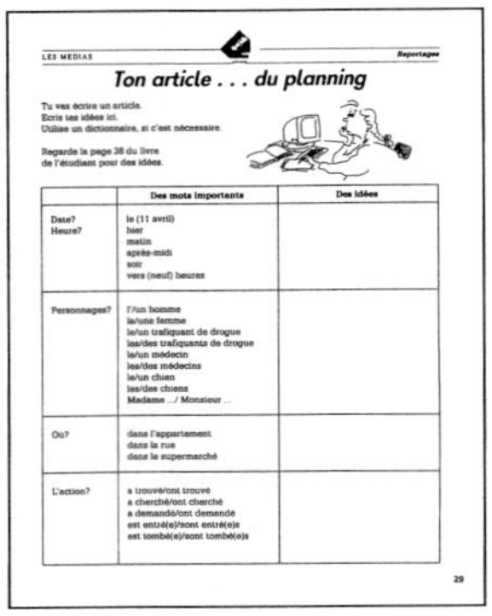
LES MEDIAS Reportages

Ton article . . . du planning

Tu vas écrire un article.
Ecris tes idées ici.
Utilise un dictionnaire, si c'est nécessaire.

Regarde la page 38 du livre de l'étudiant pour des idées.

	Des mots importants	Des idées
Date? Heure?	le (11 avril) hier matin après-midi soir vers (neuf) heures	
Personnages?	l'/un homme la/une femme le/un trafiquant de drogue les/des trafiquants de drogue le/un médecin les/des médecins le/un chien les/des chiens Madame .../ Monsieur ...	
Où?	dans l'appartement dans la rue dans le supermarché	
L'action?	a trouvé/ont trouvé a cherché/ont cherché a demandé/ont demandé est entré(e)/sont entré(e)s est tombé(e)/sont tombé(e)s	

29

- At this stage, some preparation for the writing of students' own articles might begin. Go through an example of each category on the *Cahier d'activités*, with students referring to the work already done. These lists are to be added to, as students progress through the unit.
- *Livre de l'étudiant*, page 39. This provides more reading, listening and speaking practice of the kind of language used for describing crimes. Students first look at the crime photos, then identify which photo is being talked about for each of the phone-ins on the cassette.

Answers

1 = B   2 = A   3 = A   4 = B

For transcript see page T 5.

- R 12 In the pairwork that follows, students build up a testimony, imagining they were at the scene of one of the crimes photographed above. This will be a speaking activity which may be taped. The snippets on repromaster 12 refer back to the language that has so far been practised and heard, and offers support for this activity.

- Now is an appropriate point to go back to the planning of students' own articles, with reference to *Cahier d'activités*, page 28. This is undoubtedly a challenge, though the planning page does offer the students the opportunity to think about the structure of such a piece of writing and offer them alternatives. Following the completion of each of their own planning pages, group discussion, redrafting, teacher correction and editing of the student versions will need to occur.

Follow-up ideas

- Students may find it interesting to compare different publications of magazines and newspapers in both languages in the following way: *Quelle publication britannique correspond à quelle publication française? Par exemple*:

Sunday People   *Ici Paris*

IT suggestions

- Using a package such as *Quelle Tête*, students could revise personal descriptions.
- CK 6 Using CK6, devise reinforcement activities to revise personal descriptions, for example: *il a un grand nez, une petite bouche*. You could also devise an activity where students press the pictures of criminals to discover what crimes they have committed.
- Students could use scanned images, or cut-and-paste pictures to create a wanted criminal poster.
- Using WP or DTP, students could create a simple police statement form for witnesses to complete.
- R 13 Simple articles could be produced using WP, including a spell-check facility, if available. The articles could be put onto DTP or a cut-and-paste activity could form a news sheet for students' files, sale, or wall display. The final products may be written or wordprocessed onto the formatted page: repromaster 13. This is designed to look like the page of a newspaper. Several articles may be pasted onto these pages. They could also be stuck together to look like a whole spread from a newspaper.

1 Regarde les deux reconstitutions photographiques.

2 Ecoute la cassette.
Quatre personnes ont téléphoné au studio.
La personne 1 a parlé de quelle reconstitution?
Et les personnes 2, 3 et 4?

Voici le studio de **Crime . . . Stop!**

A

Le 18 septembre
la rue Montjean

B

Le 23 septembre
la rue de la Paix

3 Travaille avec un/une partenaire.

Partenaire A: tu habites dans la rue de la Paix.
Tu as vu l'attaque du 23 septembre.
Explique tout à la police.

Partenaire B: prends des notes.

cahier d'activités, pages 30–31

Télémaniaques

1 Regarde les listes d'émissions.

2 Ecoute la cassette.
C'est un jeu.
C'est à toi de jouer!

MARDI 13 AOUT

TF1

11.55 Tournez... manège.
12.30 Le Juste Prix. *Jeu.*
13.00 Journal.
13.30 Météo.
13.35 Les Feux de l'amour.
14.25 Côte Ouest.
15.20 Tribunal.
15.55 Club Dorothée vacances. *Jeunesse.*
17.25 Texas Police.
18.10 Riviera.
18.35 Une famille en or.
19.00 Santa Barbara. *Feuilleton.*
19.30 La Roue de la fortune.
19.50 Pas folles les bêtes.
20.00 Journal.
20.30 Météo.

20.35
***CINEMA*. UN ELEPHANT ÇA TROMPE ENORMEMENT.** *Film français d'Yves Robert (1976). Avec Jean Rochefort, Claude Brasseur.*
22.25 Combien ça coûte?
23.25 Chapeau melon et bottes de cuir.

ANTENNE 2

12.00 Dessinez, c'est gagné! *Jeu.*
12.30 Les Mariés de l'A2. *Jeu.*
13.00 Journal.
13.35 Météo.
13.45 Falcon Crest. *Série.*
14.30 Le Retour du Saint. *Série.*
15.20 Privé de choc. *Série.*
16.05 Flash.
16.10 Drôles de dames. *Série.*
17.00 Giga.
18.05 Des chiffres et des lettres.
18.25 Flash.
18.30 Maguy.
19.00 Question de charme. *Jeu.*
19.30 Des jours et des vies. *Série.*
20.00 Journal.
20.35 Météo.

20.45
***CINEMA*. SOLEIL ROUGE.** *Film de Terence Young (1977). Avec Charles Bronson, Ursula Andress.*
22.35 La Vie au château. *Film de Jean-Paul Rappeneau (1965). Avec Claude Sautet, Alain Cavalier.*

FR3

12.00 Estivales. *Magazine.*
12.45 Edition nationale.
13.00 Sports 3 images.
13.30 Amuse 3 vacances.
14.40 Justiciers et hors-la-loi.
15.30 La Conquête de l'Ouest.
16.20 40°C à l'ombre.
18.30 Questions pour un champion.
19.00 19/20.
19.10 Actualités régionales.
19.30 19/20 *(suite).*
20.05 La Classe.

20.45
***CINEMA 16*. LA VIEILLE DAME ET L'AFRICAIN.** *Film 16mm d'Alain Dhouailly. Avec Danielle Darrieux, Maka Kotto.*
22.15 Soir 3.
22.35 Mardi en France.
23.30 Espace francophone.

CANAL+

12.30 Flash.
12.35 Fangio.
13.30 Le Mouton à cinq pattes. *Comédie d'Henry Verneuil (1954). Avec Fernandel.*
15.10 Jerry Lewis show.
15.45 Cherry 2000. *Film américain de science-fiction de Steve de Jarnatt (1986). Avec David Andrews, Melanie Griffith.*
17.35 Sois prof et tais-toi. *Série.*
18.00 Canaille peluche.
18.10 Tiny Toons.
18.50 Top 50.
19.30 Flash.
19.35 Les Simson.
20.00 Les Nuls, l'émission.

20.30
***CINEMA*. LE LION DU DESERT.** *Drame historique américain de Mustapha Akkad (1979). Avec Anthony Quinn, Rod Steiger.*
23.05 Flash.
0.40 Le Onzième Commandement. *Thriller américain de Paul Leder (1988). Avec Bernie White, Marilyn Hasset.*

M6

12.00 Flash.
12.10 Ma Sorcière bien-aimée.
12.35 Lassie.
13.10 Cosby Show.
13.40 Dis donc, papa.
14.05 Deux ans de vacances.
15.00 Boulevard des clips.
15.40 Bleu, blanc, clip.
16.00 Flash.
16.05 Bleu, blanc, clip *(suite).*
16.45 Hit, hit, hit, hourra!
16.50 Zygo-music.
17.20 L'Homme de fer.
18.10 Mission impossible.
19.00 La Petite Maison dans la prairie.
19.54 Flash.
20.00 Cosby Show.

20.35
***TELEFILM*. COUP DE GRISOU.** *Téléfilm américain de Walter Doniger. Avec Cheryl Ladd, Peter Weller.*
22.10 Equaliser.
23.00 Culture pub.
23.25 Soixante minutes: confession d'un tueur de la mafia.

Unité 3 *Télémaniaques*

Areas of experience

A Everyday activities
E The world of communications

Context

Television listings, watching habits and preferences. Arguments for and against watching television.

Language focus

Revision of time. *Une chaîne, une émission. C'est quel genre d'émission? Les comédies, les feuilletons, les jeux, les dessins animés, les films, les informations, les documentaires, les émissions de sciences naturelles, les émissions pour les enfants. Super, (très) bien, pas mal, lent, ennuyeux, affreux. Pour, contre.* Revision of expressions of opinion.

Materials

- *Livre de l'étudiant*, pages 40–41
- *Cahier d'activités*, pages 30–31
- Cassette: *Jeu Télé Mistral; La télé: pour ou contre?*
- 14 Repromaster 14
- 15 Repromaster 15

A way in

- 14 Using repromaster 14, introduce different types of television programmes, as listed above. Use a British programme to exemplify each type.

  After some repetition and practice, students may be shown the listings on page 40 of the *Livre de l'étudiant*: call out the name of a British programme, see if they can find a French equivalent, saying what type of programme it is.

- Then, once the understanding of each of the types is consolidated, simply call out a type of programme and ask students to offer a French example of a programme of that type. It might be useful to have the different types of programmes listed on the board or OHT. You might practise the vocabulary in a quiz format: write the names of many different British programmes on separate pieces of card, labelling each one A, B, C, D, E, F, G or H, in turn. In teams, one person at a time chooses a letter and you read out one of the cards labelled with the chosen letter: *Alors, la carte C ... c'est quel genre d'émission, 'Two of a Kind'?* If they are confident with the new French examples, add some of these also. A point is scored for each correct response: *C'est une comédie.*

Suggested route

Cahier d'activités page 30

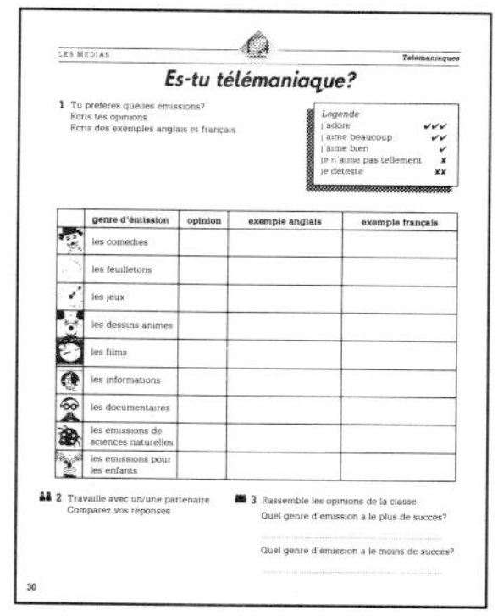
LES MEDIAS — Télémaniaques

Es-tu télémaniaque?

1 Tu préfères quelles émissions?
Ecris tes opinions.
Ecris des exemples anglais et français.

Légende
j'adore ✔✔✔
j'aime beaucoup ✔✔
j'aime bien ✔
je n'aime pas tellement ✘
je déteste ✘✘

genre d'émission	opinion	exemple anglais	exemple français
les comédies			
les feuilletons			
les jeux			
les dessins animés			
les films			
les informations			
les documentaires			
les émissions de sciences naturelles			
les émissions pour les enfants			

2 Travaille avec un/une partenaire. Comparez vos réponses.

3 Rassemble les opinions de la classe.
Quel genre d'émission a le plus de succès?
Quel genre d'émission a le moins de succès?

30

- Students are now ready to tackle this survey. They should first fill in the grid for themselves, and provide examples.

  The survey itself may be done in smaller groups. Then each group offers their own findings to the class as a whole. You collate these and students write down the most and least popular types of programmes in the class as a whole, at the bottom of the page.

- *Livre de l'étudiant*, page 40. This is a radio quiz about television programmes. Students listen to the tape which takes them through quiz questions based on the listings on this page. Included are beeps during which students should reply. If they answer the question before they hear the three beeps, they win three points, before the two beeps, two points and after one beep, just one point. The tape begins with the pronunciation of the five channels and two quiz questions are answered, to demonstrate the way the beeps work. Students can do this as a whole group or challenge each other in small teams.

  For transcript see page T 6.

- R 15 *Livre de l'étudiant*, page 41. Using repromaster 15, by way of an introduction to this debate, give each of the students in one half of the class one of the statements *pour* and *contre*. Students in the other half of the class should each be given the same statements in English. The idea is to circulate and find your "partner", the person whose statement means the same as yours in the other language. Students then form two different groups: one whose statements are for TV and the other whose statements are against.

- Before they complete the activities in the *Livre de l'étudiant*, make sure that all the class have seen the English and French statements together: perhaps OHT versions might be provided as a matching exercise for the whole class.

- The next activity encourages the students to give their own opinions on the subject. These comments may be limited to a repetition of those already given in the book. For instance: *J'aime la télé. Je suis pour, parce que c'est bien pour se relaxer. Aussi, ...* There is space on page 31 of their *Cahier d'activités* to jot down these opinions.
- Students should then listen to the cassette, and note the order in which they hear the phrases for and against television. This is a demanding task and students should be encouraged to listen to the cassette as many times as they need.

Answers

G, E, A, H, J, B, D, C, F, I

For transcript see page T 6.

Cahier d'activités page 31

- The most effective way of presenting the idea on this page is to show the class an example of this page that you have filled in. The idea is to watch a programme and to show how you react to it, at five-minute intervals and using the adjectives on the page. Perhaps, if you have a video tape of a suitable programme, or part of it, you might show it and go through the exercise in class. Alternatively, of course, students may do it at home.
- There is also space at the bottom of this *Cahier d'activités* page for students to write up their opinions for and against television.

Follow-up ideas

- Two students tape their discussion about television which you might use the tape for a listening activity either with this or another class.
- Students prepare a key to explain an evening's worth of British television to a French person, perhaps to the *assistant/e*.
- Students prepare an evening's viewing for a new French/British channel which offers programmes in both languages.
- Students could make up their own *Jeu Télé Mistral*, put it onto cassette and quiz other members of the group, or other classes in the school.

CK 7

IT suggestions

- Using CK7, devise reinforcement activities which revise vocabulary associated with television programmes, for example: *Eastenders. Trouvez un feuilleton.* Students press the symbol for a soap opera, and the computer rewards: *C'est un feuilleton.* You could also add to the CK overlay pictures of well-known stars. Devise activities where students choose stars for particular programmes or press a picture of a star for further details.
- Using WP or DTP, students could devise data collection sheets for a television programmes preference survey.
- Using WP or DTP, students could list their favourite programmes and explain in French for a French visitor what sort of programmes these are.
- Using WP or DTP, students could design a guide to television programmes, with their 'top 10 choice'.

1 Regarde ces phrases.
Quelles phrases sont 'pour'?
Quelles phrases sont 'contre'?

2 Tu es d'accord avec quelles phrases?

La télé pour ou contre ?

- **A** C'est intéressant et éducatif.
- **B** Quand on regarde la télé, on n'est pas sociable.
- **C** C'est bien pour se relaxer.
- **D** C'est amusant.
- **E** C'est important pour les informations.
- **F** La conversation est impossible devant la télé.
- **G** Beaucoup d'enfants regardent des émissions violentes.
- **H** Il y a des émissions éducatives pour les enfants.
- **I** Quand on regarde la télé, on n'est pas actif.
- **J** Les émissions sont souvent idiotes.

3 Ecoute la cassette.
C'est un débat à la radio.
Les phrases sont mentionnées dans quel ordre?

4 Travaille avec un/une partenaire.
Etes-vous pour ou contre la télé?
Pourquoi?

Ciné-clips

1 Regarde ces affiches de cinéma.
C'est quel genre de film?

2 Lis les résumés.
C'est pour quel film?

A C'est un film romantique avec Meryl Streep et Robert Redford. La scène se passe en 1914 au Kenya sur une plantation. C'est l'histoire vraie de Karen Blixen. Elle se marie avec le baron Bror von Blixen. Karen est très indépendante. Elle devient amie avec Denys Finch-Hatton. Soudain, la guerre commence…

B C'est l'histoire comique d'un policier américain, Frank Drebin. Il a arrêté mille dealers, alors il est invité à la Maison Blanche par le Président Bush. L'invité d'honneur est le Professeur Meinheimer. Il est kidnappé. L'Institut Meinheimer est dévasté par une explosion. C'est la panique à Washington.

C C'est un western et un film de guerre. Ça se passe pendant la guerre de sécession en Amérique. Kevin Costner joue le rôle du lieutenant Dunbar, un soldat américain jeune et honnête. Tout seul, il va à la frontière. Il rencontre des Indiens Sioux. Il se marie avec une Indienne. L'armée américaine le recherche.

Unité 4 *Ciné-clips*

Areas of experience

E The world of communications
G The world of the imagination and creativity

Context

Looking at different types of film, making recommendations. Describing film stars.

Language focus

Un film romantique, un film d'épouvante, un film de science-fiction, un film de guerre, un film d'aventure, un film à suspense, un film policier, un dessin animé, une comédie, un western.
Il/elle a joué dans (+ film).

Materials

- *Livre de l'étudiant*, pages 42–43
- *Cahier d'activités*, pages 32–33
- *Cassette: C'est la musique de quel genre de film?; C'est quel genre de film?*
- Repromaster 14

A way in

- Introduce the different types of films, using OHT versions of the art work from page 43 of the *Livre de l'étudiant* which are supplied on repromaster 14.

Use the usual kind of memorizing and repetition games, for instance: have all the picture clues masked and reveal them one by one, asking the students to guess what is hidden under each one. *Le numéro un, c'est une comédie ou un film d'aventure?* It does not matter that they do not know what each film category means at the guessing stage: it is simply important that they repeat the words.

Another possibility is to ask students to display the OHT cues in order of priority: their favourite kind of film at the top of the list and least favourite at the bottom. Demostrate by giving your opinions first. Then, ask all students to prioritize the list in the same way for themselves.

Ask either one person or the whole group to speculate what a certain student has written down: *Tu as écrit 'comédie' pour le numéro un?* or simply, le *1, c'est une comédie?*, and so on through the list. Out of ten guesses, each student sees how many they managed to predict correctly.

Suggested route

- *Livre de l'étudiant*, page 42. The first activity on the page simply asks students to identify what type of film is depicted in each of the posters.

Answers

Danse avec les Loups: un western

Souvenirs d'Afrique: un film romantique

Y a-t-il un flic pour sauver le Président?: une comédie

- The second activity is more demanding as students need to read through the summary of each film and say which poster matches which summary. It is intended that they read and re-read the summaries but they do not need to understand each of them thoroughly. The summaries could also be used as a basis for extension work with dictionaries however.

Answers

A: Souvenirs d'Afrique
B: Y a-t-il un flic pour sauver le Président?
C: Danse avec les Loups

- *Livre de l'étudiant*, page 43. Students listen to the cassette and first identify the film style of the three extracts of music, and then the film style of the three versions of the same dialogue.

Answers

1 un dessin animé
2 un film d'épouvante
3 un film de guerre
4 un western

1 un film romantique
2 un film policier
3 un film de science-fiction

For transcript see page T6.

- To follow up this activity, students may invent their own dialogues for different types of films or simply repeat the same given dialogue in a certain style.

Cahier d'activités page 32

LES MEDIAS
Ciné-clips
Vive le cinéma

1 C'est quel genre de film?
Ecris le bon numéro.

7 un film romantique
.... un film d'épouvante
.... un film de science-fiction
.... un film de guerre
.... un film d'aventure
.... un film à suspense
.... un film policier
.... un dessin animé
.... une comédie
.... un western

2 Fais une liste de films de toutes sortes.
Ecris le titre et le genre de chaque film dans la grille.
A qui recommandes-tu ces films?
Coche les cases appropriées (✓).

Film	genre	enfants 5–10 ans	jeunes 11–13 ans	jeunes adultes 14–17 ans	adultes
Edward Scissorhands	comédie		✓	✓	✓

32

- There is a quick checklist of all the different types of film, which students could complete from memory at this stage or might have filled in earlier in the unit as their own reference list.

Answers

7 un film romantique
4 un film d'épouvante
8 un film de science-fiction
6 un film de guerre
2 un film d'aventure
3 un film à suspense
5 un film policier
1 un dessin animé
10 une comédie
9 un western

- Students then write a list of recommended films for different audiences: children 5–10 years old, young people from 10–13, young adults 14–17, adults.

Cahier d'activités page 33

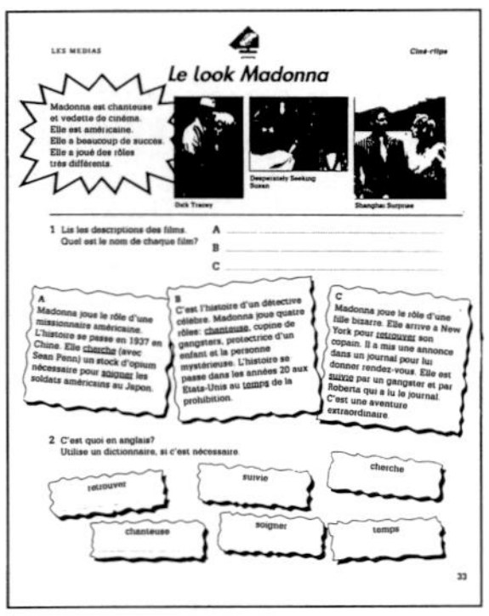

- This page outlines three different film performances by Madonna. Her three roles differ starkly from each other and by looking at the stills and reading the short description of each film, students are able to identify which film each still is taken from.

Answers

A: Shanghai Surprise
B: Dick Tracey
C: Desperately Seeking Susan

- A dictionary activity then follows. Encourage students to look up other new words and to record them on their *Page dictionnaire*.

Answers

cherche = looks for
soigner = to look after; to treat
chanteuse = singer
temps = time
retrouver = to meet
suivie = followed

Follow-up ideas

- Students plan a film festival to be held in their school or community. This might have a specific theme, for example: *Festival d'horreur, Festival franco-britannique, En noir et blanc.* This could be a group project which might involve the writing of film summaries, list of characters, publicity posters, recommendations for specific audiences, a programme, and so on.

- A follow-up pair-work activity might be to describe famous film actors, as a kind of guessing game: *Choisis une vedette de cinéma. Il/Elle a joué dans quels genres de films? Exemple:*
Personne A: "Il a joué dans un film d'aventure et aussi dans une comédie."
Personne B: " Il s'appelle Arnold Schwarzenegger?"
Personne A: "Oui"'

CK 7

IT suggestions

- Using CK7, possibly with the addition of theme tune sound effects, students could revise vocabulary for the types of programmes. By selecting from the CK overlay, students could play the role of a channel programmer, setting up a suitably balanced evening's viewing.
- Using WP or DTP, students could write short descriptions of their favourite stars for wall display. Alternatively, typed descriptions without the names of the stars could be cut up and put in a box. One student could then draw out the description and others have to guess who it is.
- Using WP, students could also try to write simple film summaries, character lists, publicity posters, film recommendations, for inclusion in a news sheet for younger pupils.
- Using WP or DTP, students could produce a *Télé Sept Jours*-style information sheet.

3 Ecoute la cassette.
C'est la musique typique de quel genre de film?

4 Ecoute la cassette.
Ecoute les trois dialogues.
C'est quel genre de film?

- Entrez.
- Bonjour.
- C'est bien vous?
- Oui, c'est moi.
- Ce n'est pas possible!
- Si, c'est possible. Je suis de retour.
- Qu'est-ce que c'est?
- C'est pour vous!

5 Travaille avec un/une partenaire.
Inventez des dialogues pour d'autres genres de films.

cahier d'activités, pages 34–36

Idoles

1 Voici quatre fans.
Regarde les photos.
Comment s'appellent les idoles?

A Un couple depuis trente ans.

Unité 5 *Idoles*

Areas of experience

B Personal and social life
E The world of communications
G The world of imagination and creativity

Context

Looking at people who are fanatical about their idols. Interviewing someone about famous people. Letter writing.

Language focus

Part I: *J'ai; j'adore; j'aime; je suis passionné(e) par...; je suis un/une fan de...*
Part II: *Quel est son nom/prénom/vrai nom/lieu de naissance/signe astrologique/poids/parfum? Quelle est sa date de naissance/situation de famille/taille? Qu'est-ce qu'il/elle préfère comme plat/boisson/musique/sport? Qu'est-ce qu'il/elle aime/déteste dans la vie? Où habite-t-il/elle? De quelle couleur sont ses yeux/cheveux?*

Materials

- *Livre de l'étudiant*, pages 44–45 + page 77
- *Cahier d'activités*, pages 34–36
- *Cassette: Idoles*
- Information, pictures, props, etc., relevant to a particular idol – see a way-in

PART I
A way in

- If you have an idol, bring in any related information, visuals or props and talk in very simple terms about your idol. For example: *Je l'aime depuis... Je suis passionné(e) par... C'est mon/ma/mes... préféré(e)(s)... Il/elle habite... Son anniversaire, c'est... Il/elle aime...* You might talk about the idol(s) without revealing their identity, to begin with and see if students can begin to guess who it might be.
- If you know of anybody in the group who has an idol of any kind, use this as your starting point instead. They might bring in the appropriate things to help you present this topic if you are asked in advance. Elicit from them the kinds of things already mentioned above.
- Do some research with younger classes and find out whom they favour as idols or heros: a sample from each year group and from some primary school-aged children would be good. Present a name or a picture and see if they can guess which class/age of pupil rated that particular person. For example: *Bon, j'ai un poster ici... C'est un poster de qui? Comment s'appelle cette personne? Qui adore cette personne/ce groupe/cette vedette à ton avis?... Qui est le/la fan typique? Un garçon ou une fille? De quelle année? De quel âge?*, etc.

Students might also say which area of entertainment or public life each person comes from: *C'est une vedette de cinéma, un acteur/une actrice, une vedette de télévision, un sportif/une sportive, un chanteur/une chanteuse, un musicien/une musicienne, un homme politique/une femme politique*, etc.

- Within the same context, find out whether anyone had a hero or idol in the past, using the same language: *Quand tu avais onze ans, toi, est-ce que tu avais un idole? ... C'était qui?... un sportif?*, etc.

Suggested route

- *Livre de l'étudiant*, pages 44–45. The first activity is to identify the stars.

Answers

A Elvis Presley	C The Beatles
B James Dean	D New Kids on the Block

- The next reading activity encourages students to look in detail at the things said by these fans. Once they have found the meanings of the words in italics, they should record them on their *Page dictionnaire*.

Answers

a = D	b = A	c = B	d = C
e = A	f = A	g = C	h = D

- This reading activity and the listening task which follows can be done independently by the students.

Answers

It is the Elvis fan (person A) talking. Three phrases are heard on the tape in the following order: b, f, e.

For transcript see page T7.

- Students might then assume the identity of any one of the four fans in the photos and using the phrases a–h on page 45 of the *Livre de l'étudiant* as models, they prepare three things to say about the chosen idol. Working in pairs, they would guess which identity they have each taken on, simply by listening to the three statements. They might prefer to be the fan of somebody else – perhaps one of the examples used in the way-in? The listener would simply need to make a few interjections for this to build up into a straightforward conversation, like the one on the tape. These might be statements and questions like:
– *Ça fait longtemps que tu as cette passion?*
– *Mais, dis donc!*
– *Tu as combien de posters?*
– *Tu as combien de disques?*
– *Ah bon?*
– *C'est marrant ça.*
You could build these into a conversation with one or two students first, as a model. Then, with any of these phrases written up, with an English version beside them, students could work out and practise their own conversation. This might turn out to be sincere and meaningful or more exaggerated and mocking in tone.

Cahier d'activités page 34

- The letter written by Gaëlle is to be read and understood well enough by the students so that they can write down an English version of it. The language in the letter carefully recycles vocabulary that they have come across and both in this unit and earlier on.

Part II
A way in

- With the profile of Julien Clerc from *Cahier d'activités*, page 35 in front of them, students should first answer your questions. These are listed in the 'Language focus'. Perhaps ask them in order first time through the text, then put the questions randomly so that students have to look carefully at the information before answering. Try it a third time with one half of the group, timing their responses. Then again with the other half of the class, seeing which team answered the quickest. Or, simply choose two opposing panels of three or four students and put the questions to each team alternately. Try this once allowing students to look at the test and then again without looking. With such a brisk, but gradual build-up, students will begin to understand the questions simply through the context and by repetition.

  Intermittently, do a quick comprehension check (*C'est quoi en anglais...?*) starting with the easier, guessable vocabulary first and working up to the more difficult. You might write up their English explanations alongside the written ones for the French question as they give it and have it on the OHT for reference.

- Ask students, either from this group or from a younger class to provide a similar profile of a different idol. The more profiles the better, but this will work if only one example is found and then photocopied for everyone to use. The profile may stay in English or can be put into French by the students or by you. If it retains the format of the one in the *Cahier d'activités*, it may well be within the capabiilities of the students to provide the information in French, particularly if you allocate just one or two details for each student to research.

- Then, set up a similar two-panel quiz format, using the new profile and a student as the quiz host. Alternatively, a Mastermind version of the quiz would work with just one student as the expert contestant on their chosen idol.

Suggested route
Cahier d'activités page 35

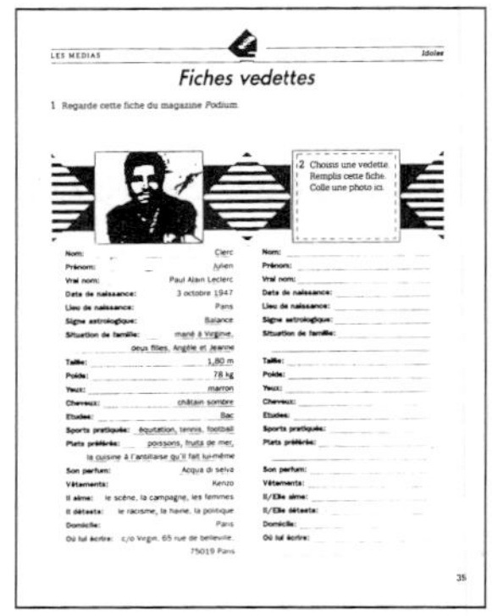

- The pro-forma 'fiche-vedette' should now be filled in.
- *Livre de l'étudiant*, page 77. Students should then try this quiz on famous idols.

Answers

1 = b	2 = c	3 = c	4 = c
5 = b	6 = c	7 = b	8 = c

Cahier d'activités page 36

- Using the types of questions in the quiz on *Livre de l'étudiant*, page 77, students should invent a quiz on idols of their choice. This could be for other members of the class, or for younger pupils in the school.

Follow-up ideas

- Students write a fan letter to an idol of their choice. They could do this for display and, taking on a fictitious identity, their letters could be as exaggerated or sincere as they want them to be.

IT suggestions

- You or the students could create data collection forms about idols from the pop or screen world.
- The data thus collected could be entered into a database and graphs produced. Fields could be as simple as the names of some well known people, or more complicated so as to include their personal details.
- Using WP or DTP, students could edit the descriptions of idols from the *Livre de l'étudiant* or make up their own descriptions about current pop idols.
- Using WP or DTP and graphics or scanned images, students from various classes could create their own pop magazine for distribution to younger pupils. The magazine could also include a pop quiz.
- Using DTP and graphics, students could create their own horoscope or a horoscope page for the magazine.
- Using WP, students could type out their fan letters.

an français, 28 ans, c'est sa passion.

2 Lis les phrases.
Cherche les mots *en italique* dans un dictionnaire.
Qui parle? La personne sur la photo A, B, C ou D?

a Je *craque* pour Jordan.
b J'ai une chambre *consacrée* à Elvis.
c J'ai cette *pièce* où habite Jimmy.
d J'ai *toujours* John dans la tête.
e Je regarde Elvis et j'*oublie* tous mes problèmes.
f Je l'aime *depuis* trente ans.
g Ces quatre garçons, ce sont ma *vie.*
h Je suis *passionnée* par la musique américaine et c'est mon groupe préféré.

3 Ecoute la cassette.
Quelle personne parle de son idole?
Tu entends quelles phrases (a-h)?

4 Travaille avec un/une partenaire.
Inventez d'autres conversations avec les autres fans.

5 Regarde la page 76.
Fais le quiz idoles.

C Beatlemanie!

D Elle a cinq copains.

Contrôle 3

Ecris tes réponses dans ton cahier d'activités, page 58

A

Ecoute la cassette.
Un critique parle des films.
Quelle est son opinion?

Exemple: Martin Guerre = **a**

B

Lis l'article de journal.
Décris le suspect.
Ecris cinq phrases en anglais.

Exemple: He is quite fat.

Télégramme de l'Ouest

Faits Divers Faits Divers

AU VOLEUR!

Le bureau de tabac de l'avenue Pasteur cambriolé dans la nuit du 17 au 18 août! La police recherche un homme. Environ 25 ans, assez gros et petit. Il porte un t-shirt blanc, un jean à trous, une casquette de base-ball, et des baskets blanches.

Contrôle 3

NOTE

A

1 b 2 a 3 a 4 c 5 a

5

B

1 He's about 25 years old.
2 He's small / short.
3 He's wearing a white T-shirt.
4 He's wearing jeans (with holes).
5 He's wearing a baseball cap.
Also: He's wearing white trainers.

5

C

1
2
3 See guidelines overleaf
4
5

5

D

Journal parlé See guidelines overleaf

5

OBSERVATIONS

TOTAL

Date:

Signature de l'étudiant:

Signature du professeur:

20

CASSETTE 1 FACE 2

Contrôle 3
Livre de l'étudiant, page 46
Cahier d'activités, page 58

Un critique parle de films

– Alors, voyons... les films de la semaine

Le Retour de Martin Guerre. Un film à suspense. C'est super.

Un Thé au Sahara. Un film italo-américain. C'est un drame. Une bonne musique. Pas mal. Vraiment pas mal du tout.

Le Retour de la Panthère Rose. Moi, je suis une fan de Peter Sellers. C'est un film comique. Excellent. J'adore.

Bons Baisers de Russie. Un vrai James Bond. Plein d'aventures. musique dramatique. Je ne résiste pas. C'est super. J'adore.

Tilaï. Un film franco-suisse. Bof, pas formidable. Une histoire d'amour impossible. Pas bien. Je n'aime pas.

Le Grand Bleu. Un film pour les jeunes. Sensationnel. Musique formidable. Images superbes. Mon film préféré de l'année. J'adore.

Writing task guidelines (task C)

Each answer is worth one mark. The tasks are open ended so that there are no 'right' answers. Answers should be marked positively. Students should have the opportunity to refer to their books and a dictionary, to check spellings. With this in mind, if a student successfully communicates a relevant message, a mark should be awarded. A mark should not be awarded if the spelling is so awry that a sympathetic native speaker would be unlikely to understand the message.

In certain instances, where a student has severe handwriting difficulties, he/she may be offered the option of dictating and spelling out answers for you to transcribe. Similarly, answers might be word-processed and then pasted into the answer pages of the *Cahier d'activités*.

Possible answers to task C

1 C'est un film d'épouvante/un film à suspense.
2 C'est une comédie.
3 C'est un film romantique.
4 C'est un western.
5 C'est un dessin animé.

Speaking task guidelines (task D)

Ideally, these contributions will be recorded onto a student's own individual tape which may also included other items from the course. Otherwise a class tape on which all students record their answers could be used.

A mark should be awarded for each relevant utterance understood by the listener. The example in the *Livre de l'étudiant* gives some guidance as to what the speaker may be expected to say.

National Curriculum assessment

Task A	AT 1, level 2(b)
Task B	AT 3, level 3(a)
Task C	AT 4, level 3(a)
Task D	AT 2, level 3(b)

C'est quel genre de film?
Ecris une phrase pour chaque poster.

Exemple:
C'est un film de science-fiction.

Les films de la semaine

Journal parlé

Choisis une émission que tu aimes à la télé.
Donne:

- le titre
- le jour
- l'heure
- le nom d'un acteur/ une actrice
- le genre

Exemple:

- J'aime *Eastenders*.
- C'est le mardi et le jeudi,
- à 7 heures et demie.
- Il y a une actrice qui s'appelle Wendy Richard.
- C'est un feuilleton anglais.

CHANGE
CHANGE

GEORGE V
TOM SELLECK
L'AUSTRALIEN
Schwarzenegger
UN FLIC à la maternelle
DOLBY STEREO
Vincent et moi
SELECTION OFFICIELLE

Café · Brasserie
LE MISTRAL

Attention!
Ne mets pas tes mains sur la porte: tu risques de te faire pincer très fort.

AUBERGE de JEUNESSE
YOUTH HOSTEL

PARC
Astérix

hamburger Quick restaurant

l'officiel des spectacles
cette semaine
N° 2357 2 F
Ville à Vendre

forum des halles

LES CAMPINGS D'ILE DE FRAN
A VOTRE SERVICE
BIENVENUE A PARIS
BUREAU D'INFORMATIONS
BUREAU DE CHANGE
NAVETTE CAMPING/METRO
VISITE DE PARIS EN BUS
SNACK BAR
ALIMENTATION-SOUVENIRS
PHOTOS-DROGUERIE
LAVERIE AUTOMATIQUE
WELCOME IN PARIS
INFORMATIONS DESK
CHANGE OFFICE
SHUTTLE BUS CAMPING/METRO
SIGHTSEEING IN PARIS BY BUS
SNACK BAR
MARKET/PHOTOS
AUTOMATIC LAUNDRY
SOUVENIRS
BENVENUTI A PARIGI
UFFICIO D'INFORMAZIONI
UFFICIO CAMBIO
SERVIZIO PULLMAN CAMPEGGIO/METRO
VISITA DI PARIGI COL PULLMAN
BAR/TAVOLA CALDA
DROGUERIA/LAVANDERIA AUTOMATICA
WILKOMMEN

PARIS

Le Guide Mistral

Bon voyage!

En route!

INFOS VOYAGES

National Express
Londres: 071 730 0202
Glasgow: 041 332 4100
Manchester: 061 228 3881

Air Travel Advice Bureau
Londres: 071 636 5000

British Rail
Londres: 071 834 2345

SNCF
Paris:
010.33.1.45.82.50.50

Sealink
Ashford: 0233 647047

Brittany Ferries
Portsmouth:
0705 827701

Introduction

- This module is project-based and concentrates on survival French for the student as potential tourist in Paris. It intends to put familiar language to a creative end, nevertheless. The format is unlike any other in **Mistral**: students should work at their own pace and should be encouraged to work on the different parts of the module in whichever order they wish in order to compile their own teenage guide to Paris. They should decide for themselves what the target readership would be interested in and what they might need to know. The *Livre de l'étudiant* pages, the *Cahier d'activités* tasks, and the *A l'écoute* sheets should be used for introduction and practice of the key language, and as a resource for students to dip into as they create their own guide.
- You may wish to present the language at the outset of each topic. The teacher's notes focus on ways of presenting the key language of each topic area. Students at this level of ability will have difficulty recalling specific language items or structures but they should be encouraged to draw upon whatever existing knowledge they may have.

A way in

- Before you embark upon this module, introduce students to the project as a whole. It may well be that you do this in English. Make sure students are aware of the resources offered:
  – The *Livre de l'étudiant* is a resource offering students ideas and information useful to them in the compilation of their own guide. You and the students may have extra authentic resources and real maps which you prefer to use.
  – The pages in the *Cahier d'activités* provide reading, writing, and speaking practice of the key language. There is also guidance as to when the *A l'écoute* sheets should be tackled.
  – The nine *A l'écoute* sheets are to be found at the back of this book. The scenes are transactional, not unlike those found in the GCSE syllabus. These activities are designed for students to work through on their own, at each relevant stage, and to decide which spoken language might be useful to the readers of their guide. Students should decide for themselves how best to record the key language in their own guide. They might, for example, decide to make a written note, in a phrase-book format. They may see the advantage of making a cassette to go with their guide, using the conversations on the cassette as a model. Encourage students to consider how best to make their cassette user-friendly; by providing an introduction in English, and/or providing counter numbers to help locate the various extracts, etc. Students should build up the cassette gradually as they work through the module, so that there is less likelihood of pronunciation going awry.
  17 18 – Repromasters 17–18 can be used to provide a framework for the students' own guide pages.
- The students' first task might be to simply brainstorm the kind of situations that they could envisage a *Guide Mistral* traveller having to tackle. They could then add to their list by looking in the *Livre de l'étudiant*.

Unité 1 *Bon voyage!*

Areas of experience

D The world of education, training and work
F The international world
G The world of imagination and creativity

Context

Getting to Paris. Buying a ticket at a railway station. Money equivalents, budgeting, changing money. Travelling within Paris.

Language focus

Part I: *en car, en voiture, par le train, en avion, par le ferry, en aéroglisseur. Un aller simple, un aller-retour, fumeur, non-fumeur, je voudrais réserver, une place, pour* (+ destination), *part* (+ times), *ça fait* (+ prices). *Je voudrais, un ticket, un carnet, une carte orange, un plan de métro, un plan des autobus.*

Part II: *je voudrais changer* (+ money), *une pièce d'identité, un passeport.*

Materials

- *Livre de l'étudiant*, pages 50–51
- *Cahier d'activités*, pages 37–38
- *Cassette: A la gare; Au bureau de change*
- E 1 *A l'écoute: feuille numéro 1*
- E 2 *A l'écoute: feuille numéro 2*
- R 17 R 18 Repromasters 17–18

PART I
A way in

- Students should make use of the map on *Livre de l'étudiant*, page 50, to plan and research travel to Paris.

Suggested route

Cahier d'activités page 37

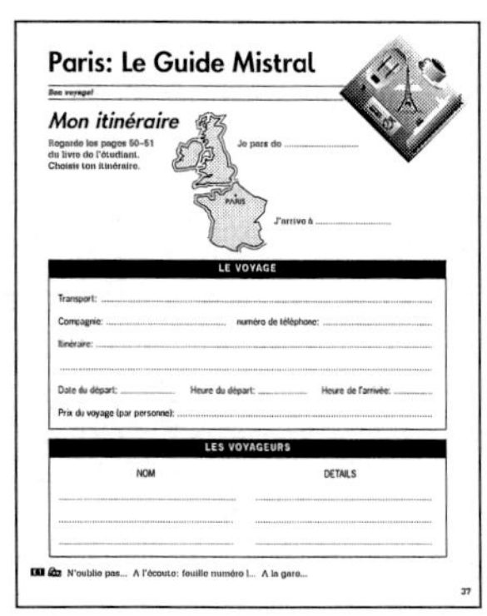

- Once they have researched and costed their journey, students fill in the itinerary information.

- Now introduce the key language for buying a rail ticket. **E 1** Make an OHT of the symbols on *A l'écoute* sheet 1. Use the symbols to build up the dialogue. Once you have built up the conversation, direct each half of the class to repeat the A or B parts together as a choral repetition exercise. Change over after a while so that everyone will have drilled each part of the conversation. You might give students a copy of the symbols cut up so that they can try the conversations in pairs. They might also try testing their partner by holding up the symbols.
- Once students are familiar with the conversation, give different pairs different roles to try out while rehearsing the same conversation. One of them is the ticket clerk and the other has a role card on which is written one of the following or similar:
  You have lost your contact lens; You have just robbed a bank; You find the ticket clerk funny; You are a famous person; You are absent-minded; You are a compulsive eater.
- Pairs then become groups of four. Each pair performs their scene to the other and the opposing pair has to guess what is written on the role card. It is likely that the dialogue will not change from that which is familiar but the actions and tones of voice should enliven it.
- *A l'écoute: feuille numéro 1*: students are ready to tackle the first of the independent listening activities. **E 1** They should listen to the tape as many times as they need and should work at their own pace.

For transcript see page **T 7**.

Answers

1: Paris; 18h ; aller simple, non-fumeur, 200 FF 2: Versailles; 9h; aller-retour; non-fumeur; 150 FF
3: Boulogne; 9h ; aller-retour; fumeur; 165 FF

un aller simple = a single ticket; un aller-retour = a return ticket; fumeur = smoking; non-fumeur = non-smoking; je voudrais réserver = I'd like to reserve; une place dans le train pour Paris = a seat on the Paris train; qui part à dix-huit heures = which leaves at 18.00 hours; ça fait deux cents francs = that's 200 francs.

- Page 51 of the *Livre de l'étudiant* provides information about travelling by bus and métro within Paris. Ask students to find the sentences on the page that include the following key words: *valable, les environs, gratuits, toutes, jours.* Students discover the meanings of these words from the context or they will refer to their dictionaries for help.
- Students could decide on five requests in the form of statements or questions which would be useful for a tourist travelling within Paris: a sentence asking for a book of tickets or a request for a map of the métro, and so on. Use page 51 of the *Livre de l'etudiant* as well as any existing knowledge.

PART II
A way in

- For preparatory work on exchanging money you might use a list of duty-free goods to practise converting sterling into francs. Students will need a calculator to do this and discussion with your maths department could stand you in good stead.
- Make a list of goods you want to buy at the duty free giving the sterling price listed. Give the students the current exchange rate and ask them to work out how much you would pay in francs. Explain that the number of francs equals the number of £ multiplied by the current exchange rate.

Suggested route

***Cahier d'activités* page 38**

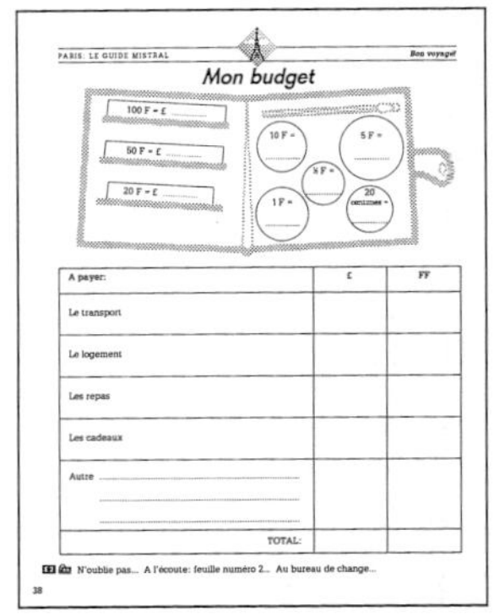

- Once students are familiar with the notion of an exchange rate and have had practice in switching from one currency to another, they should plan their budget for a stay in Paris.
- *A l'écoute: feuille numéro 2*: this sheet provides additional practice and model conversations for **E 2** changing money in France.

For transcript see page **T 7**.

Answers

DM: Allemagne; £: Grande-Bretagne; L: Italie; Sch: Autriche; Dr: Grèce; FF: France; Pes: Espagne; FB: Belgique; FS: Suisse; FL: Pays-Bas; Esc: Portugal

1: pesetas; 2000. 2: livres sterlings; 50.
3: deutschmarks; 100.

je voudrais changer = I'd like to change; une pièce d'identité = proof of identity; voilà mon passeport = here is my passport.

Follow-up ideas

- Having decided on the target readership for their own **R 17** guide, students are now ready to begin this project. **R 18** Having worked through this unit, students are equipped to write a section on travelling to and within Paris. Repromasters 17–18 provide border outlines and headings which students may use.

IT suggestions

- Using WP, students could type out the key phrases of the unit onto cue cards to use in the conversations.
- Using DTP and graphics or scanned images from authentic material, students could produce their own tickets, simple timetables or even French money.
- Using WP, students could make list of goods available in an imaginary duty-free shop and give the prices in French francs and pounds sterling for wall display.

Enfin à Paris!

Prenez le métro!
Les trains sont fréquents.
Cherchez cette pancarte:

◀ Les autobus sont aussi fréquents. Il y a un plan à chaque arrêt d'autobus. La nuit, les autobus arrivent à la Place Châtelet toutes les 60 minutes.

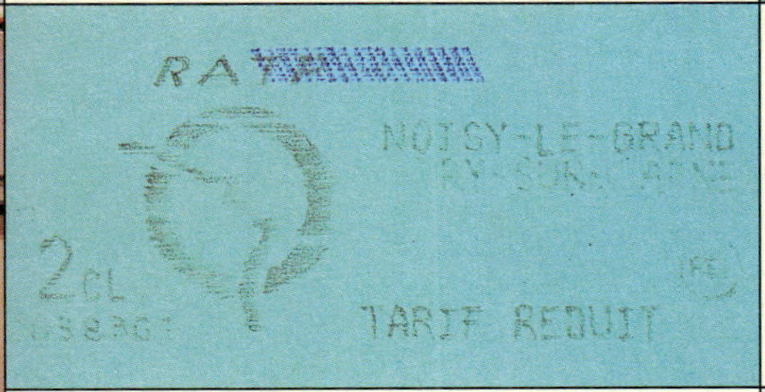

▶ Les plans de métro et des autobus sont gratuits.

▲ Vous pouvez acheter un ticket ou un carnet (10 tickets).
Un ticket est valable en autobus, en métro et en train RER.

▼ Vous pouvez acheter une Carte Orange (métro + autobus pour 7 jours).
Attention – une photo est nécessaire.

▼ Les trains RER.
Prenez un train RER pour visiter les environs de Paris.
Cherchez cette pancarte:

Bienvenue!

OFFICES DE TOURISME

Ecrivez à cette adresse avant votre départ:
French Tourist Office
178 Piccadilly, London. W1.

A Paris:
Office de Tourisme de Paris
127 avenue des Champs-Elysées.
Ouvert de 9h à 20h tous les jours.

Vous pouvez demander des listes des hôtels, des plans, des brochures et des renseignements sur les monuments, les marchés, les magasins, les musées et des idées pour les excursions...

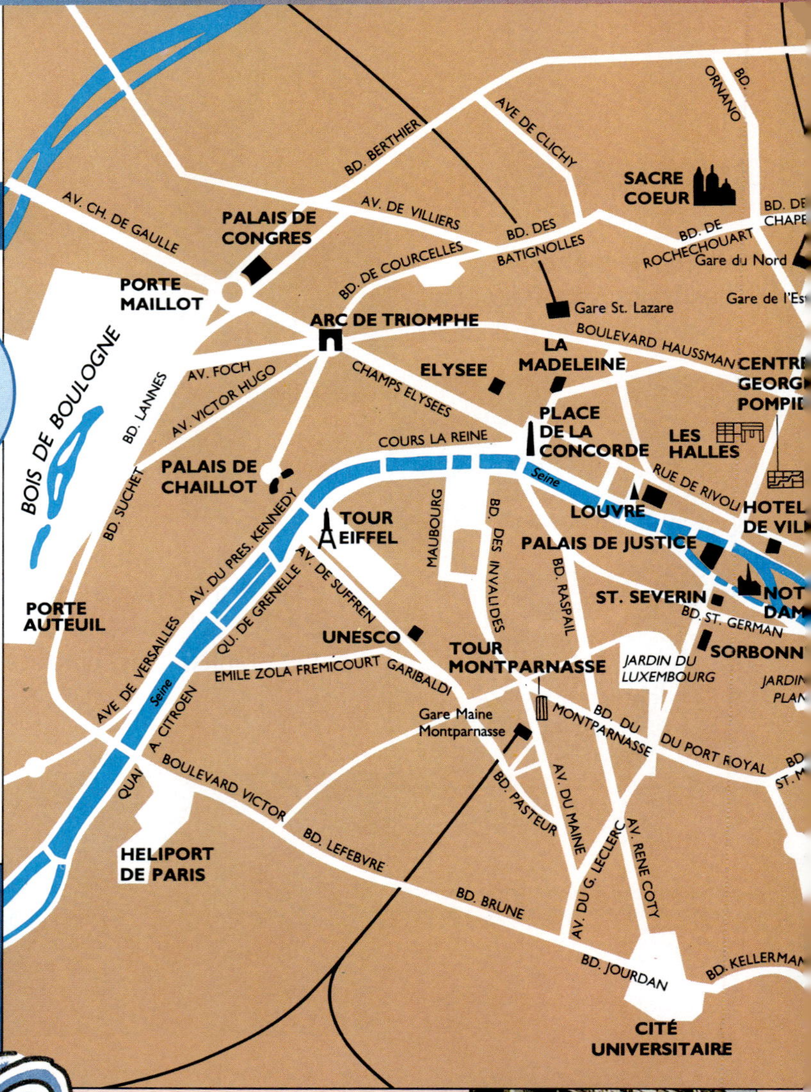

HÔTEL NATIONAL***

224, rue du Faubourg Saint-Denis
75010 Paris - Tél. 46.07.99.56
Métro Gare du Nord ou
La Chapelle

Situé à proximité de la gare du Nord et de la gare de l'Est. 56 chambres équipées de douche ou bains/W.C., télévision et téléphone direct.

▶ Il y a un grand choix d'hôtels. Demandez une liste des hôtels à l'office de tourisme.

HÔTEL BRITTANY**

3 et 5, rue Saint-Lazare 75009
Paris - Tél. 48.78.44.50
Métro Notre-Dame-de-Lorette

Situé entre l'Opéra et le Sacré Cœur, à 10 minutes des grands magasins, l'hôtel offre 44 chambres insonorisées, toutes équipées de douche ou bains/W.C., télévision couleur, radio. Bar et salons.

RATP

Unité 2 *Bienvenue!*

Areas of experience

D The world of education, training and work
E The world of communications
F The international world
G The world of imagination and creativity

Context

Choosing and checking in at suitable accommodation. Writing letters to book accommodation in advance. Using a tourist office.

Language focus

Part I: *Je voudrais/avez-vous... Une chambre pour une/deux personne/s, avec douche. Une place, une nuit, un emplacement. C'est combien par nuit? Où est/sont ...? Une tente, une caravane. C'est à quel nom? C'est pour combien de nuits/ personnes? Comment ça s'écrit? Vous désirez?*

Part II: *J'ai besoin de... Une liste des hôtels, campings, excursions, monuments importants, musées. Un horaire des autobus/trains. Un plan de la ville.*

Materials

- *Livre de l'étudiant*, pages 52–53
- *Cahier d'activités*, pages 39–40
- *Cassette: Le logement; A l'office de tourisme*
- *A l'écoute*: *feuille numéro 3*
- *A l'écoute*: *feuille numéro 4*
- Repromasters 17–18

3 4 17 18

PART I
A way in

3
- *A l'écoute: feuille numéro 3:* students could use this sheet as their lead-in to the language for finding the right accommodation and booking it. The activities allow them to access the transcript by themselves.

For transcript see pages T7 – T8.

Answers

1: hôtel
2: auberge de jeunesse
3: camping
4: hôtel

– Bonjour, madame
– Bonjour, monsieur. Vous désirez?
– Je voudrais une chambre pour deux personnes, s'il vous plaît.
– C'est pour combien de nuits?
– Trois nuits.
– Vous désirez une chambre avec salle de bains ou douche?
– Avec douche, s'il vous plaît.
– C'est combien par nuit, s'il vous plaît?
– C'est trois cents francs par nuit.
– Très bien.
– C'est à quel nom?
– Jones.
– Comment ça s'écrit?
– J-O-N-E-S.
– C'est la chambre quarante-quatre. Voici votre clé.
– Merci.
– De rien, monsieur.

- Alternatively, start by playing the first conversation to the class cold, asking students to note down any word or phrase at all that they can understand, regardless of spelling. Pool these and write up their suggestions on the board. Then, ask students to work out a short conversation using all these words or phrases.

Suggested route

- Once students are familiar with the key phrases, they should practise them in role-play situations, which they themselves write. There are ways of adding a note of unpredictability to such a conversation and therefore of making a role-play activity more interesting. For instance, one of the two roles could be played with the student portraying a certain mood. It is then up to the second person in the pair or indeed another pair of students altogether to guess which mood comes across. We acknowledge Barry Jones for the idea of presenting a selection of moods in a grid, for students to choose from. Like this:

Choisis une émotion.
Répète la conversation en jouant ce rôle.

furieux furieuse	impatient impatiente
paresseux paresseuse	content contente
de bonne humeur de mauvaise humeur	poli polie
inquiet inquiète	impoli impolie
malheureux malheureuse	gentil gentille
froid froide	pressé pressée

- By now, students will be familiar with the different types of accommodation available and also will be able to book in to a chosen hotel, campsite or hostel with confidence.

Cahier d'activités page 39

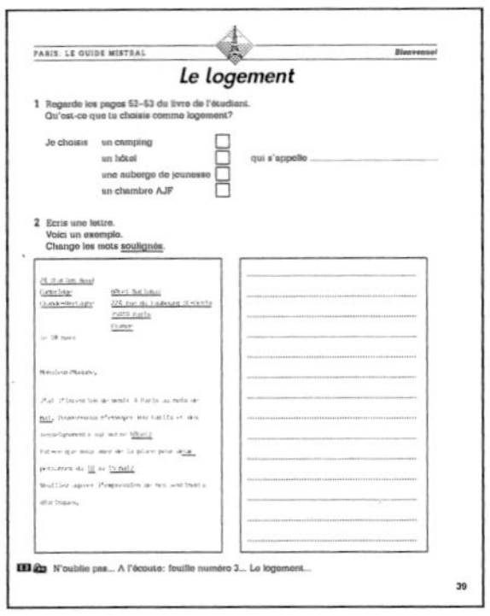
PARIS: LE GUIDE MISTRAL Bienvenue!

Le logement

1 Regarde les pages 52–53 du livre de l'étudiant. Qu'est-ce que tu choisis comme logement?

Je choisis un camping / un hôtel / une auberge de jeunesse / un chambre AJF — qui s'appelle ...

2 Ecris une lettre. Voici un exemple. Change les mots soulignés.

N'oublie pas... A l'écoute: feuille numéro 3... Le logement...

39

- This page allows for writing practice: students choose from a range of accommodation listed on pages 52–53 of the *Livre de l'étudiant* and then write a letter of reservation, based on the model provided.

PART II
Suggested route

- *A l'écoute: feuille numéro 4:* these listening activities introduce students to the key language needed to obtain information at the tourist office. Most students will find the vocabulary easy to understand, though you may like to go over it with them.

E 4

For transcript see page **T 8**.

Answers

1: une liste des hôtels
2: un plan de la ville
3: un horaire des autobus
4: une liste des campings
5: une liste des excursions + une liste des hôtels
6: un horaire des trains + un plan de la ville
7: une liste des monuments + une liste des musées

Cahier d'activités page 40

PARIS: LE GUIDE MISTRAL Bienvenue!

Bienvenue à Paris

Regarde les pages 53–54 du livre de l'étudiant. Complète ton plan de Paris.

1 Marque ton logement sur le plan.
2 Identifie les monuments. Complète la légende.
3 Trace un chemin touristique sur le plan.

Légende

N'oublie pas... A l'écoute: feuille numéro 4... A l'office de tourisme...

40

- Students can use this page to record which places they have decided to visit.

Follow-up ideas

- The information in the *Livre de l'étudiant* and the activities in the *Cahier d'activités* are to be exploited by the students and used for their own purposes in their own guide.

R 17 R 18

IT suggestions

- Using WP, students could write letters to book accommodation or edit the letter in the *Cahier d'activités*.
- Using DTP and graphics or scanned images, students could prepare their own Paris posters for wall display or for use in a simulated tourist office scene.
- Using a facility like *Chatter,* where two computers are linked, students could try taking turns at booking accommodation via computer.
- Using Minitel, students could enquire about accommodation in Paris.

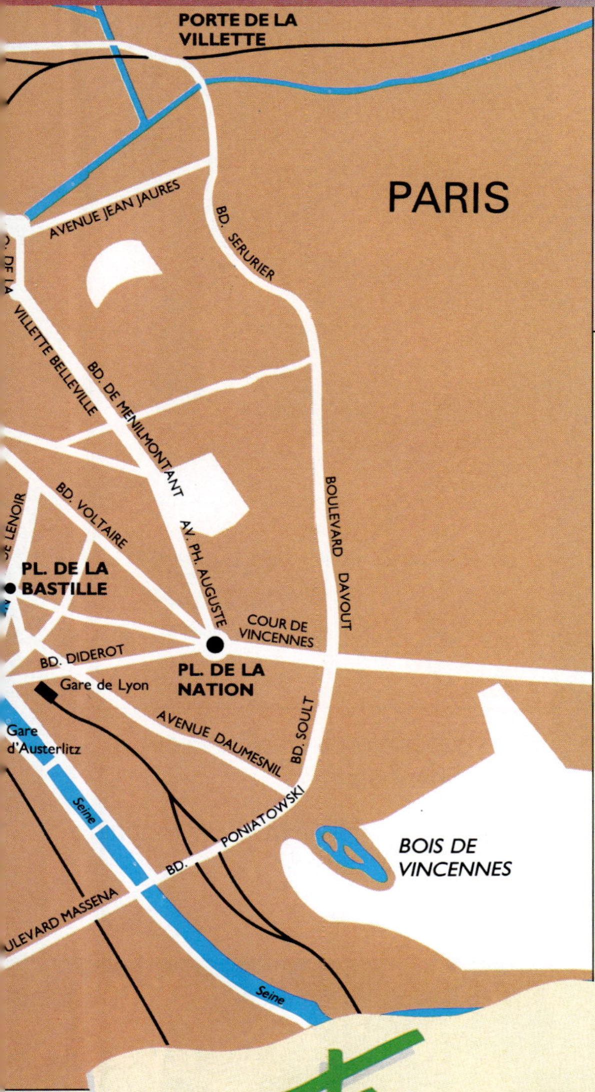

FEDERATION UNIE DES AUBERGES DE JEUNESSE

euil des Jeunes en France (AJF)

r les chambres propres et pas chères, voici
adresses utiles:

idence Bastille,
avenue Ledru-Rollin, Paris 11e.

ourcy,
e de Fourcy, Paris 4e.

auconnier,
rue de Fauconnier, Paris 4e.

a un restaurant pas cher dans tous les AJF.

▶ Il y a deux Auberges de Jeunesse:

Jules Ferry,
8 boulevard Jules Ferry, Paris 11e.

D'Artagnan,
80 rue Vitruve, Paris 20e.

▼ l'Auberge de Jeunesse du D'Artagnan vous propose:

- une capacité d'hébergement de 400 lits, en chambres à 2 lits, 3 lits, et 8 lits. Douches et WC à l'étage, chambres à 2 et 8 lits entièrement équipées
- un restaurant self-service
- un bar-cafétéria-discothèque
- 2 salles de réunion
- un amphithéâtre
- un lavomatique

20e
Auberge de jeunesse
Porte de Bagnolet M

▶ Vous préférez camper?
Il y a trois campings à l'Est de Paris.

Camping du Tremblay,
Quai de Polangis,
Champigny-sur-Marne.

Camping du Camp des Cigognes,
Bord-de-Marne, Créteil.

Camping de Paris-Est,
Boulevard des Alliés,
Champigny-sur-Marne.

▶ Il y a un camping au
Bois de Boulogne aussi.

Bon appétit!

▲ Cherchez un menu à prix fixe - c'est moins cher!

Il y a le fast-food à Paris!

▶ Vous préférez un pique-nique? Les supermarchés:

As Eco Félix Potin Monoprix
Franprix Prisunic

Unité 3 *Bon appétit!*

Areas of experience

A Everyday activities
F The international world
G The world of imagination and creativity

Context

Food in Paris. Choosing an eating place. Reading a menu and ordering a meal. Shopping for food.

Language focus

Parts I + II: *je voudrais, je prends, pour moi, vous désirez? Et à boire? Et avec ça? C'est combien? Un kilo de; 500 grammes de. Une tranche de, une bouteille de, une boîte de* (+ food).

Materials

- *Livre de l'étudiant*, pages 54–55
- *Cahier d'activités*, page 41
- *Cassette: Au restaurant; Les courses*
- *A l'écoute: feuille numéro 5*
- *A l'écoute: feuille numéro 6*
- Repromasters 17–18

E5 E6 17 18

Note

The language of food and drink will be familiar to students to some extent: they are likely to bring with them much existing knowldege. It turns up in a variety of contexts and was a feature of **Mistral 1** where the emphasis was on healthy/unhealthy eating habits.

PART I
A way in

- An easy way of presenting food items is to think about which course a particular food would be served in. Take the French menu on page 41 of the *Cahier d'activités* as your stimulus. Write up the items on strips of acetate or pieces of paper. Students should guess or predict whether each item is a starter (*entrée*), main course (*plat principal*), or dessert (*dessert*) and assemble the items in appropriate groups. To exploit the same menu further, give students the Italian equivalents of each item and see if they can pair them up with the correct French.
- Once students have sorted and matched these words, they should choose three items from the menu that they would eat or drink. Each person should read out their list and the rest of the group will listen carefully and see if they have made exactly the same choices.

Equally, students may predict what you and anyone else in the group has chosen from the menu. They might also use their knowledge of French and British currency values and try to put a price in francs to each of the items. Explain that there is no right answer, but encourage students to compare their prices and find who has pitched theirs at the most realistic level.

Suggested route

- *A l'écoute: feuille numéro 5:* these activities provide a context for language already met: simple restaurant dialogues. These are independent listening activities and students should be encouraged to listen as many times as they need. Students finish by inventing similar dialogues.

E5

For transcript see page T8.

Answers

1: The customers did not order two coffees or two tomato salads. They only ordered one homemade tart. In addition, they ordered one strawberry ice cream.

1 œuf mayonnaise
1 poulet rôti
1 salade verte
1/2 bouteille de vin blanc
1 glace au chocolat
1 café

1 melon
1 truite
1 salade verte
1 bouteille d'eau minérale
fromage

- Once students have become familiar with the language of the menu and of ordering a meal in a restaurant, they might design their own menus, in groups. Each group of, say, three students, should produce cards to go with their menu, each of which outlining a certain dietary or food-related requirement. For instance:
  – you are allergic to fish
  – you are vegetarian
  – you only have 100 francs to spend in the restaurant
  – you are on a low-cholesterol diet
  – you are extremely greedy
  – you only eat orange food
- Groups can then offer each other their menus and present 'a customer' one of the cards. By looking at the menu, a third group of students or the rest of the class should guess what the card says.
- At some point, once the students have listened to the tape and practised the language, you might communally put together a list of useful phrases and present these for reference in a phrase-book, French/English, style. Oversize versions of the phrases may go up on the wall or notice-board for the duration of this work.

Cahier d'activités page 41

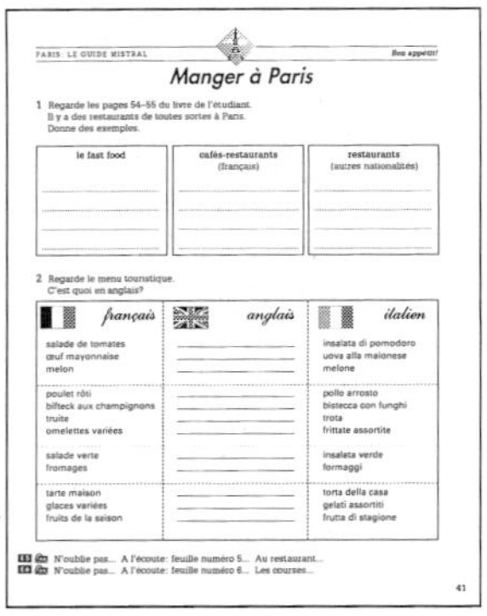
PARIS: LE GUIDE MISTRAL — Bon appétit!

Manger à Paris

1 Regarde les pages 54–55 du livre de l'étudiant.
Il y a des restaurants de toutes sortes à Paris.
Donne des exemples.

le fast food	cafés-restaurants (français)	restaurants (autres nationalités)

2 Regarde le menu touristique.
C'est quoi en anglais?

français	*anglais*	*italien*
salade de tomates œuf mayonnaise melon		insalata di pomodoro uova alla maionese melone
poulet rôti bifteck aux champignons truite omelettes variées salade verte fromages		pollo arrosto bistecca con funghi trota frittate assortite insalata verde formaggi
tarte maison glaces variées fruits de la saison		torta della casa gelati assortiti frutta di stagione

N'oublie pas... A l'écoute: feuille numéro 5... Au restaurant...
N'oublie pas... A l'écoute: feuille numéro 6... Les courses...

41

- This page directs students to pages 54–55 of the *Livre de l'étudiant* and together with the menu activity at the bottom of the page provides comprehension practice of types of restaurant and menus.

Answers

Le fast food: MacDonalds, Quick, Hollywood Canteen.
Café-restaurants (français): crêperie, le Quasimodo.
Restaurants (autres nationalités): Matsuya, Pizza, restaurant chinois.

Tomato salad
Egg mayonnaise
Melon
Roast chicken
Steak with mushrooms
Trout
Variety of omelettes
Green salad
Cheeses
Homemade tart
Variety of ice-creams
Fruit

PART II
A way in

- The context of eating out is widened here to include shopping for food and drink. Students will probably feel confident enough to tackle the activities without too much help as much of the language will be familiar to them. Nevertheless, revision of language appropriate to scenes in the market, bakery and delicatessen might be helpful to students before they begin to work independently.
- Use props or visuals to revise products typically bought on holiday. Demonstrate the meanings of: *un kilo de, 500 grammes de, une tranche de, une bouteille de, une boîte de* and combinations of these and various products. Some combinations make sense, others are clearly incorrect: *Une bouteille de Coca. Ça va? Ben, oui... c'est correct. Une tranche de pêches... c'est correct, ca? Non! Alors, écoutez bien. Je vous donne trois phrases. Une n'est pas correcte. Laquelle? Alors... un kilo de vin, un kilo de pommes, un kilo de tomates.*
- This can be done as a writing exercise. A version of this activity could be done in pairs or small groups, using sets of mini-flashcards made by the students themselves. They should have half a set of cards with quantities written on them and the other half with products.

Suggested route

- *A l'écoute, feuille numéro 6:* this provides model conversations in the market, bakery and delicatessen.
E6 Students are encouraged to listen to these models as many times as they wish and then to use them to make up their own similar dialogues.

For transcript see pages T8 – T9.

Answers

1: 1 kilo peaches; 13FF
2: 2 croissants; 1 pain au chocolat; 1 baguette
3: cheese; 500g tomato salad

1: Marché
2: Boulangerie/Pâtisserie
3: Charcuterie

Follow-up ideas

- Students are now ready to use any information from this unit to continue with their own guide. It is appropriate at this stage to check that students have begun to compile a phrase-book section of useful phrases in French and English. There is a suitable
R 17 heading for such a section to be found on
R 18 repromaster 18.

IT suggestions

- Using DTP and graphics or scanned images, students could produce their own menus or advertisements for eating places.
- Using WP or DTP, students could produce the cards with dietary requirements (referred to in this unit).
- Using WP and graphics, students could produce a list of useful phrases for classroom wall display.

Quelques marchés parisiens:

ue de Buci
ue de Mouffetard
oulevard Port-Royal
oulevard de Belleville

Il y a des restaurants de toutes sortes!

▲ **une crêperie**

▼ **un restaurant chinois**

▲ **un restaurant japonais**

▼ **un restaurant italien**

Si vous voulez manger un snack, allez dans un café, un bar ou une brasserie.

▼ Vous aimez les cafés?
Voici de bons endroits:

Boulevard Montparnasse
Boulevard St. Germain
Boulevard St-Michel
Les Halles
La Bastille

Ville vivante!

▼ Château de Versailles

▼ Centre Georges Pompidou

CLUB 18–25 WEEK-END A PARIS

vendredi

18.30 Cocktails. *Hôtel Paradis.*
20.00 Dîner. *Chez André*, 12 rue Marbœuf.
22.30 Café-théâtre *Bravissimo* ,116 bis Champs Elysées.

samedi

10.00 Promenade en hélicoptère. Départ de l'Héliport.
12.30 Déjeuner. *Hôtel Paradis.*
14.00 Tour de Paris en car: la tour Eiffel, le centre Pompidou, Notre Dame de Paris, les égouts de Paris, Montmartre.
16.00 Centre de Loisir, rue Louis-Armand. (Tennis, squash, golf, gymnasium, bowling, billard, parc aquatique, bars, boutiques.)
20.00 Dîner. *Hôtel Paradis.*
22.00 Paris la nuit. Visite en car.
23.00 *Discophage*,11 passage du Clos-Bruneau.

dimanche

11.00 Promenade en bateau-mouche. Départ du Pont de l'Alma.
12.30 Déjeuner. *Hôtel Paradis.*
15.00 Visite de Versailles. Départ en car.
18.00 Retour à Paris.

Unité 4 *Ville vivante!*

Areas of experience
A Everyday activities
D The world of education, training and work
F The international world
G The world of imagination and creativity

Context
Shopping. Choosing souvenirs. What to do in Paris.

Language focus
Part I: *je voudrais, je prends. C'est combien? Je voudrais envoyer. Quelle taille?*

Part II: revision of what you can do in Paris – vocabulary for main sights and places to visit, etc.

Materials
- *Livre de l'étudiant*, pages 56–57
- *Cahier d'activités*, pages 42–43
- *Cassette: Le shopping (1); Le shopping (2)*
- E 7 *A l'écoute: feuille numéro 7*
- 16 Repromaster 16
- 17 18 Repromasters 17–18
- A disconnected telephone (optional)

PART I
A way in
- The lesson before you want to present the shopping dialogue ask students to jot down in English all of the phrases they can think of which would enable them to communicate in a shop. This should not include a list of products but the type of thing a tourist might find him/herself needing to look up in a phrase book.
- Take the bits of paper away with you and arrive next lesson with the list of French phrases they asked for. Write them up and ask the class to consider whether there are enough phrases there to get them through a simple conversation in a shop: *C'est assez pour une conversation dans un magasin?* Add any that they feel are missing.
- Once students have all of the phrases in random order in front of them on the board ask them to discuss with a partner which of them the customer would say and which the assistant would say.
- E 7 *A l'écoute: feuille numéro 7*: students are now ready to tackle these independent listening activities.

For transcript see page T 9.

Answers

1 = C	4 = D	7 = E
2 = A	5 = H	8 = G
3 = I	6 = B	9 = F

1: t-shirt
2: voudrais
3: s'il vous plaît
4: combien
5: prends
6: deux
7: vous
8: stylo
9: préfère

1: t-shirt; rouge; grand; grand; 50FF
2: crème solaire; 35FF
3: 2 timbres (lettres); 3 timbres (cartes postales); 11.50FF

Suggested route
- Once this is complete divide the class into two groups, shop assistants and customers and organize the tables into horse-shoe formation. The shop assistants sit behind the tables and each customer stands opposite a shop assistant. The shop assistants need to have in front of them the little pictures of souvenirs which they have already seen on *A l'écoute* sheet 7. These should be cut out by the shop assistant so that they may be handed to customers. (E 7)

When you start the activity the pairs begin a conversation in which the customer is buying a souvenir. If the shop assistant has a picture of the item requested he/she must hand it to the customer who keeps it. A simple: *Non je regrette* will suffice if the assistant is out of stock.

When you shout: *Changez!* the customers must move anti-clockwise to the next 'shop' and begin another conversation with the next shop assistant regardless of whether they managed to complete the transaction or not. The object of the exercise is for the customers to buy as many items as they can in the time you allow the activity to last.

Cahier d'activités page 42

Des souvenirs
LISTE DES RAYONS

- This works well as an independent activity but you might like to use it to reinforce dictionary skills using any of the games described in the introduction to this book.

PART II
A way in

- The double-page spread on pages 48 and 49 of the *Livre de l'étudiant* provides an excellent resource for investigating things to do in Paris. Any of the activities suggested on page vii of the introduction will familiarize students with the names of the places and what you can do in them. The captions referred to on page vii are available on repromaster 16. For reference, imagine each of the photos numbered 1 to 35, from left to right:

R 16

1 un bureau de change
2 un cinéma
3 un café
4 dans le métro
5 la Pyramide au musée du Louvre
6 un plan de métro
7 un menu à emporter
8 une auberge de jeunesse
9 Notre Dame et la Seine
10 un parc de loisirs – le Parc Astérix
11 les jardins des Tuilleries
12 un jardin publique
13 un marché
14 le Centre Pompidou
15 le restaurant Quick
16 la rive gauche
17 l'Arche de la Défense
18 l'Arc de Triomphe
19 une gare
20 le musée d'Orsay
21 la tour Eiffel
22 le magazine *L'Officiel des Spectacles*
23 près du Centre Pompidou
24 le Forum des Halles, un centre commercial
25 un camping
26 un marché aux puces
27 le grand magasin, Galeries Lafayette
28 une colonne Morris
29 le basilique Sacré Cœur
30 des bateaux mouches
31 la Géode, à la cité des Sciences et de l'Industrie, la Villette
32 la Défense
33 une station de métro
34 le marché des antiquaires
35 un cirque

Suggested route

- Students study the itinerary on page 56 of the *Livre de l'étudiant* and try to identify as many of the places mentioned as possible. They might refer back to the double-page spread to help them.

Cahier d'activités page 43

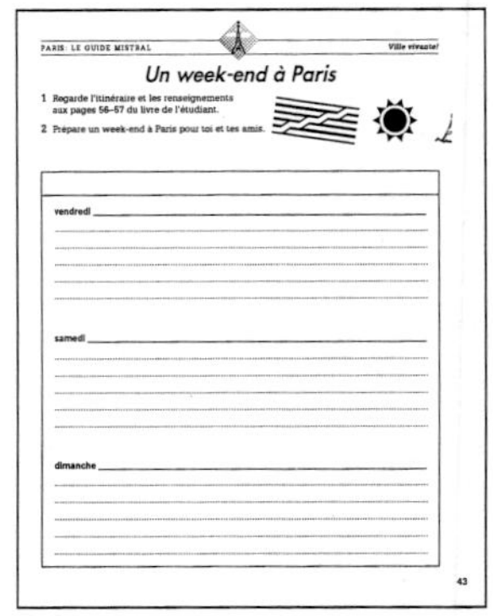

- Students use all the information gathered to plan their own weekend in Paris and write out the itinerary, following the style of the example on page 56 of the *Livre de l'étudiant.*

Follow-up ideas

- With reference to this unit and any other appropriate resources (maps, brochures, guides), students now add to their guide recommendations of places to go to and things to see. They may choose to work out an itinerary and plot a suitable walk on a map.

R 17
R 18

IT suggestions

CK 8

- Using CK 8, devise activities based on the monuments of Paris and what there is to do in Paris. Devise activities where students press on the map to discover the names of famous sights, or where students press to gather more tourist information.
- Using WP or DTP and a graphics package or database, students could produce their own diary of weekend activities, including times of the day. Students could then be asked to check diary appointments and times of events.
- Using graphics or catalogue cut-outs on a CK overlay or on DTP, students could make a list of typical souvenirs.
- Using DTP, students could write useful phrases for wall display.

Château Vaux le Vicomte ▲

▲ Parc Asterix

Musée de l'Air et de l'Espace ▼

▼ Musée du Cheval, Chantilly

▼ Palais de la Découverte

Tour Eiffel ▼

▼ Galeries Lafayette

ACTIVITES SPORTIVES

Piscine des Halles, niveau — 3 du nouveau Forum des Halles, Porte du Jour, 10 place de la Rotonde, 42 38 98 44, M° Les Halles. Ent. 20 F, enfants: 15 F.

Patinoire d'Evry, pl. de l'Agora, 69 91 58 91. SNCF Evry-Courcouronnes, RN 7 et A 6. Le soir jeux de lumières. Ambiance discothèque, animations. Ent. : 23,50 F ou 17,50 F, — 16 ans : 20 F ou 15,50 F. Location patins : 13 F.

Aquaboulevard de Paris, 4 rue Louis-Armand. 40 60 10 00. Tennis, squash, golf, gymnasium. Village provençal, bowling, billard, bridge, club courses PMU. Tir, parc aquatique, espace verts. Restaurants, bars, boutiques. Ent. parc aquatique. : 4h : 68 F. 10 F par heure supplémentaire. — 12 ans : 49 F. — 3 ans : gratuit.

Bowling de Paris, Jardin d'Acclimatation, Bois de Boulogne. 40 67 94 00.

GOLF MINIATURE:

Châlet du Lac, Orée du bois de Vincennes, M° Saint-Mandé-Tourelles, 43 28 09 89. Ven., sam. de 22h à l'aube, dim. de 15h à 19h30. Parcours de 18 trous : 17 F. Selon météo.

KARTING et 4 x 4:

Racing Kart Buffo, Les Etards R.N. 19. 77390 Tél.: 64 07 62 97. Fermé lun. mat. et mar. tte la journée. Tarif semaine 53 F 10' — 67 F 15' — 119 F 30'. Tarifs week-end et jours fériés : 66 F 10' — 85 F 15' — 148 F 30'.

MUSEUM NATIONAL D'HISTOIRE NATURELLE

PARC ZOOLOGIQUE DE PARIS

BOIS DE VINCENNES

53, avenue St-Maurice - 75012
Tél. : 43.43.84.95

cahier d'activités, page 44

Face à face

1 Ecoute la cassette. Regarde les scénarios rouges.

2 Ecoute la cassette. Regarde les scénarios verts.

Unité 5 *Face à face*

Areas of experience

A Everyday activities
B Personal and social life
E The world of communications
F The international world
G The world of imagination and creativity

Context

Introducing oneself. Taking the initiative in a conversation. Open and closed conversations. Inviting people out; suggesting where to go, what to do, etc.

Language focus

Part I: revision of personal details. *Comment tu t'appelles? Tu es en vacances ici? Tu voudrais boire quelque chose? Tu es britannique? C'est ta première visite en France? Tu habites à Paris? Je m'appelle... J'habite...*

Part II: *si on allait ...? A quelle heure? Quand? On se retrouve où? Tu veux sortir? Je veux bien. Non, je ne peux pas. Je suis occupé/occupée.*

Materials

- *Livre de l'étudiant*, pages 58–59
- *Cahier d'activités*, page 44
- *Cassette: Les scénarios rouges; Les scénarios verts; Questions et réponses; Conversation avec Jacqueline; On sort?*
- *A l'écoute: feuille numéro 8*
- *A l'écoute: feuille numéro 9*
- Repromasters 17–18
- Repromaster 19

PART I
A way in

- Introduce the idea of having your first conversation with a French-speaker of their age on their trip to France. You could perhaps refer to the photo which appears in **Mistral 1**, repromaster 6, and use this as a stimulus: *Imaginez votre première conversation avec la fille ou le garçon de ce couple. Donnez-moi une question... votre première question... donnez-moi une idée...* You might offer an example at this stage: *Par exemple, 'Comment tu t'appelles?'... 'Où habites-tu?'...*
- Accept any ideas given by the students, even if they are in English. Write these up in French. Students then try to prioritize these statements and questions: *Qu'est-ce que vous préférez comme première question... comme question d'introduction?* Number the ideas in a suitable order for a conversation, as agreed by the students. At this point, a student might try to use the language pooled so far to try and sustain a conversation with you or with the foreign language assistant: this should be a short, simple activity which allows students to repeat and begin to practise the language.
- Now introduce the idea of keeping a conversation going. One way of doing it, is to repeat the last phrase heard by the speaker:
  – Comment tu t'appelles?
  – Je m'appelle Guy.
  – Guy? Ah. bon!
  – C'est ta première visite en France?
  – Oui, c'est ma première visite.
  – C'est ma première visite aussi.
- E 8 *A l'écoute: feuille numéro 8*: use the questions and answers on *A l'écoute* sheet 8 in this way: choose some of them and see if students are able to continue the short dialogues by repeating the key phrases. Students should then tackle the independent listening activities.

For transcript see page T 9.

Answers

1 Comment tu t'appelles?
C Je m'appelle Guy.

2 Tu es en vacances ici?
B Oui, je suis en vacances avec ma famille.

3 Tiens, comment tu t'appelles?
I Martyn.

4 Tu voudrais boire quelque chose?
E Merci, je veux bien.

5 Tu aimes Paris?
D Oui, j'adore Paris.

6 Tu es britannique?
A Oui, c'est ça. Je suis de Birmingham.

7 C'est ta première visite en France?
F Oui, c'est ma première visite.

8 Tu connais la Grande-Bretagne?
G Oui, je connais Londres un peu.

9 Tu habites à Paris?
H J'habite à Poissy, tout près de Paris.

Suggested route

- Pages 68–69 of the *Livre de l'étudiant* show how conversations are blocked: they often do not develop, they are not sustained. Work on the red conversations on the left-hand side first, by making sure that the green conversaions on the right-hand side are covered up. Student read these conversations and taking one conversation per group or pair, they try to keep the conversation going. They should then feedback their ideas, listen to conversations on the tape and follow the text.

For transcript see page T 9.

Introduce the idea of using natural conversation 'fillers' or noises. For example:
– *Ben, oui.*
– *C'est vrai?*
– *Ah, non.*
– *Ah, bon?*
– *Hein?*
– *Comment?*

- Students then go through the green conversations on the right-hand side of the *Livre de l'étudiant*, adding to them any such noises or conversation 'fillers'. Can they beat the clock and sustain a conversation for a whole minute?

For transcript see page T 9.

Cahier d'activités page 44

- Students should now be ready to continue the conversations in writing on page 44 of the *Cahier d'activités*.

PART II
A way in

- To practise the basic conversation for arranging to go out begin with the question: *Tu veux sortir?* Put a list of ten suggestions on the board of famous people the students might or might not like to go out with, for example: *Tu veux sortir avec Paul Gascoigne?* Ask the class to predict the answer that five named students in the class might give to some of the questions. Interview a one of these students using the questions on the board and the class see who was right in their predictions.
- To extend this to include places first pool all of the names of places they already know and add any venues which they might want to go out to. The question is: *Tu veux venir... avec moi* (at this level we suggest not getting over concerned about the accuracy of *au*, *à la*, etc.). The students must decide on one place that they want to go to. They must find as many people in the class as they can who have want to go to the same place. They are not allowed to leave their seats for this activity so they will need to shout to each other across the room: *Tu veux venir... avec moi?* The noise level will be dreadful but short lived! If you or your neighbouring colleagues cannot tolerate noise then the same activity can be managed with students moving around the room.

- R 19 You might now try presenting a sample dialogue through a series of symbols which you gradually build up on the OHT (in the same way as for unit 1). You will find some symbols on repromaster 19.
- Once students are familiar with the dialogue you might try this idea using two telephones which, as far as we know, originates from St Martin's College PGCE course. Students sit in a circle and pass a telephone around. As in 'Pass the Parcel' you stand with your back to the circle. When you make a telephone ringing sound, the person holding the phone must pick it up and start the conversation with you. Another student may take over your role or you might introduce another telephone into the circle so that students take over both sides of the conversation.

Suggested route

- E 9 *A l'écoute: feuille numéro 9*: all the activities on this listening sheet consolidate the language practised in this unit so far.

For transcript see pages T 9 – T 10.

Answers

1: bowling; mercredi; neuf heures; café; oui
2: concert de jazz; mardi; neuf heures; club Rex; oui
3: théâtre; samedi; —; café; non

How about going...? = Si on allait...?
I'd like to. = Je veux bien.
When? = Quand?
What time? = A quelle heure?
Where shall we meet? = On se rencontre où?

Follow-up ideas

- R 17 R 18 This unit's language lends itself well to students compiling a phrase-book section for their guide. There is a suitable heading to be found on repromaster 18 for this purpose.

IT suggestions

- Using graphics or scanned images of suitable places to go, students could devise party invitations, for example, to the cinema, disco, etc.
- Using WP or DTP, students could write messages or fan letters to famous stars to arrange a meeting.
- Using *Chatter*, or two linked computers, students could simulate a situation where two people arrange a meeting (to include place, date and time).
- Using a database of well known stars, students could set up a dating agency and try to match up the stars.

Oh, pardon. Excusez-moi.
Ne vous inquiétez pas. Pas de problème, hein.

Oh, je suis désolée!
Ça va...
graffiti
8 AVRIL

Excusez-moi... C'est libre?

Oui... bien sûr...

Merci. Je m'appelle Thierry... et vous?

Salut! Tu loges ici?

Oui, je suis avec un groupe scolaire. Et toi?
Je suis en vacances avec des amis.

Salut.
Tu veux sortir avec nous?
D'accord...

Contrôle 4

Ecris tes réponses dans ton cahier d'activités, page 59

A

Ecoute la cassette.
Une marchande parle au marché.
Coche la bonne case "quantité".
Ecris les prix et le total.

	quantité			prix
	1 kg	2 kg	3kg	
Pommes	✓			5F 50
Tomates				
Pêches				
			Total:	

B

Lis le menu en français.
Ecris le menu en anglais.

Exemple:
1 = egg mayonnaise

Brasserie Mistral

Menu touristique

75f

Oeuf mayonnaise 1
ou
Salade de tomates 2
****

Steak 3
ou
Poulet rôti 4
****
Légumes 5
ou
Frites 6
****
Tarte aux pommes 7
ou
Yaourt 8
****
Café 9
Service compris 10

Contrôle 4

NOTE

A

	quantité			prix
	1 kg	2 kg	3kg	
Pommes	✓			5F 50
Tomates		✓		18F
Pêches	✓			19F 50
			Total:	43F

5

B

1 Egg mayonnaise
2 Tomato salad
3 Steak
4 Roast chicken
5 Vegetables
6 Chips
7 Apple pie
8 Yogurt
9 Coffee
10 Service included

5

C

Journal parlé

See guidelines overleaf

5

D

9h ....
10h ....
11h ....
12h ....
13h ....
14h ....
15h ....
16h ....
19h ....
20h ....

See guidelines overleaf

5

OBSERVATIONS

TOTAL

Date:

Signature de l'étudiant:

Signature du professeur:

20

CASSETTE 2 FACE 1

Contrôle 4
Livre de l'étudiant, page 60
Cahier d'activités, page 59

– Allez allez messieurs dames, mes pommes, là, toutes belles, toutes bonnes! 5 F 50 le kilo. Pas cher! Voilà, oui, madame, 1 kilo de pommes. Ça fait 5F 50 le kilo... Et avec ça? Oui des petites tomates bien mûres, bien rouges. Combien? 2 kilos? Voilà... 2 kilos de tomates. Ça fait 18F. 18F pour 2 kilos de tomates, c'est pas cher! C'est tout?... Vous ne voulez pas de mes pêches? Regardez, elles sont belles... et délicieuses! D'accord, allez, madame, 1 kilo de pêches! Voilà! 1 kilo de pêches. Ça fait 19F 50... Tout ça, ça fait... ben... 43F. 43F tout rond.

Speaking task guidelines (task C)

Ideally, these contributions will be recorded onto a student's own individual tape which may also included other items from the course. Otherwise a class tape on which all students record their answers could be used.

A mark should be awarded for each relevant utterance understood by the listener. Here is some guidance as to what the speaker may be expected to say:

Je voudrais une chambre... avec un grand lit/avec une douche/avec salle de bains... pour quatre personnes... pour deux nuits... du 6 août au 7 août...

Writing task guidelines (task D)

Each answer is worth one mark. The tasks are open ended so that there are no 'right' answers. Answers should be marked positively. Students should have the opportunity to refer to their books and a dictionary, to check spellings. With this in mind, if a student successfully communicates a relevant message, a mark should be awarded. A mark should not be awarded if the spelling is so awry that a sympathetic native speaker would be unlikely to understand the message.

In certain instances, where a student has severe handwriting difficulties, he/she may be offered the option of dictating and spelling out answers for you to transcribe. Similarly, answers might be word-processed and then pasted into the answer pages of the *Cahier d'activités.*

National Curriculum assessment

Task A	AT 1, level 3(b)
Task B	AT 3, level 2(a)
Task C	AT 2, level 3(a)
Task D	AT 4, level 3(a)

C

Journal parlé

Tu téléphones à l'Hôtel Floréal.
Fais une réservation.

Exemple:

Je téléphone de la part de mes parents, Monsieur et Madame X. Je voudrais...

D

C'est ton premier jour à Paris.
Tu écris ton journal.
Ecris cinq phrases en français.

Exemple:

scénario /senarjo/ *n.m.* scenario.

scène /sɛn/ *n.f.* scene; (*estrade, art dramatique*) stage. **mettre en ~,** (*pièce*) stage.

drame /dram/ *n.m.* drama.

pays /pei/ *n.m.* country; (*région*) region; (*village*) village. **du ~,** local.

feuilleton /fœjtɔ̃/ *n.m.* (*à suivre*) serial; (*histoire complète*) series.

voisinage /vwazinaʒ/ *n.m.* neighbourhood; (*proximité*) proximity.

RIVIERA, LE FEUILLETON QUI VAUT 21 MILLIARDS AF !

LA FAMILLE LAMBERT :
Ils ont une secrète revanche à prendre sur les Courcey

Fortune, passion et jalousie...

Sam et Elizabeth Layton : derrière le sourire du frère et de la sœur, une implacable férocité...

LA FAMILLE LAYTON :
2 Américains aux dents longues qui vont s'introduire chez les puissants Courcey

LA FAMILLE MARQUES :
Clara et Diego forment un couple diabolique qui ne recule devant rien...

endroit /ɑ̃drwa/ *n.m.* place; (*de tissu*) right side. **à l'~**, the right way round, right side out.

accessoire /akseswar/ *a.* secondary. —*n.m.* accessory; (*théâtre*) prop.

personnage /pɛrsɔnaʒ/ *n.m.* character; (*important*) personality.

Feuilleton

FEUILLETON AMÉRICAIN.

SANTA BARBARA

Carmen (Marisol Rodriguez).

Robin Wright : *Kelly* ● Ross Kettle : *Jeffrey* ● Nancy Grahn : *Julia* ● Kristen Meadows : *Tori* ● Lane Davies : *Mason* ● Scott Jaeck : *Cain* ● Marcy Walker : *Eden* ● A. Martinez : *Cruz* ● Justin Deas : *Keith* ● Nicolas Coster : *Lionel* ● Todd McKee : *Ted* ● Susan Marie Snyder : *Laken* ● Sherilyn Wolter : *Eleanor/Elena* ● Stacy Edwards : *Hayley* ● Marisol Rodriguez : *Carmen* ● Robin Mattson : *Gina* ● Richard Eden : *Brick* ● Jed Allan : *Channing* ● Jane Sibbett : *Jane* ● Judith McConnell : *Sophia* ● Rick Edwards : *Jake* ● Robert Thaler : *Pearl.*

Elena (Sherilyn Wolter) téléphone à l'hôpital pour se renseigner sur les médicaments que prend **Cain** (Scott Jaeck), puis dépose une boîte de comprimés chez les Capwell. Mais **Carmen** (Marisol Rodriguez), qui a surpris son coup de téléphone, en parle à **Pearl** (Robert Thaler)...

cahier d'activités, pages 46–47

Le voisinage

1 *Mistral-sur-Rhône* est un nouveau feuilleton.
Regarde les photos.
Fais une liste des endroits principaux.

2 Ecoute la cassette.
Les deux feuilletonistes de *Mistral-sur-Rhône* parlent.
Ils discutent des endroits principaux.
Regarde ta liste. C'est correct?

Unité 1 *Le voisinage*

Areas of experience

B Personal and social life
C The world around us
E The world of communications
G The world of imagination and creativity

Context

Deciding on a setting for a soap opera. Typical settings, countries of origin, describing areas. Different types of soap opera.

Language focus

Les endroits principaux. Un café-tabac, un pub, une épicerie, une maison de la presse, des maisons, des appartements, un immeuble, un marché, une boulangerie, une église, un supermarché. Un quartier. Une rue moderne, une vieille rue, une grande ville, un village. Le sud des Etats-Unis, l'Australie, le nord de l'Angleterre, la France, la Grande-Bretagne. Rural, chic, calme, animé, riche, sympa.

Materials

- *Livre de l'étudiant*, pages 64–65
- *Cahier d'activités*, pages 46–47
- *Cassette: Le voisinage; La musique des feuilletons*
- Repromaster 20

A way in

- Introduce the idea of the soap opera by giving an example, Eastenders: *c'est un feuilleton britannique*. Ask for other examples including those other than British. Find out the group's preferences and watching habits: *Qui aime ...? Qui regarde ...?* Students may take over the questioning here. They may like to guess how long each soap has been running.
- Having established the meaning of *feuilleton*, ask the group to come up with the principal places in each soap mentioned: *Quels sont les endroits principaux de Neighbours?* Write these on the board or OHT. Ask for other places they know the French for (revision from **Mistral 1**).
- Using repromaster 20, photocopy the soap opera settings onto OHT and ask students to help build up a plan of a new soap town, Mistral-sur-Rhône. Draw a rough plan of a town and ask students to supply the details. Encourage them to be precise using the points of the compass: *C'est où le café, au nord, au nord-est, à l'est* etc?. Students should then look at *Livre de l'étudiant*, pages 64–65, to see what the key places in Mistral-sur-Rhône actually are. You could then revise the plan to match.

Suggested route

- *Livre de l'étudiant*, pages 64–65. Students first list the focal points in Mistral-sur-Rhône and then listen to the two script writers to see if their list is correct.

Answers

un supermarché
un marché
un café-tabac (avec une terrasse)
une église
un hôtel
une boulangerie
des appartements
un immeuble
des maisons

For transcript see page T 10.

- Students then identify the famous soap operas and match the descriptions to the photographs.

Answers

A: *Coronation Street*
B: *Neighbours*
C: *Dallas*

- ***Cahier d'activités* page 46**

FEUILLETON Le voisinage

Feuilletons: êtes-vous experts?

1 Regarde la page 65 du livre de l'étudiant.
Donne les détails pour *Mistral-sur-Rhône*.

Endroits principaux: ....

Situation: ....

Pays d'origine: ....

2 Donne les détails pour trois autres feuilletons.
Remplis les cases 1, 2 et 3.

	Titre	Endroits principaux	Situation	Pays d'origine
1				
2				
3				
4				
5				

3 Et en classe?
Cherche des experts de deux autres feuilletons.
Pose des questions.
Remplis les cases 4 et 5.

46

- Having matched up the descriptions of famous soap operas with the photos, they then write a similar description for *Mistral-sur-Rhône*.

Answers

Endroits principaux: un supermarché, un café-tabac, un immeuble et des maisons, un hôtel, une boulangerie, une église, un marché.
Situation: un faubourg de Lyon.
Pays d'origine: la France.

- Students are then asked to gather information about current soap operas. To prepare for this you might ask the set of questions with reference to those soaps on the *Livre de l'étudiant* (or any others that they watch and can detail in the same way). This could be a memory test if students do not look back at the book.

Cahier d'activités page 47

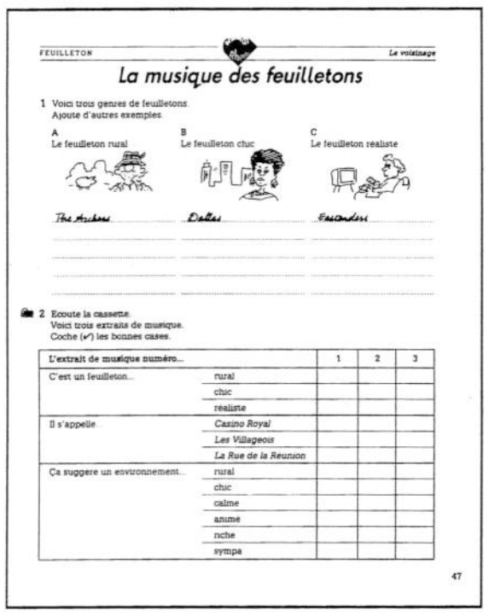
La musique des feuilletons

- This activity focuses on different types of soap opera, and their signature tunes. Students are first asked to list examples of different types of soap opera.
- They then listen to the cassette, and complete the grid, choosing a suitable title and type of setting for the three types of soap opera. They first have to decide on the type of soap each piece of music is probably for.

For transcript see page T 10.

Answers

L'extrait de musique numéro...		1	2	3
C'est un feuilleton...	rural			✓
	chic	✓		
	réaliste		✓	
Il s'appelle...	*Casino Royal*	✓		
	Les Villageois			✓
	La Rue de la Réunion		✓	
Ça suggère un environnement...	rural			✓
	chic	✓		
	calme			✓
	animé	✓	✓	
	riche	✓		
	sympa		✓	✓

Follow-up idea

- Students may like to invent their own French soap opera. At the end of each unit they could add details. At this juncture they might decide on the name, location and focal points. They could draw up a plan.

IT suggestions

CK 9

- Using CK9, devise reinforcement exercises which revise the soap opera place names and settings.
- The countries of origin could be added on the screen or this CK could be combined with a listening activity which includes the signature tunes of the most popular soaps.
- You or the students may prefer to make up your own CK using coloured pictures of current soap opera stars in order to revise vocabulary for descriptions.
- Using WP or DTP, students could prepare data collection forms about soap opera preferences.
- Students could enter the data thus collected into a simple database that incorporates the field names of popular soaps.

3 Voici trois feuilletons célèbres.
Tu les reconnais?
Quel est le titre de chaque feuilleton?

4 Lis les descriptions.
Quelle description va avec quel feuilleton?

A
Endroits principaux: un café, un pub, l'épicerie du coin, une maison de la presse, des maisons.
Situation: une vieille rue dans le nord de l'Angleterre.
Pays d'origine: la Grande-Bretagne.

B
Endroits principaux: un café, des maisons, un hôtel.
Situation: une rue moderne.
Pays d'origine: l'Australie.

C
Endroits principaux: un ranch, un bureau.
Situation: une grande ville dans le sud des Etats-Unis.
Pays d'origine: les Etats-Unis.

Et pour *Mistral-sur-Rhône*?	la France un supermarché un café-tabac
Endroits principaux?	un immeuble et des maisons un hôtel
Situation?	une boulangerie une église un marché
Pays d'origine?	un faubourg de Lyon

cahier d'activités, pages 48–49

Les personnages

1 Travaille dans un groupe de trois personnes.
Regardez ces acteurs et actrices.
Ils auditionnent pour le feuilleton *Mistral-sur-Rhône*.

Vincent Blois 26.4.65

Joseph Moutier 3.6.46

Patrick Foncier 3.3.72

Jean-Louis Pitel 27.6.32

Fernand Janteau 2.3.48

Olivier Machet 12.3.79

Richard Deneuve 15.5.66

Gilles Pons 12.12.71

Marco Guigin 28.10.78

Thierry Colin 1.8.56

Michel Jonsac
- 15 ans
- frère de Nicolas Jonsac
- très sympa
- beaucoup d'amis
- sénégalais

Nicolas Jonsac
- 13 ans
- sympa mais il aime faire des bêtises
- adore son frère Michel
- sénégalais

Antoine Merville
- 17 ans
- parents morts
- habite chez ses grands-parents, rapports difficiles
- en apprentissage chez le plombier, Gilles Jonsac
- l'esprit indépendant

Stéphane Durrant
- 59 ans
- mari de Geneviève Durrant
- concierge de l'immeuble

Robert Desjardins
- 25 ans
- célibataire
- beau, charmant et arrogant
- malhonnête
- homme d'affaires

Yann Belfort
- 34 ans
- mari de Julia Belfort
- médecin
- Julia et Yann sont riches et matérialistes

Gilles Jonsac
- 46 ans
- habite une maison ordinaire avec sa femme, Marie, et leurs deux fils
- plombier
- heureux et amusant
- sénégalais

Unité 2 *Les personnages*

Areas of experience

A Everyday activities
B Personal and social life
G The world of imagination and creativity

Context

The casting agency, types of characters found in typical soap operas. Choosing actors and actresses for suitable roles. Stereotypes.

Language focus

Les personnes âgées, le couple BCBG, une famille solide et stable, le personnage malhonnête, le groupe de jeunes, la famille monoparentale, les gens de passage, la femme fatale.
Revision of personal descriptions.

Materials

- *Livre de l'étudiant*, pages 66–67
- *Cahier d'activités*, pages 48–49
- *Cassette: Les personnages*
- 21 Repromaster 21

A way in

- 21 To introduce the different types of characters normally found in soap operas, use repromaster 21. This gives illustrations of each type as a caricature. Use them either as OHTs or flashcards so that you build them up gradually. When you have introduced them you might say each type and the students must name a soap opera character which fits the type.
- Then reverse rôles – students say the type and you name the character or ask students to do this with a partner.
- Once students are familiar with the language ask them to fit a label to each type so that they can see the written version. You might make this into a mini-flashcard game where each pair of students has a set of pictures and labels. Using these they might test each other on the French, name a character to fit the type or play pelmanism.
- Depending on the group of students you might give them the following short dialogue as an audition piece and pairs must audition by choosing a character type each. The audience must watch and guess which type each was auditioning for.

This will not work for all of the types so it might be an idea to list those possible. Read the script through first. They are likely to need to look up or ask the meaning of *cambriolage*.

– Bonjour, Pascal(e)
– Bonjour. Ça va.
– Oui, merci.
– As-tu vu Madame Voisine ce matin?
– Madame Voisine?
– Oui.
– Pourquoi?
– Son appartement!
– Son appartement?
– Oui ... C'est terrible ... Un cambriolage.
– Non!
– La police est là.
– Ah bon! Et Madame Voisine, ça va?
– Oui, oui, ça va.

Suggested route

Cahier d'activités page 48

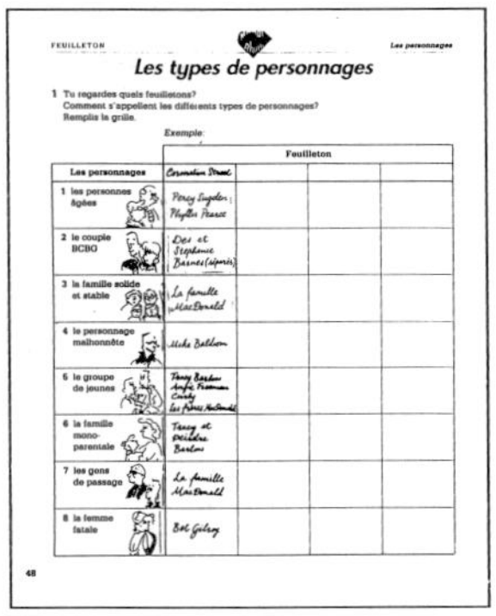

- This activity asks students to match types of character to soap opera characters which they know. It attempts to show that script writers work to a formula and that a mix of types makes for a successful soap.
- *Livre de l'étudiant*, pages 66–67. Before doing this activity where students decide which actors they would choose for each character you might ask them to categorize the characters under three headings: *MALHONNETE/SYMPA/ON NE SAIT PAS.*
- The listening activity then asks students to work out which rôles are being auditioned.

Answers

1 Nicolas Jonsac
2 Geneviève Durrant
3 Hélène Blanchard

For transcript see page T 10.

Cahier d'activités page 49

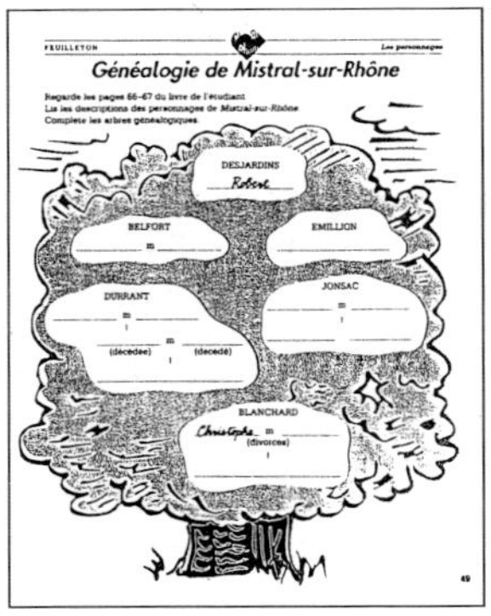

- This page also involves a close reading of pages 66–67 of the *Livre de l'étudiant*; students need to re-read the text about the characters and complete the family trees.

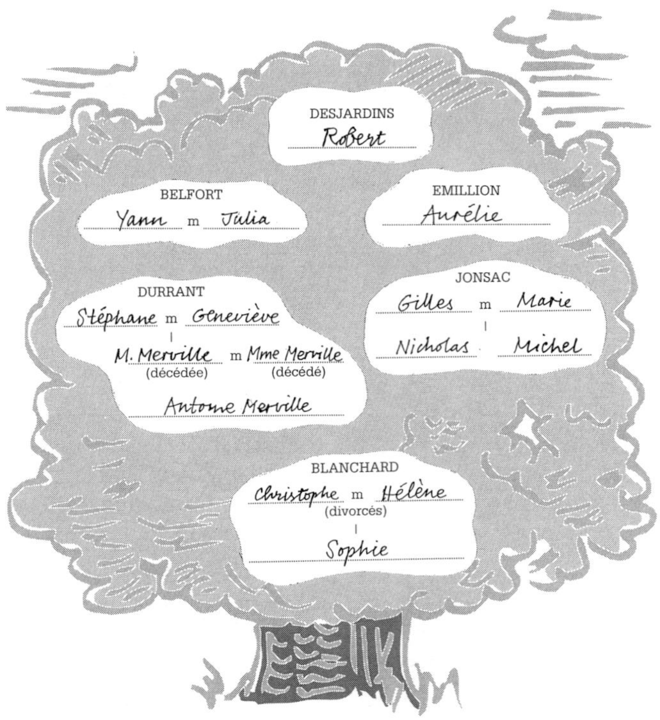

Follow-up idea

- If students have started their own soap opera from the previous unit it is at this point that they invent a series of characters following the list of types covered in this unit. They could also create cards for the characters, as on *Livre de l'étudiant*, pages 66–67, and family trees.

IT suggestions

- Using WP or DTP and scanned images, students could write short descriptions of their favourite soap opera characters.
- Using E-mail, they could conduct a survey into which soap stars are liked by the partner school's students.
- Using WP or DTP and graphics or scanned images, students could then invent descriptions for their own soap opera characters, using the guidelines suggested in the *Livre de l'étudiant*. These descriptions could then be made into a news sheet for a magazine.

2 Lisez les descriptions des personnages de *Mistral-sur-Rhône*. Choisissez les acteurs et les actrices.

Exemple: Richard Deneuve joue le rôle de Robert Desjardins.

Sophie Blanchard
- 16 ans
- lycéenne
- amusante et sympa
- habite avec sa mère

Julia Belfort
- 35 ans
- femme de Yann Belfort
- sans enfants
- habite une grande maison de grand standing
- notaire

Geneviève Durrant
- 59 ans
- femme de Stéphane Durrant
- concierge de l'immeuble
- habite avec son mari et leur petit-fils, Antoine
- bavarde et curieuse

Marie Jonsac
- 47 ans
- femme de Gilles Jonsac
- institutrice
- Marie et son mari sont bien respectés
- sénégalaise

Hélène Blanchard
- 36 ans
- divorcée
- habite avec sa fille, Sophie, dans un appartement
- secrétaire
- très sympa et gentille

Aurélie Emillion
- 19 ans
- indépendante et mystérieuse
- habite seule dans un studio
- travaille dans un bureau

3 Comparez vos choix avec un antre groupe.

4 Ecoute la cassette. Quel acteur auditionne pour quel rôle?

cahier d'activités, pages 50–51

En scène

1 Ecoute la cassette.
Des acteurs jouent dans une scène.
Lis le texte.
Quels sont les accessoires
pour cette scène?

Au Café

Mistral sur Rhône

Michel: Tiens, tu l'as?
Aurélie: Oui oui... c'est dans le sac.
Michel: Tu as vu le journal?
Aurélie: Quoi?
Michel: Le journal. Il y a sa photo dans le journal.
Aurélie: Une photo. Ben, dis donc, si on ...
Barman: Salut! Qu'est-ce que je vous sers?
Aurélie: Euh, oui. Euh, un ... un whisky avec de l'eau, s'il te plaît.
Barman: Oui, d'accord. Et pour toi, Michel?
Michel: De l'eau.
Barman: Tu ne veux pas un sandwich?
Michel: Non, non. Merci.
Aurélie: Eh, bien. Dis, la photo, c'est...
Antoine: Aurélie, tu dois te sauver. Vite. Il y a une voiture de police devant ton appartement et...
Aurélie: Zut, c'est la photo.
Barman: Elle est partie? Aah, elle a laissé son sac ... Mais qu'est-ce que c'est que ça?
Michel: Euh... donne-moi le sac. Donne moi ça.
Barman: Un revolver!... Et l'addition? Tu n'as pas payé!

2 Travaille avec un/une partenaire.
Jouez les rôles des personnages.

Unité 3 *En scène*

Area of experience

A Everyday activities
C The world around us
G The world of imagination and creativity

Context

Soap opera sets and script. Stage props.

Language focus

Des accessoires. Un miroir, des posters, des disques, une chaîne hi-fi, des vêtements, des coussins, des étagères, des fleurs, des plantes, un téléviseur, un calendrier, une addition, des sandwiches, un chapeau, un journal, des verres, une bouteille, un sac, un revolver. Revision of prepositions: *à droite, à gauche, entre, en face, à côté de, devant, derrière.*

Materials

- *Livre de l'étudiant*, pages 68–69
- *Cahier d'activités*, pages 50–51
- *Cassette: Au café*
- A recently recorded episode of a soap opera. You might ask one of the students or a cooperative member of your form to make a recording for you.

A way in

- You will ideally need to have video recorded a recent episode of a soap opera. Failing this you will need photographs of soap opera sets from a magazine. The idea is to look at the stage props used in some of the sets.

Show a clip of your video and freeze frame on the most interesting set (a house interior, a pub or café interior). Students must imagine that they are responsible for the props used in the programme (*responsable des accessoires*). You may feel that this is best done in English or use objects around you to illustrate what you mean: *Ça, c'est un accessoire* (showing your bag) *mais ça, non* (showing table).

Students then make a list of all of the props needed in that scene. Explain that a prop is anything on the set that is portable, not furniture. This will work best in small groups and with a time limit. Fast forward to another set and repeat the exercise. Each group now joins another and comes up with a composite list for each scene. They may require the use of dictionaries for this activity. Finally make a class list from contributions from the different groups.

- You may feel that this activity is too difficult for your group, in which case you might prepare the list yourself and include props which don't actually appear, give it to them, they then watch the clips, and tick the props from the list you have provided.
- To revise prepositions using this context draw a rough plan on the board or OHT of one of the rooms you have just seen, including the main features, for example the bar if it is a pub. Students must then try to remember where all of the props were so that you, or another student, may mark them on the plan. If students have difficulty remembering the prepositions it might be an idea to do the activity at the bottom of page 51 of the *Cahier d'activités* first. They can then check with the video recording to see if they were right.

Suggested route

- *Livre de l'étudiant*, pages 68–69. Students listen to this part of an episode of *Mistral-sur-Rhône* and read the script. They must decide what props are needed for this scene.

For transcript see page T11.

Answers

un sac
un journal
des verres
des sandwiches
un revolver

- Some groups might like to act out this scene, though this will not be a suitable activity for all.
- The final activity is to look closely at the photo of the scene, and to decide if the list of props is correct.

Answers

It's not correct; the following are <u>not</u> needed:
un calendrier
un chapeau
une bouteille de vin

Cahier d'activités page 50

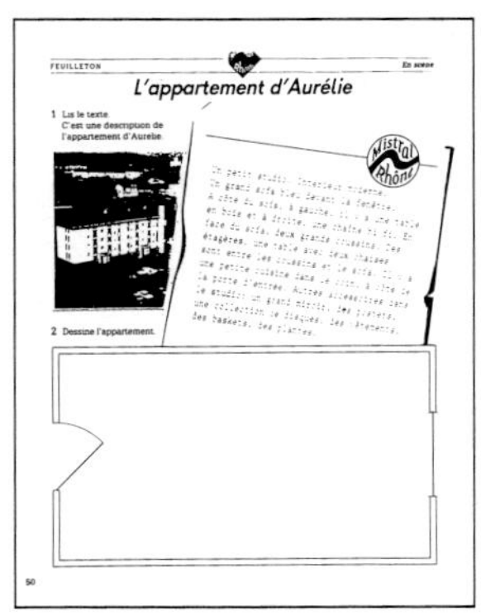

- Students read the description of the studio flat of Aurélie and then draw a plan.

Answers

The plan must include the following:
- a large blue sofa in front of a window
- a wooden table to the left of the sofa
- a hi-fi system to the right
- two large cushions opposite the sofa
- a table and two chairs between the cushions and the sofa
- a small kitchen in a corner, next to the entrance
- shelves, a large mirror, posters, records, clothes, trainers, plants

Cahier d'activités page 51

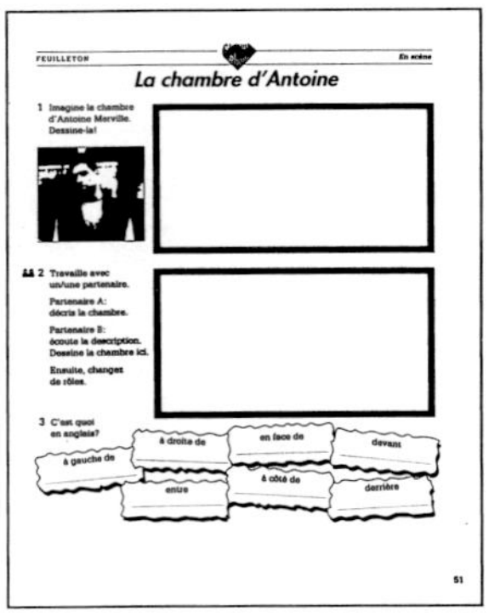

- Students imagine the room of Antoine Merville, draw it, and then describe it to a partner who then draws what they say without seeing the original. They compare drawings to see if the partner has understood the description.
- Students then complete the definitions at the bottom of the page, using a dictionary if necessary.

Answers

à gauche de = to the left of
à droite de = to the right of
entre = between
en face de = opposite
à côté de = next to
devant = in front of
derrière = behind

Follow-up idea

- If students have started their own soap opera in the previous units it is at this point that they decide on their sets and write their props lists. They could also add plans of rooms, main sets, etc.

IT suggestions

- Using a package such as *Quelle Tête* or *Jeu des Ménages,* students could revise terms which will be useful for placing furniture items on set.
- Using a graphics package, students could design a television set for their own soap opera and label all items on set.
- CK 10 Using CK10 devise activities to reinforce the vocabulary for props. Students could decide what props are needed for various scenes.
- Using WP or DTP, students could devise simple props lists for their production.

1 Un téléviseur
2 Un calendrier
3 Une addition
4 Des sandwiches
5 Un chapeau
6 Un journal
7 Des verres
8 Une bouteille de vin
9 Un sac
10 Des fleurs

3 Regarde la liste des accessoires pour la scène sur la photo. C'est correct?

cahier d'activités, pages 52–53

L'action

1 Ecoute la cassette.
Regarde la photo du mariage de Robert et Hélène.
Madame Durrant observe la scène et bavarde.

2 Identifie les huit personnes qui habitent Mistral-sur-Rhône.

Exemple: **10** = Nicolas Jonsac

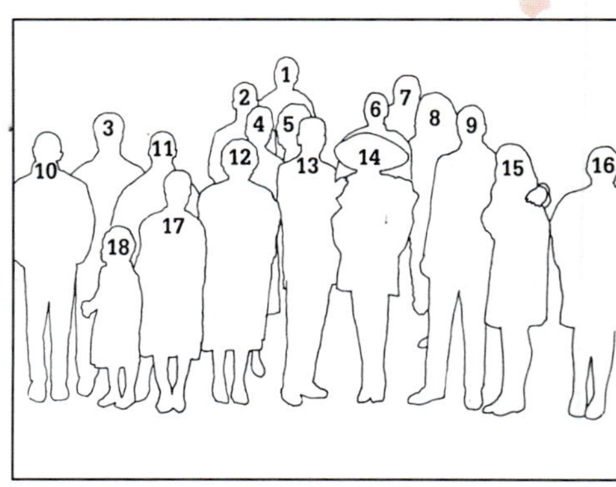

Unité 4 *L'action*

Area of experience

B Personal and social life
E The world of communications
G The world of imagination and creativity

Context

Story lines for a soap opera.

Language focus

Present tense using the idea if planning what is going to happen in a series of episodes. *X se marie, X va en vacances, X gagne de l'argent, X a un bébé, X meurt, X se dispute avec..., X rencontre Y, X part, X a un accident, X a une liaison avec Y, X divorce.*

Materials

- *Livre de l'étudiant*, pages 70–71
- *Cahier d'activités*, pages 52–53
- *Cassette: Le mariage de Robert et Hélène; Le drame du retour*

A way in

- This unit lends itself to students working independently and at their own pace. Your input might come towards the end of the unit, *Cahier d'activités* pages 52–53, as they work out what different characters might be doing in several on-going episodes. You will probably need to give quite a lot of help with the language but emphasize that the outline of the episodes may be written as jotted notes rather than full sentences.
- If you have copies of **Mistral 1** available, encourage students to look back at *Histoire Vraie* (module 2) where they prepared and wrote short photo romances. Give them time to look through the *Livre de l'étudiant* as well as their *Cahier d'activités*, if available, to find as many phrases or sentences which tell you a part of the action of a story. You may prefer to choose the sentences from **Mistral 1** yourself, give the students the English and ask them to find the French. Brainstorm these and put them on the board or OHT.

You may want to add to this list some of the following as being more suitable for the soap opera *context: X se marie, X va en vacances, X gagne de l'argent, X a un bébé, X meurt, X se dispute avec..., X rencontre Y, X part, X a un accident, X a une liaison avec Y, X divorce.* Try where possible to think of instances from current soaps so that you can add names. A discussion in English with you tutor group will help if your knowledge is patchy. Failing that colleagues may be able to help.

Suggested route

- *Livre de l'étudiant,* pages 70–71. Students should begin with this. They are to listen to a discussion about the wedding in *Mistral-sur-Rhône* and identify the people on the wedding photograph. They will probably have to refer back to *Livre de l'étudiant*, pages 66–67.

For transcript see page T 11.

Answers

3 = Gilles Jonsac
9 = Antoine Merville
10 = Nicolas Jonsac
11 = Michel Jonsac
12 = Marie Jonsac
13 = Robert Desjardins
14 = Hélène Blanchard
15 = Sophie Blanchard

- Students then listen to the scene of the return of the newly weds, and decide which strip of pictures illustrates the scene.

For transcript see page T 11.

Answer

B

Cahier d'activités page 52

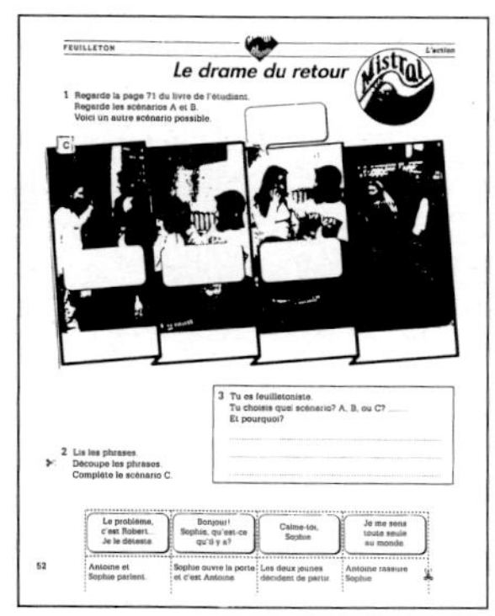

- Students complete the third version of the scene of the return of the newly weds, and then choose the version they feel is the most suitable.

Answers

Sophie ouvre la porte et c'est Antoine.

"Bonjour! Sophie, qu'est-ce qu'il y a?"

Antoine et Sophie parlent.
"Le problème, c'est Robert ... Je le déteste."

Antoine rassure Sophie.

"Je me sens toute seule au monde."
"Calme toi, Sophie."

Les deux jeunes décident de partir.

Cahier d'activités page 53

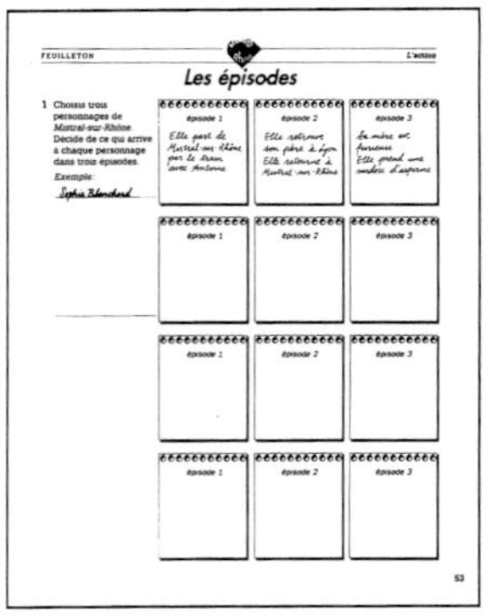

- We suggest that you follow the 'way in' to prepare students for this activity, writing episodes for different characters.

Follow-up idea

- If students have been preparing their own soap opera in previous units they should now choose some of the story lines they have just been working on but substitute names from their own list of characters.

IT suggestions

- Using WP or DTP, students could devise a story line for their own soap opera, using the words and phrases in the *Livre de l'étudiant* and on the cassette. Photocopiable transcipts are available for reference.
- Using WP or DTP, students could then edit the script that they or another group have produced.

Le drame du retour

3 Ecoute la cassette.
Robert et Hélène rentrent après leur voyage de noces.
C'est le drame.
Regarde les photos.
C'est A ou B?

A

B

cahier d'activités, pages 54–55

Moments à suspense

1 Ecoute la cassette.
Lis ces exemples de scénarios.

Unité 5 *Moments à suspense*

Area of experience

A Everyday activities
B Personal and social life
E The world of communications
G The world of imagination and creativity

Context

Cliffhangers at the end of an episode of a soap opera. Looking at various possibilities.

Language focus

Personal preferences: *aime, n'aime pas.*

Materials

- *Livre de l'étudiant*, pages 72–73
- *Cahier d'activités*, pages 54–55
- *Cassette: Moments à suspense; A suivre...*

A way in

- This unit is designed mainly to show students another technique that soap opera writers use: the cliffhanger at the end of the episode.

  The unit requires them to have some knowledge of the characters so far in *Mistral-sur-Rhône*. They might like to refer back to pages 66–67. First ask some general questions about what we already know about some of the characters; their ages, personalities, family circumstances and type: *Il/elle est jeune? Il est le père/elle est la mère de qui? Il/elle est comment? Sympa? Il/elle représente quel type de personnage*?

- Now ask them to use facts if they know them or their imagination to decide who gets on with whom in *Mistral-sur-Rhône*: *Qui aime qui? X aime ou n'aime pas Y?* First build up a list of all the characters they have so far met. Begin to construct a sociogramme on the board or OHT.

  This is an idea taken from page 43 of *L'immeuble* by Francis Debyser. It consists of a large circle around the edge of which you write the names of the characters. You may prefer two circles one for *Les jeunes*, the other for *Les moins jeunes* allowing for overlaps between circles, if appropriate. You then join one character to another by a line the type of line you draw indicates if the character gets on with the other or not. So a line like this ++++++ indicates that they do not get on well, a dotted line - - - - - - indicates that they do. Some characters may not join up with anyone else, or perhaps with only one or two people. Students may like to do the sociogramme on the spare page at the beginning of the module in their *Cahier d'activités*.

Suggested route

- *Livre de l'étudiant*, pages 72–73. This is a listen-and-read activity in which students are asked to consider which, of a series of cliffhangers, is the most passionate, the most tragic and so on.

  For transcript see page T 11.

Cahier d'activités page 54

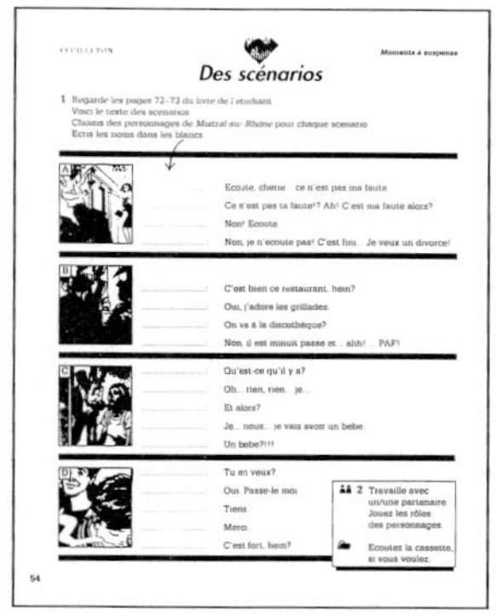
FEUILLETON — Moments à suspense

Des scénarios

1 Regarde les pages 72–73 du livre de l'étudiant.
Voici le texte des scénarios.
Choisis des personnages de *Mistral-sur-Rhône* pour chaque scénario.
Ecris les noms dans les blancs.

A
........: Ecoute, chérie... ce n'est pas ma faute.
........: Ce n'est pas ta faute!? Ah! C'est ma faute alors?
........: Non! Ecoute...
........: Non, je n'écoute pas! C'est fini... Je veux un divorce!

B
........: C'est bien ce restaurant, hein?
........: Oui, j'adore les grillades.
........: On va à la discothèque?
........: Non, il est minuit passé et... ahh! ... PAF!

C
........: Qu'est-ce qu'il y a?
........: Oh... rien, rien... je...
........: Et alors?
........: Je... nous... je vais avoir un bébé.
........: Un bébé?!!!

D
........: Tu en veux?
........: Oui. Passe-le moi.
........: Tiens.
........: Merci.
........: C'est fort, hein?

2 Travaille avec un/une partenaire. Jouez les rôles des personnages.
Ecoutez la cassette, si vous voulez.

54

- This follows on directly from the above but this time they are given a written version of the scenarios and they have to decide for themselves which *Mistral-sur-Rhône* characters might be involved in each. Their sociogramme should come in useful here.
- Students could also act out the scenes, and record them onto cassette or perform them to the rest of the group.

Cahier d'activités page 55

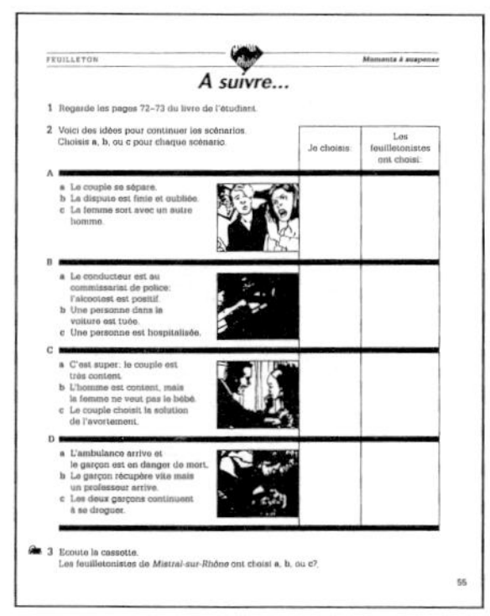
FEUILLETON — Moments à suspense

A suivre...

1 Regarde les pages 72–73 du livre de l'étudiant.

2 Voici des idées pour continuer les scénarios.
Choisis a, b, ou c pour chaque scénario.

	Je choisis:	Les feuilletonistes ont choisi:
A a Le couple se sépare. b La dispute est finie et oubliée. c La femme sort avec un autre homme.		
B a Le conducteur est au commissariat de police: l'alcootest est positif. b Une personne dans la voiture est tuée. c Une personne est hospitalisée.		
C a C'est super: le couple est très content. b L'homme est content, mais la femme ne veut pas le bébé. c Le couple choisit la solution de l'avortement.		
D a L'ambulance arrive et le garçon est en danger de mort. b Le garçon récupère vite mais un professeur arrive. c Les deux garçons continuent à se droguer.		

3 Ecoute la cassette.
Les feuilletonistes de *Mistral-sur-Rhône* ont choisi a, b, ou c?

55

- This is a multiple choice activity in which students are asked to predict the next scene for each of the scenarios detailed in the *Livre de l'étudiant*. They have three possible options for each and they must decide on one of them. They then listen and see which was actually chosen by the script writers.

  For transcript see pages T 11 – T 12.

Answers

A = c B = a C = b D = a

Follow-up idea

- If the students have been inventing their own soap opera they may now like to add some cliffhangers to their plans taken from this unit.

IT suggestions

- Using WP or DTP, students could create the sociogramme (referred to in the way in to this unit).
- Using WP or DTP, students could also devise their own cliffhangers for the ends of episodes, following closely the suggestions given.
- Using WP or DTP, students could then edit the script they have produced.

2 Travaille avec un/une partenaire.
Quel est le moment ...

a) le plus passionnant? b) le plus triste? c) le plus réaliste? d) le plus tragique?

3 Comparez vos choix avec un autre groupe.

Contrôle 5

Ecris tes réponses dans ton cahier d'activités, page 60

A

Ecoute la cassette.
Coche (✓) la bonne case.
Ces personnages sont heureux ou malheureux en amour?

Exemple:

B

Lis ces notes.
Complète le plan de la scène.

- Une voiture de police devant la banque.
- Un policier derrière la voiture de police.
- Un café en face de la banque.
- Un couple à la terrasse du café.
- Un supermarché à côté de la banque.

Contrôle 5

NOTE

A

1 ☺ ☐ ☹ ☑   2 ☺ ☑ ☹ ☐

3 ☺ ☐ ☹ ☑   4 ☺ ☑ ☹ ☐   5 ☺ ☐ ☹ ☑

5

B

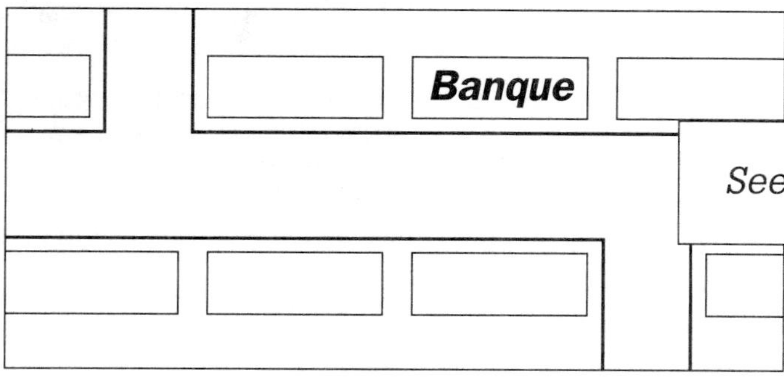

See answers overleaf

5

C

1 ....

2 ....

3 ....

4 ....

5 ....

See guidelines overleaf

5

D

Journal parlé

See guidelines overleaf

5

OBSERVATIONS

TOTAL

Date:

Signature de l'étudiant:

Signature du professeur:

20

CASSETTE 2 FACE 2

Contrôle 5
Livre de l'étudiant, page 74
Cahier d'activités, page 60

Exemple

– Oui, c'est vrai. C'est bien, hein? Je sors avec Robert. Oui... Robert! Il est sympa! Tu sais, je crois que je suis amoureuse de Robert.

1

– Mon grand malheur: j'aime Nicole. Mais elle ne me regarde pas! Je pense à Nicole. Je rêve de Nicole... Je dis bonjour à Nicole... Rien! Pas de réaction.

2

– Allô! Claude, salut! Je te téléphone pour dire merci pour les fleurs! Je t'aime, tu sais...

3

– Allô, mademoiselle? Georges est avec vous? Je suis la fiancée de Georges. Dites à Georges s'il vous plaît que c'est cassé. C'est fini. C'est terminé! Je ne l'aime plus.

4

– Alors on sort ce soir ma Julie? A huit heures, devant le cinéma. Je t'embrasse ma Julie, je t'adore. A ce soir.

5

– Caroline est enceinte mon vieux. Oui, c'est moi le père. C'est une catastrophe. C'est épouvantable.

Answers to task B

The sketch should include the following details:
A police car in front of the bank.
A policeman behind the police car.
A café opposite the bank.
A couple sitting outside the café.
A supermarket next to the bank.

Writing task guidelines (task C)

Each answer is worth one mark. The tasks are open ended so that there are no 'right' answers. Answers should be marked positively. Students should have the opportunity to refer to their books and a dictionary, to check spellings. With this in mind, if a student successfully communicates a relevant message, a mark should be awarded. A mark should not be awarded if the spelling is so awry that a sympathetic native speaker would be unlikely to understand the message.

In certain instances, where a student has severe handwriting difficulties, he/she may be offered the option of dictating and spelling out answers for you to transcribe. Similarly, answers might be word-processed and then pasted into the answer pages of the *Cahier d'activités.*

Possible answers to task C

une plante
des coussins
des livres
des étagères
des disques
des posters
des tableaux
un sofa
une table

Speaking task guidelines (task D)

Ideally, these contributions will be recorded onto a student's own individual tape which may also included other items from the course. Otherwise a class tape on which all students record their answers could be used.

A mark should be awarded for each relevant utterance understood by the listener. The example in the *Livre de l'étudiant* gives some guidance as to what the speaker may be expected to say.

National Curriculum assessment

Task A	AT 1, level 4(a)
Task B	AT 3, level 3(a)
Task C	AT 4, level 2(b)
Task D	AT 2, level 3(b)

Regarde la photo.
C'est le salon de la famille Jonsac.
Quels sont les accessoires?
Donne cinq exemples en français.

Exemple: Un miroir

C

EastEnders

Journal parlé

Choisis un personnage de feuilleton.
Donne cinq détails en français.

Exemple:

J'aime Michelle dans *Eastenders*.

Elle est gentille.

Michelle aime Clyde.

Elle a les cheveux bruns.

Sa mère s'appelle Pauline.

D

Transcripts

CASSETTE 1 FACE 1

TOUS LES JOURS
Unité 1: Tout le confort moderne
Livre de l'étudiant, page 8

La liste de mariage

- Tiens, Alain regarde!
- Ah oui, c'est joli, cette parure de lit.
- Il y a une housse de couette en coton. C'est très simple et si beau. Et tu as vu les taies d'oreiller? Comme c'est élégant, tout ça!
- C'est de la part de Jacqueline, n'est-ce pas?
- Oui, c'est bien ça.
- Ah, et... ça, c'est un cadeau de mémé.
- Qu'est-ce que c'est?
- C'est... ah... une cafetière...
- Une cafetière? Oh, chouette!
- Une cafetière à piston. Sans filtre, ni électricité... un délicieux café vite fait. Super, hein?
- J'adore ces verres à vin. En verre bleu, c'est original, n'est-ce pas?
- Ah oui, c'est super, ça. Passe-moi la boîte là-bas, Elisabeth.
- Voilà, c'est lourd, hein?
- Je crois que c'est de Julien. Oui, oui... c'est bien ça.
- C'est quoi? Oh, ça doit être l'horloge.
- Je ne sais pas... Non... Attends un moment... C'est, ah, c'est le service que nous avons demandé. Le service Fantaisie.
- Fais-moi voir, Alain... Oh, c'est merveilleux, ça! Tu vois... il y a des tasses, des soucoupes... et un sucrier, un plateau... et un pot à lait.

Unité 1: Tout le confort moderne
Cahier d'activités, page 6

Encore une invention!

- Mesdames et messieurs, je vous présente tout le confort moderne. Voici une invention superbe! Si on tire la corde 1, un téléviseur descend. Et la corde 2, c'est pour la télécommande. Si on tire la corde 3, avec le pied, du bain moussant tombe dans la baignoire. C'est formidable! Vous avez soif? Pas de problème... Si on tire la corde 4, du vin tombe dans un verre. Vous avez faim? Dans le placard 1, vous trouvez des choses délicieuses, un hamburger, de la limonade – tout ce que vous voulez. Et dans le placard 2, vous trouvez des serviettes de bain... C'est incroyable, n'est-ce pas? Eh bien, mesdames et messieurs, ce système formidable coûte seulement 5 millions de francs!

Unité 2: Le travail n'est jamais fini
Cahier d'activités, page 7

Dispute en famille

- Marilyne?... Marilyne?... Oh, ça m'énerve... Marilyne!
- Oui, papa?
- Viens ici.
- Comment?
- V-i-e-n-s i-c-i!
- Un moment... j'arrive!
- Tu descends immédiatement!
- Oui, papa?
- J'en ai marre. Tu ne fais r-i-e-n en ce moment.
- Quoi?
- Tu écoutes tes disques. C'est tout.
- Ce n'est pas vrai, papa. En ce moment, je fais mon lit. Allez, monte! Tu vas voir.
- Ah oui, tu fais ton lit. Extra! Et quoi d'autre, euh? C'est tout, hein?
- Ben... je fais la vaisselle tous les jours...
- Ah! Quelle merveille! Tu fais la vaisselle! Oh... C'est bien gentil!
- Oui... et, samedi, j'ai fait le ménage.
- Oui, d'accord, mais...
- Et je fais toute ma lessive et, vendredi, j'ai fait la cuisine puis...
- Oui, oui mais...
- Et toi, papa?
- Quoi... moi?
- Qu'est-ce que tu fais, toi?
- Ecoute...
- Tu fais la lessive?... Non... La vaisselle? Non jamais... La cuisine? Ah, tu parles! Le ménage?...
- Ça y est, hein? Tu ne respectes jamais tes parents! C'est toujours pareil! Et ta musique... ça m'énerve!!

Unité 2: Le travail n'est jamais fini
Livre de l'étudiant, page 11

Monsieur Madame

- Bonsoir à tous. Voici notre premier couple, les Guiguin.
- Bonsoir.
- Bonsoir.
- Il fait souvent la vaisselle?
- Non, jamais!
- Il fait souvent la cuisine?
- Ah! Non, jamais!
- Il fait souvent le ménage?
- Non, non!
- Vous faites souvent la vaisselle, la cuisine, le ménage?
- Oui, toujours!!
- Zéro!
- Menteur! Idiot!

Unité 3: Agendas
Livre de l'étudiant, page 12

Un week-end avec le Président de la République française

Scène 1

- Voilà ton dessert préféré, chérie. Ferme les yeux et devine ce que c'est.
- Oui, mamie, devine, devine.
- Oh là là! Euh... Ça sent un peu comme des fraises.
- Non, non!
- Un gâteau au chocolat...?
- Non, ce n'est pas ça!
- Attends... Une tarte aux pommes?
- Oui, oui, c'est ça!!
- Silence, silence, s'il vous plaît. Allez, on chante tous ensemble...
- Joyeux anniversaire...

Scène 2

- Monsieur le Président, vos costumes sont presque prêts. Vous avez ces cinq-là pour votre voyage au Japon. Toutes des couleurs claires.
- Ahhh là là, je n'aime pas du tout les couleurs claires. Surtout pas le beige... Le gris, ça va, mais le beige... oh...
- Oui, monsieur, mais il faut penser au climat. Il va faire chaud!
- Je sais, mais ces couleurs là!!
- Le beige est à la mode, Monsieur le Président...
- Oui, mais je ne suis pas à la mode. Et qu'est-ce que c'est que cette cravate multicolore? Il y a du rouge là-dedans. Beurk!
- Voulez-vous essayer la veste, Monsieur le Président?
- Oui, oui d'accord.
- Ça vous va très bien, monsieur. Très très élégant.

Scène 3

- Je profite de cette session du Parlement Européen pour assurer l'assemblée que notre pays soutient la Convention des droits de l'enfance. A notre avis, l'enfant a le droit à l'éducation, le droit à une nationalité... L'enfant a aussi le droit à...

Unité 3: Agendas
Livre de l'étudiant, page 13

Clémentine en Tunisie

- Tu veux voir mes photos? C'était bien chez mon oncle Hédi. Il habite Houmt Souk. C'est dans l'Ile de Djerba au sud-est de la Tunisie. Regarde celle-là!
- Celle-ci?
- Oui. Tu vois... Ça, c'est le moment où j'ai acheté un tapis. C'est chouette, hein? C'était un magasin de souvenirs. Mais il est joli, le tapis, hein? Rouge, bleu, jaune, vert... Il est dans ma chambre maintenant.
- Ah, oui, c'est très joli!
- Tu vois... Ça, c'est le moment où j'ai essayé une djellaba. C'est chouette comme robe, hein?
- Très élégante, ma chère!
- Alors celle-là, c'est le moment où j'ai mangé du couscous pour la première fois! Tu as déjà mangé du couscous, toi?
- Non, jamais...
- C'est spécial, mais rudement bon. Il y a de la viande, des légumes – des carottes et tout ça... avec une sauce très épicée.
- Mmm, ça a l'air bon!
- Alors, celle-là, c'est le moment où je suis montée sur un chameau pour la première fois! Ridicule, hein? Qu'est-ce qu'il était méchant cet animal! Tu ne peux pas imaginer.
- C'est toi, ça?
- Bien sûr que c'est moi! Mais alors, ça pue, les chameaux, ah là là! Et il y a des mouches partout!
- Ah, ma pauvre!
- Ça, c'est l'oasis dans le désert. C'est comme un jardin. C'est fantastique. J'ai vu beaucoup de palmiers. C'est très beau.
- Ah oui, c'est super!!
- Ah, ça c'est mon cousin – il est complètement fou, mais je l'adore. Il fait ça pour les touristes. C'est bien, hein? Un, deux, trois, quatre pichets en équilibre. Il peut le faire avec six! Mais deux secondes après, il a tout cassé!
- Complètement fou, ton cousin!!!
- On a pris cette photo un dimanche matin au café. C'est moi avec mon oncle Hédi...
- Tu as de la chance! J'aimerais bien aller en Tunisie!

Unité 4: Une journée de Jean-Denis
Cahier d'activités, page 12

Métro boulot dodo

Métro... boulot... dodo...
Ah! C'est pas possible!
Ah! C'est pas possible!
Lève-toi, Monique! Lève-toi!!

Métro... boulot... dodo...
Mm le café... mm les cornflakes.
Ah! Regarde l'heure!

Métro... boulot... dodo...
Le numéro 6 vite vite!

Métro... boulot... dodo...
Salut Sandrine, salut Marilyne, salut Francine!

Métro... boulot... dodo...
J'adore les sandwiches, moi et du Coca.
Frites, steak et ananas.

Métro... boulot... dodo...
Oui, madame. J'arrive, monsieur.
Allô, ne quittez pas...
Oui, madame. J'arrive, monsieur.
Allô, ne quittez pas...

Métro... boulot... dodo...
Fatiguée! Oh, mes pieds!
C'est pas possible!

Métro... boulot... dodo...
Ouf! zzz... dodo dodo dodo dodo.
Métro... boulot... dodo...

Ah! C'est pas possible!
Ah! C'est pas possible!
Lève-toi, Monique! Lève-toi!!
Métro... boulot... dodo...

(backing track follows, for students who want to invent their own words)

Unité 4: Une journée de Jean-Denis

Je suis toujours pressée

(sound effects to go with poem on repromaster 5: brushing teeth; eating breakfast; drinking tea; catching a bus; hurrying up the stairs; entering office; someone saying 'Oh zut!')

Unité 5: La vie à deux
Livre de l'étudiant, page 17

C'est quelle scène?

Scène 1

- Oh non! Ce n'est pas possible.
- Bonsoir, madame. Je peux vous aider?
- Ah bonsoir, monsieur... Euh je ne sais pas...
- Allez, madame, je peux regarder?... Mmm... Mmm...
- C'est grave, monsieur?
- Grave, madame? Non non non, c'est une question d'essence!! Les voitures ont besoin d'essence, vous savez? De l'essence... on achète ça chez Esso, chez Shell... vous savez?
- Oh non! Excusez-moi. Quelle idiote! Mais je suis dingue, complètement stupide... Excusez moi... Quelle idiote!
- Allez, madame... Il y a une station-service Shell à 100 mètres. Pas de problème.

Scène 2

- Oh là là là, je suis fatigué!
- Oui, moi aussi.
- Chérie, tu peux me passer une bière, s'il te plaît?
- Oui, chéri... Tiens.
- Merci. Qu'est-ce qu'il y a pour le dîner?
- Mm... Tu préfères une omelette ou un steak frites?
- Oh, je suis trop fatigué... C'est toi qui décides, chérie... Un steak frites peut-être... et de la soupe?... Et peut-être une petite tarte aux pommes pour finir.
- Une tarte aux pommes?!
- Ohh non, chérie, ne t'inquiète pas. C'est trop, hein? Tu es fatiguée.
- Non, non chéri. Si tu veux une tarte aux pommes, je vais t'en faire une. Une demi-heure, ça va?
- Oui oui, chérie... Tu peux me passer une autre bière?

Scène 3

- Allez, au revoir, chéri. Au revoir, les enfants. A ce soir.
- Oui... Tu rentres à quelle heure?
- Oh... Je ne sais pas. 8 heures, 8 heures et demie. Je ne sais pas exactement.
- Tu sais que ta mère arrive ce soir...
- Oui oui, je sais, je sais, mais c'est mercredi! J'ai une réunion...
- Oui, mais c'est ta mère. Tu pourrais au moins... Chut minette... Allez... Chut!
- Ecoute, je te téléphone. D'accord?
- Oui... Mais... 8 heures, alors?
- Oui... Je te téléphone...

Contrôle 1
Livre de l'étudiant, page 18
Cahier d'activités, page 56

- Jean, tu peux m'aider à ranger les affaires, s'il te plaît?
- Ohh! Pitié... non!
- Allez, allez, pas de discussion. Tu m'aides. C'est tout! Donne-moi la cafetière, là... et puis, passe-moi les couteaux... là... et les cuillères. Non! Pas les fourchettes! J'ai dit les couteaux et les cuillères.
- Excuse-moi.
- Bon... Maintenant les verres... Merci! Et les bols là dans le coin. Et les tasses à café. D'abord les tasses... Attention là... Et les soucoupes... Attention!... Oh! Ce n'est pas vrai. Mes soucoupes! Jean, tu exagères. Fais attention! Maintenant, je n'ai plus de soucoupes. Tu es maladroit, vraiment. Quel maladroit!
- Pardon maman, je suis désolé. Je suis vraiment très désolé.

L'ECOLO
Unité 1: Nous, les consommateurs
Livre de l'étudiant, pages 22–23
Cahier d'activités, page 15

Les années 30 et les années 90

1
- Mets ça dans le frigo, tu veux bien, Stéphane?

2
- Maman, je peux avoir un Coca?
- Oui.

3
- Le lundi, c'est pénible. C'est toujours pareil. Quelle horreur! Cette lessive que c'est long!

4
- 200 grammes de farine... 100 grammes de beurre... de l'eau...
  un kilo de pommes...

5
- Paul! Paul... viens ici! Tu vas faire la vaisselle, hein?
- Oh, non, c'est toujours moi qui...
- Je ne t'écoute pas... c'est ton tour, vas-y!
- Ça y est, il n'y a plus de liquide!

6
- Prends le fromage dans la boîte en plastique rouge, là devant toi.

Unité 2: Les ressources naturelles
Livre de l'étudiant, page 24

La vie d'une boîte de Coca

- Voici le bon ordre des phrases:
  Nous exploitons la Terre.
  Nous fabriquons la boîte.
  Nous achetons le produit.
  Nous buvons le Coca.
  Nous jetons la boîte.
  Nous recyclons la boîte.

Unité 2: Les ressources naturelles
Cahier d'activités, page 19

La vie d'un journal

- Voici le bon ordre des phrases:
  Nous plantons des arbres.
  Nous coupons des arbres.
  Nous transportons les arbres au moulin.
  Nous fabriquons du papier.
  Nous transportons le papier chez l'imprimeur.
  Nous achetons le journal.
  Nous lisons le journal.
  Nous jetons le journal.
  Nous recyclons le journal.

Unité 2: Les ressources naturelles
Livre de l'étudiant, page 25

Des jeunes dans la rue

1
- Non aux armes!

2
- Défendons les animaux!

3
- Sauvons nos rivières!

4
- Non à la pollution!

5
- Protégeons notre ville!

Unité 3: Le recyclage
Livre de l'étudiant, page 26
Cahier d'activités, page 20

La décharge publique

- Alors vous, les 3èmes B, qu'est-ce que vous faites pour protéger l'environnement? Le recyclage, par exemple... Qu'est-ce que vous recyclez chez vous? Le papier, par exemple?
- Chez nous, madame, mon père achète du papier hygiénique recyclé.
- Eh ben... nous, on a trois poubelles. Une pour le plastique, une pour le verre... et une pour les ordures ménagères.
- Oui, nous aussi, on a trois poubelles.
- On peut recycler les journaux aussi!
- Oui c'est vrai. Encore des idées?
- On peut recycler le métal.
- Oui, quoi par exemple?
- Les boîtes – les boîtes de Coca!
- Les boîtes de conserve aussi!
- Et on peut recycler le verre – les bouteilles de vin, de bière!
- Oui. Et quoi d'autre?
- Ben... chez moi, ma mère, elle garde tous les vieux pull-overs.
- Oui, on peut recycler les vêtements.
- Et le plastique aussi! Les sacs en plastique, les bouteilles en plastique!
- Attendez, on va faire une liste. Alors qu'est-ce que j'écris?... En titre: Le recyclage... Les boîtes, les journaux, le plastique, les vêtements, les bouteilles, le métal...

Unité 4: Les amis de la Terre
Cahier d'activités, page 22

Bois-Tout

- Voici Bois-Tout, le personnage principal de l'histoire. Il s'appelle Bois-Tout parce qu'il boit beaucoup. Sa boisson préférée n'est pas le Coca, non, ni le whisky, ni la bière, ni le thé. Non! Sa boisson préférée, c'est le pétrole. Mm... Il adore ça! Il boit le pétrole de la Terre. Il y a des gisements de pétrole partout. Voilà un puits. Il y entre et il boit le pétrole. Il murmure, "J'ai soif... Mmm, gloup, gloup, mmm. Comme c'est délicieux!"

De loin, il voit un autre puits. Il s'approche. Il entre dans le puits et il boit le pétrole. Il boit des millions de litres de pétrole. Il pousse et il pousse. Il devient gros... Très très gros. Il devient énorme, archi-énorme!

Le temps passe. Un jour, il s'approche d'un puits mais le gisement de pétrole est très petit. Il s'approche d'un autre puits, et le gisement de pétrole est minuscule. Il a soif. Il n'y a plus de pétrole. Bois-Tout devient de plus en plus faible. Il n'y a plus de pétrole à boire. Le pauvre Bois-Tout! Maintenant il est mort.

Unité 4: Les amis de la Terre
Livre de l'étudiant, page 28

La dernière aventure de Bouffe-Tout

- Bouffe-Tout est une machine qui adore manger.
- La voilà dans une forêt au fond d'une vallée.
- Elle commence à manger.
- Super chouette! Miam, miam, ah! Ces arbres!
- Elle regarde derrière. Il n'y a plus d'arbres.
- Miam slapslafl, cronchcrunch, gnap gnap slurp gloup.
- Elle arrive au sommet.
- Miam miam scrontch scrontch glop glop slip slip.
- Encore, encore. Je veux encore des arbres.
- Elle regarde la vallée.
- Ho ha mmmm encore une forêt! Super!
- Elle descend.
- Srontch scrontch.
- Mais elle est fatiguée. Elle ferme les yeux et elle dort.
- Ron ron ron zzz.
- Horreur! Il pleut!
- La terre coule. C'est un torrent furieux.
- Glouglouglousplaf.
- Bouffe-Tout est fichue! Elle est morte!

CASSETTE 1 FACE 2

Unité 4: Les amis de la Terre
Livre de l'étudiant, page 29

L'écocide

On dit que la forêt partout disparaît,
On dit que la Terre perd ses poumons,
On dit que la mer devient une poubelle,
Et qu'on tue les dauphins en tuant les thons.

On dit qu'il existe un trou dans l'ozone,
On dit quand il pleut, il pleut de l'acide,
On dit que le monde est tombé malade,
Et voilà comment on fait l'écocide.

Tant pis! N'oublie pas:
Nous sommes riches,
Nous sommes riches,
Et je m'en fiche,
Car nous sommes riches!

On dit qu'on fabrique trop de voitures,
On dit que les puits de pétrole s'épuisent,
On dit qu'on a faim dans un pays lointain,
On dit que la Ville des Anges est en crise.

Tant pis! N'oublie pas:
Nous sommes riches,
Nous sommes riches,
Et je m'en fiche,
Car nous sommes riches!

Tant pis! N'oublie pas:
Nous sommes riches,
Nous sommes riches,
Et je m'en fiche,
Car nous sommes riches!

Unité 5: Quiz éco
Livre de l'étudiant, pages 30–31

- Voici comment jouer:
1 L'arbitre pose les questions.
2 Choisis une réponse.
3 Mets un trombone, si tu n'es pas très sûr/sûre.
4 Mets deux trombones, si tu es sûr/sûre.
5 Mets trois trombones, si tu es absolument sûr/sûre.
6 L'arbitre donne la réponse.
7 Tu gagnes? Prends tous les trombones.
- Voici les questions:

1 Quel est le total des ordures produites par un bébé en un an?
a 20kg **b** 200 kg **c** 250kg **d** 500kg

2 Quel est le total des ordures produites par un Européen en une vie?
a 300 tonnes **b** 450 tonnes **c** 650 tonnes **d** 655 tonnes

3 Quel est le pourcentage de l'eau par rapport à la Terre?
a 40% **b** 50% **c** 71% **d** 70%

4 Quel est le nombre de poubelles remplies par un Britannique en un an?
a 50 **b** 100 **c** 75 **d** 85

5 Quel est le nombre d'arbres consommés pour le papier par un Français en un an?
a 1 **b** 2 **c** 3 **d** 4

6 Quel est le total des boîtes de conserve jetées en un an, par personne?
a 90 **b** 30 **c** 200 **d** 10

7 Quel est le total des bouteilles jetées en un an par personne?
a 50 **b** plus de100 **c** 40 **d** 30

8 Quel est le nombre de kilos de plastique jetés en un an par personne?
a 6 **b** 25 **c** 45 **d** 15

9 La couche d'ozone est à combien de kilomètres de la Terre?
a 18–48 kilomètres **b** 12–15 kilomètres **c** 5–10 kilomètres **d** 2–4 kilomètres

10 Quelle est la date de la découverte du trou dans la couche d'ozone?
a 1922 **b** 1968 **c** 1985 **d** 1840

11 Il y a combien d'arbres affectés par la pluie acide en Grande-Bretagne par an?
a 200 millions **b** 450 millions **c** 2 millions **d** 2000

12 Combien d'espèces de fleurs ont disparu entre 1900 et 1992?
a 20 **b** 5 **c** 17 **d** 19

13 Une chasse d'eau consomme combien de litres d'eau?
a 12 litres **b** 20 litres **c** 11 litres **d** 15 litres

14 Un bain consomme combien de litres d'eau?
a 200 litres **b** 40 litres **c** 50 litres **d** 100 litres

15 Une douche consomme combien de litres d'eau?
a 200 litres **b** 40 litres **c** 50 litres **d** 100 litres

Contrôle 2
Livre de l'étudiant, page 32
Cahier d'activités, page 57

- Tu es copine avec Jacques, toi?
- Oui, moi je le trouve sympa! Pas toi?
- Ben... non... Je ne l'aime pas beaucoup! Il n'est pas écolo du tout, tu sais. Pas comme toi, ou moi.
- Ah bon? Jacques n'est pas écolo? Ça alors! Jacques n'est pas écolo! Pourquoi tu dis ça?
- Ecoute, d'abord, il jette ses papiers de chewing-gum par terre! Ce n'est pas très bien...
- Oui, d'accord. Tiens, c'est vrai, il ne vient pas à la réunion des Amis de la Terre aujourd'hui.
- Exactement! Il préfère regarder le foot à la télé! Et puis... Il va au Fast Food et il achète des frites dans des boîtes en plastique! Et il jette la boîte par terre!
- Il jette la boîte par terre!?
- Oui! Il jette la boîte par terre. Et il jette sa boîte de Coca par terre aussi!
- Hé ben!
- Il achète des aérosols aussi. Il ne pense pas à la couche d'ozone!
- Il achète des aérosols!
- En plus, il ne recycle pas ses journaux!

LES MEDIAS
Unité 1: J'aime lire
Cahier d'activités, page 26

La presse: les préférences

Interview 1

- Excusez-moi, monsieur. Euh... je suis étudiant britannique. Je fais un exposé sur la presse. Je peux vous poser quelques questions?
- O.K! I can speak in English, yes?
- In English? Fine. Right, do you prefer reading newspapers, books, magazines or cartoon strips?
- Euh... magazines.
- Do you read regularly?
- Ah. I read magazines one time every week.
- How long do you spend reading, generally?
- About half an hour.
- And where do you usually do your reading?
- Ah usually, I read in the train when I go to work.
- And may I ask your age? Are you aged between 15 and 20? 21 to 30?
- I am 22 years old.
- Well, thank you very much. Merci, monsieur!
- Euh, well, bye bye.

Interview 2

- Excusez-moi, madame. Je suis étudiant britannique. Je fais un exposé sur la presse. Je peux vous poser quelques questions?
- Oui, oui ça va.
- Bien, vous préférez lire des journaux, des livres, des magazines ou des bandes dessinées, madame?
- Des livres. Je préfère les livres.
- Et vous lisez régulièrement?
- Oui, tous les jours.
- Merci, et vous passez combien de temps à lire, en général?
- Oh, je ne sais pas... euh, environ une heure, je suppose.
- Et vous lisez où?
- A la maison, au lit ou dans le jardin.
- Merci bien. Et je peux vous demander... Vous avez quel âge, madame? Entre 21 et 30 ans? Plus de 30 ans?
- Plus de 30 ans, malheureusement!
- Merci... Au revoir.

Interview 3

- Excusez-moi, mademoiselle. Je suis étudiant britannique. Je fais un exposé sur la presse. Je peux vous poser quelques questions?
- D'accord.
- Vous préférez lire des journaux, des livres, des magazines ou des bandes dessinées?
- Bof, je ne sais pas moi. Des magazines.
- Et vous lisez régulièrement?
- Pas très souvent, hein. Une fois par mois.
- Et vous passez combien de temps à lire, en général?
- Euh quinze minutes, je ne sais pas.
- Vous lisez où?
- Euh, devant la télé.
- Et vous avez quel âge, mademoiselle?
- J'ai dix-sept ans.
- Merci beaucoup.

Unité 1: J'aime lire
Livre de l'étudiant, pages 36–37

1

- Au nom du ciel! Tintin, soyez prudent!...
- Ça ira!
- HÊ-Ê-EK!
- Tintin! De grâce, faites attention!...
- Soyez tranquille, je...
- CRÂC!
- !

2

- Stop!
- !!??!!
- Dangereux!
- Défendu! Verboten! Prohibited!! On peut pas!
- Confisqué!
- Na!
- Confisqué!??
- !!!

3

- Toi, à gauche! Toi, là! Et toi, schtroumpfe-lui sur les épaules! Toi...
- Une heure plus tard...
- Parfait! Ne schtroumpfez plus!
- !
- Dites, c'est marrant, j'ai oublié la pellicule!
- !
- !!

Unité 2: Reportages
Livre de l'étudiant, page 38

Bulletin à la radio

- Aujourd'hui, à Lyon, s'est terminée la longue histoire Renier. Ils habitaient à deux, Philippe Renier et sa mère, Liliane. Philippe a 19 ans et demi et sa maman l'adore. Aujourd'hui, Philippe est en prison. C'est une histoire de désespoir. Lorsque Philippe avait 16 ans, Liliane a trouvé ses seringues et de grandes sommes d'argent à la maison. Elle était terrorisée. Philippe a expliqué franchement à sa mère qu'il était trafiquant d'héroïne.
- Dès ce moment, j'étais tourmentée. Mon Philippe... trafiquant de drogue! Que faire?
- Philippe se transformait peu à peu en zombie et il était souvent absent de la maison. Liliane Renier trouvait ça insupportable. Et enfin, elle a téléphoné à la police.
- C'était une décision difficile... mais, c'était nécessaire. Je voudrais dire à Philippe que je l'aime.
- Pour l'instant, Philippe n'a pas de message pour sa mère. Il refuse toute discussion avec Liliane.

Unité 2: Reportages
Livre de l'étudiant, page 39

Crime... Stop!

1

- Notre premier appel était de la part d'une voisine. Elle a vu une voiture bleue près de la maison vers minuit, le 23 septembre. Alors, une voiture bleue. C'est confirmé.

2

- Un monsieur a téléphoné. Il a vu trois jeunes gens dans la rue Montjean, le soir du 18 septembre. Ils sont entrés au bar 'Flamant Rose' à 22 heures. Les trois hommes portaient un jean et un blouson. Si vous avez d'autres renseignements, appelez-nous immédiatement au 43 42 00 00...

3

- Et encore des nouvelles importantes! Une troisième téléspectatrice a téléphoné à propos de ce crime. Elle habite tout près de la maison Vauvert. Tout récemment, elle a trouvé dans son jardin une montre et une cassette-vidéo qui correspondent aux descriptions des objets volés. Elle a aussi confirmé la présence de trois jeunes gens dans le quartier Montjean à dix heures et demie, le 18 septembre.

4

- Encore une description importante. Un monsieur a vu un homme, âgé de 30 à 35 ans dans la rue de la Paix, vers minuit dix. Il avait les cheveux noirs, et il portait un jean et des baskets blanches. Une écharpe, et une casquette sur la tête...

Unité 3: Télémaniaques
Livre de l'étudiant, page 40

Jeu Télé Mistral

- Bienvenue au Jeu Télé Mistral. D'abord les noms des chaînes. Regardez la page 40 de votre livre de l'étudiant. Il y a cinq chaînes: TF1, A2, FR3, Canal+, M6... Et pour les points: vous donnez la réponse avant les 3 bips et vous avez 3 points. Vous donnez la réponse avant les 2 bips et vous avez 2 points. Vous donnez la réponse avant 1 bip et vous avez 1 point. Regardez bien les programmes proposés pour le mardi 13 août. Ecoutez les questions. Voici deux exemples...
- Première question: qu'est-ce qu'il y a sur TF1 à 17 heures 25?... Allez, vite, pour 2 points...
- *Texas Police.*
- Oui, c'est correct, *Texas Police*. Vous avez gagné 2 points, 2 points, super! Deuxième question: *Coup de Grisou* sur M6 à 20 heures 35, c'est quel genre d'émission?
- C'est un téléfilm américain.
- Oui, c'est ça! 1 point!
- Alors donnez la réponse avant les 3 bips et vous gagnez 3 points. Donnez la réponse avant les 2 bips et vous gagnez 2 points. Donnez la réponse avant 1 bip et vous gagnez 1 point.
- *Le Lion du Désert* sur Canal+ à 20 heures 30, c'est quel genre d'émission?
- C'est un drame historique.
- Qu'est-ce qu'il y a sur A2 à 20 heures?
- C'est le journal.
- *Cherry 2000* sur Canal+ à 15 heures 45, c'est quel genre d'émission?
- C'est un film américain de science-fiction.
- Qu'est-ce qu'il y a sur FR3 à 13 heures?
- C'est le sport.
- Qu'est-ce qu'il y a sur M6 à 20 heures?
- C'est le Cosby Show.
- *Santa Barbara* sur TF1 à 19 heures, c'est quel genre d'émission?
- C'est un feuilleton.
- Qu'est-ce qu'il y a sur A2 à 20 heures 35?
- C'est la météo
- Et la dernière question sur Jeu Télé Mistral: *Le Juste Prix* sur TF1 à 12 heures 30, c'est quel genre d'émission?
- C'est un jeu.
- Comptez vos points! Bien joué et à bientôt. Au revoir.

Unité 3: Télémaniaques
Livre de l'étudiant, page 41

La télé: pour ou contre?

- Bonjour à tous. Le sujet de discussion de cette semaine est... la télévision. Aujourd'hui, 48 millions et demi de personnes la regardent. Mais vous, que pensez-vous de la télévision? Vous êtes pour? Ou vous êtes contre? Avez-vous la télévision chez vous? Avez-vous des enfants qui la regardent? Combien d'heures par semaine? Téléphonez au 34.67.48.12 et dites-nous tout!
- Voici notre premier appel. Il vient de Monsieur Grancher, de Lomeneur. Bonjour, monsieur.
- Bonjour. Je suis père de deux enfants...
- Et vous avez la télévision?
- Nous avons la télévision bien sûr, mais je trouve que c'est affreux. Il y a toujours des émissions dangereuses. Beaucoup d'enfants regardent les émissions violentes. Je travaille le soir. J'ai toujours peur que mes enfants regardent des émissions comme ça...
- Des émissions violentes...
- Oui, des émissions violentes, faites pour des adultes, quoi?
- Merci, monsieur. La violence à la télévision est un problème. C'est certain. Ecoutons maintenant une auditrice, Madame Richard de Paris... Bonjour, madame.
- Bonjour, moi, je trouve que la télé est très importante pour les informations. C'est tout ce que je regarde...
- Bon, merci, madame. Et maintenant, Michel Lebrun, vous êtes là?
- Oui, je suis d'accord avec Madame Richard. La télé, c'est intéressant et très éducatif. Il y a beaucoup d'émissions éducatives pour les enfants, c'est bien ça. J'ai deux enfants et c'est très important pour leur éducation, je trouve.
- Merci, monsieur. Et maintenant nous avons un appel de Bordeaux.
- Bonjour, oui, je suis Kathy MacFarlane... je suis britannique. J'habite en France depuis dix ans. Je ne regarde pas souvent la télé. Je trouve que les émissions sont souvent idiotes.
- Vous parlez de la télé française?
- Oui, mais de la télé britannique aussi. C'est stupide, je trouve, de passer des heures devant la télé. Quand on regarde la télé on n'est pas sociable. En plus, la plupart du temps, on passe des émissions vraiment idiotes.
- Merci, Madame MacFarlane. Notre prochain auditeur vient de Calais. Monsieur Jambon, vous êtes là?
- Oui, oui. Mais dites donc, je ne suis pas d'accord avec Madame MacFarlane. Pour moi, la télé est un divertissement très important. C'est amusant. C'est indispensable et c'est bien pour se relaxer.
- Merci. Et pour finir, écoutons Madame Martigne de Saint-Malo.
- J'ai une chose à dire. Quand on regarde la télé, la conversation est impossible... Ce n'est pas bien, on reste là, devant la télé. On ne parle pas. On n'est pas actif...
- Bon, eh ben, c'est tout pour cette semaine. Merci à tous et à la semaine prochaine!

Unité 4: Ciné-clips
Livre de l'étudiant, page 43

- Ecoute la cassette.
  C'est la musique typique de quel genre de film?

1
(cartoon music)
2
(horror film music)
3
(war film music)
4
(western music)

Unité 4: Ciné-clips
Livre de l'étudiant, page 43

- Ecoute la cassette.
  Ecoute les trois dialogues.
  C'est quel genre de film?

1
(romance style)
- Entrez.
- Bonjour.
- C'est bien vous?
- Oui, c'est moi.
- Ce n'est pas possible!
- Si, c'est possible. Je suis de retour.
- Qu'est-ce que c'est?
- C'est pour vous!

2
(police film/thriller style)
- Entrez.
- Bonjour.
- C'est bien vous?
- Oui, c'est moi.
- Ce n'est pas possible!
- Si, c'est possible. Je suis de retour.
- Qu'est-ce que c'est?
- C'est pour vous!

3
(science fiction style)
- Entrez.
- Bonjour.
- C'est bien vous?
- Oui, c'est moi.
- Ce n'est pas possible!
- Si, c'est possible. Je suis de retour.
- Qu'est-ce que c'est?
- C'est pour vous!

Unité 5: Idoles
Livre de l'étudiant, pages 44–45

C'est quel fan?

- Entrez, entrez...
- Mais, dites donc!
- C'est bien, hein?
- Oui, c'est incroyable. Vous avez combien de posters?
- Deux cents, à peu près.
- Ce n'est pas croyable!
- Oui, j'ai une chambre consacrée à Elvis.
- Dites donc! Vous avez combien de disques?
- Trois cents, et cinq cents photos. Je passe dix heures par semaine à ma collection.
- C'est marrant ça.
- Oui, c'est marrant, mais c'est ma passion!
- Ça fait longtemps que vous avez cette passion?
- Voyons... je l'aime depuis trente ans. Je regarde Elvis et j'oublie mes problèmes.
- Ah bon?
- Oui, c'est lui qui me guide!

Contrôle 3
Livre de l'étudiant, page 46
Cahier d'activités, page 58

Un critique parle de films

- Alors, voyons... les films de la semaine...

Le Retour de Martin Guerre. Un film à suspense. C'est super.

Un Thé au Sahara. Un film italo-américain. C'est un drame. Une bonne musique. Pas mal. Vraiment pas mal du tout.

Le Retour de la Panthère Rose. Moi, je suis un fan de Peter Sellers. C'est un film comique. Excellent. J'adore.

Bons Baisers de Russie. Un vrai James Bond. Plein d'aventures. Musique dramatique. Je ne résiste pas. C'est super. J'adore.

Tilaï. Un film franco-suisse. Bof, pas formidable. Une histoire d'amour impossible. Pas bien. Je n'aime pas.

Le Grand Bleu. Un film pour les jeunes. Sensationnel. Musique formidable. Images superbes. Mon film préféré de l'année. J'adore.

CASSETTE 2 FACE 1

PARIS: LE GUIDE MISTRAL
Unité 1: Bon voyage!
A l'écoute: feuille numéro 1

A la gare

Conversation 1

- Je voudrais réserver une place dans le train pour Paris qui part à 18 heures, s'il vous plaît.
- Oui, madame. Un aller simple ou un aller-retour?
- Un aller simple, s'il vous plaît.
- Fumeur ou non-fumeur?
- Non-fumeur, s'il vous plaît.
- Ça fait 200 francs en tout, s'il vous plaît.
- Voilà.
- Merci.

Conversation 2

- Je voudrais réserver une place dans le train pour Versailles qui part à 9 heures, s'il vous plaît.
- Oui, madame. Un aller simple ou un aller-retour?
- Un aller-retour, s'il vous plaît.
- Fumeur ou non-fumeur?
- Non-fumeur, s'il vous plaît.
- Ça fait 150 francs en tout, s'il vous plaît.
- Voilà.
- Merci.

Conversation 3

- Je voudrais réserver une place dans le train pour Boulogne qui part à 9 heures, s'il vous plaît.
- Oui, monsieur. Un aller simple ou un aller-retour?
- Un aller-retour, s'il vous plaît.
- Fumeur ou non-fumeur?
- Fumeur, s'il vous plaît.
- Ça fait 165 francs en tout, s'il vous plaît.
- Voilà.
- Merci.

Des phrases utiles

- je voudrais réserver
- le train qui part à dix heures
- un aller simple
- un aller-retour
- fumeur
- non-fumeur
- ça fait deux cents francs

Unité 2: Bon voyage!
A l'écoute: feuille numéro 2

Au bureau de change

Conversation 1

- Je voudrais changer 2000 pesetas, s'il vous plaît.
- Oui, monsieur... Vous avez une pièce d'identité?
- Voilà...
- Merci. Alors, 2000 pesetas espagnoles...

Conversation 2

- Bonjour... Je voudrais changer 50 livres sterling en francs, s'il vous plaît.
- Bien sûr, madame. Votre passeport, s'il vous plaît.
- Voilà... et voilà les livres sterling.
- Merci.

Conversation 3

- Je peux vous aider?
- Oui, je voudrais changer 100 Deutschmarks, s'il vous plaît.
- Bien sûr... Je peux voir une pièce d'identité, s'il vous plaît?
- Voilà mon passeport.
- Merci. Alors, 100 Deutschmarks, ça vous fait...

Des phrases utiles

- je voudrais changer
- voilà mon passeport
- une pièce d'identité

Unité 2: Bienvenue!
A l'écoute: feuille numéro 3

Le logement

Conversation 1

- Bonjour, madame.
- Bonjour, monsieur. Vous désirez?
- Je voudrais une chambre pour deux personnes, s'il vous plaît.
- C'est pour combien de nuits?
- Trois nuits.
- Vous désirez une chambre avec salle de bains ou douche?
- Avec douche, s'il vous plaît. C'est combien par nuit, s'il vous plaît?
- C'est trois cents francs par nuit.
- Très bien.
- C'est à quel nom?
- Jones.
- Comment ça s'écrit?
- J-O-N-E-S.
- C'est la chambre quarante quatre. Voici votre clé.
- Merci.
- De rien, monsieur.

Conversation 2
- Bonjour.
- Oui. Vous désirez?
- Avez-vous quatre places, s'il vous plaît?
- C'est pour combien de nuits?
- Une nuit.
- Vous êtes quatre filles?
- Oui, ç'est ça.
- Euh, une nuit... quatre... oui, ça va.
- C'est combien par nuit, s'il vous plaît?
- C'est cinquante francs par nuit. C'est à quel nom?
- Vincent.
- Comment ça s'écrit?
- V-I-N-C-E-N-T.
- Vous êtes dans le dortoir numéro cinq.
- Très bien. Merci. Où est la caféteria, s'il vous plaît?
- A gauche. Par là.
- Où sont les douches, s'il vous plaît?
- A droite.
- Merci.

Conversation 3
- Bonjour, monsieur.
- Oui, madame. Vous désirez?
- Je voudrais un emplacement, s'il vous plaît.
- C'est pour une tente ou une caravane?
- C'est pour une tente.
- C'est pour combien de personnes?
- Deux personnes.
- C'est pour combien de nuits?
- Cinq nuits. C'est combien par nuit, s'il vous plaît?
- C'est trente francs par nuit. C'est à quel nom?
- Martineau.
- Comment ça s'écrit?
- M-A-R-T-I-N-E-A-U.
- C'est l'emplacement numéro vingt.
- Il y a un supermarché?
- Oui. A côté des toilettes.
- Merci.
- De rien.

Conversation 4
- Bonjour, madame.
- Bonjour, monsieur. Vous désirez?
- Je voudrais une chambre pour trois personnes, s'il vous plaît.
- C'est pour combien de nuits?
- Deux nuits.
- Vous désirez une chambre avec salle de bains ou douche?
- Avec salle de bains, s'il vous plaît. C'est combien par nuit, s'il vous plaît?
- C'est cent cinquante francs par nuit.
- Très bien.
- C'est à quel nom?
- Hogan.
- Comment ça s'écrit?
- H-O-G-A-N.
- C'est la chambre numéro cent deux. Voici votre clé.
- Merci.

Des phrases utiles
- un camping
- un hôtel
- une auberge de jeunesse
- une chambre pour deux personnes
- le dortoir
- c'est pour trois nuits
- une chambre avec douche
- une chambre avec salle de bains
- voici votre clé
- un emplacement
- les douches

Unité 2: Bienvenue!
A l'écoute: feuille numéro 4

A l'office de tourisme

1
- J'ai besoin d'une liste des hôtels, s'il vous plaît.

2
- Je voudrais un plan de la ville, s'il vous plaît.

3
- Avez-vous un horaire des autobus, s'il vous plaît?

4
- Je voudrais une liste des campings, s'il vous plaît.

5
- J'ai besoin d'une liste des excursions et une liste des hôtels, s'il vous plaît.

6
- Je voudrais un horaire des trains s'il vous plaît... et un plan de la ville.

7
- Avez-vous une liste des monuments importants, et aussi, j'ai besoin d'une liste des musées, s'il vous plaît.

Des phrases utiles
- j'ai besoin de...
- une liste
- des campings
- des hôtels
- des monuments importants
- un horaire
- un plan de la ville

Unité 3: Bon appétit!
A l'écoute: feuille numéro 5

Au restaurant

Conversation 1
- Bonjour, monsieur-dame. Vous désirez?
- Je voudrais une omelette, s'il vous plaît.
- Et pour moi, le bifteck aux champignons, s'il vous plaît.
- Oui... et à boire?
- Je prends une bouteille de vin rouge. Tu veux de l'eau minérale?
- Oui, je veux bien.
- Alors, monsieur-dame. Vous prenez un dessert?
- Oui, pour moi... une tarte maison, s'il vous plaît.
- Et, moi, je prends une glace à la fraise.
- D'accord.

Conversation 2
- Bonjour, monsieur. Vous désirez?
- Je voudrais un œuf mayonnaise, s'il vous plaît.
- Oui, et avec ca?
- Un poulet rôti... et une salade verte, s'il vous plaît.
- Oui... et à boire?
- Je prends un demi de vin blanc.
- Alors, monsieur... Vous prenez un dessert?
- Mm... oui... une glace au chocolat, s'il vous plaît.
- D'accord. Et vous prenez un café, monsieur?
- Oui.

Conversation 3
- Bonjour, madame. Vous désirez?
- Je voudrais un melon, s'il vous plaît.
- Oui, et avec ça?
- Une truite... et une salade verte, s'il vous plaît.
- Oui... et à boire?
- Je prends de l'eau minérale.
- Alors, madame. Vous prenez un dessert?
- Du fromage, s'il vous plaît.
- D'accord. Et vous prenez un café, madame?
- Non merci.

Des phrases utiles
- vous désirez?
- je voudrais
- je prends
- et à boire?
- et avec ça?

Unité 3: Bon appétit!
A l'écoute: feuille numéro 6

Les courses

Conversation 1
- Madame, s'il vous plaît... un kilo de pêches.
- Un kilo de pêches... voilà. Treize francs, s'il vous plaît.
- Merci, au revoir.

Conversation 2
- Bonjour...
- Bonjour... euh, je voudrais deux croissants, s'il vous plaît.
- Et avec ça?
- Un pain au chocolat et... une baguette, s'il vous plaît.
- Voilà... deux croissants, un pain au chocolat et une baguette... Alors, ça vous fait euh...

Conversation 3
- Bonjour. Je voudrais une tranche de fromage, s'il vous plaît. Celui-ci...
- Oui... voilà. C'est tout?
- Non, je voudrais aussi 500 grammes de salade de tomates, s'il vous plaît.
- Voilà... du fromage... et de la salade de tomates. Alors euh... ça fait... voyons...

Des phrases utiles
- je voudrais
- et avec ça?
- je prends...
- c'est combien?
- un kilo de...
- 500 grammes de...

Unité 4: Ville vivante!
A l'écoute: feuille numéro 7

Le shopping (1)

1
- Avez-vous un t-shirt avec la tour Eiffel dessus?

2
- Je voudrais le petit nounours, s'il vous plaît.

3
- Je prends le petit flacon de parfum, s'il vous plaît.

4
- Ça coûte combien, cette paire de boucles d'oreilles, s'il vous plaît?

5
- Je prends les chocolats belges.

6
- Je voudrais deux torchons comme ça, s'il vous plaît.

7
- Avez-vous d'autres porte-clés?

8
- Je peux voir le stylo là-bas?

9
- Je préfère la petite tour Eiffel, s'il vous plaît.

Unité 4: Ville vivante!
A l'écoute: feuille numéro 7

Le shopping (2)

Conversation 1
- Je voudrais un t-shirt rouge comme ça, s'il vous plaît. Vous en avez?
- Oui, quelle taille?
- Grand, s'il vous plaît.
- En voilà un grand.
- C'est combien?
- 50 francs.

Conversation 2
- Monsieur?
- Je prends cette crème solaire, s'il vous plaît.
- Et avec ça?
- C'est tout, merci.
- Bon... ça vous fait 35 francs pour la crème solaire.

Conversation 3
- Je voudrais envoyer deux lettres et trois cartes postales en Grande-Bretagne.
- Alors, deux lettres et trois cartes postales ... voilà... ça fait onze francs cinquante.

Des phrases utiles
- je voudrais
- quelle taille?
- je prends...
- c'est combien?
- je voudrais envoyer

Unité 5: Face à face
Livre de l'étudiant, pages 58–59
Cahier d'activités, page 44

Les scénarios rouges

1
- Oh, pardon. Excusez-moi.
- Ne vous inquiétez pas. Pas de problème, hein.

2
- Excusez-moi... C'est libre?
- Non, c'est occupé.
- D'accord.

3
- Salut. Tu loges ici?
- Oui, c'est ça. Salut.
- Salut.

Unité 5: Face à face
Livre de l'étudiant, pages 58–59
Cahier d'activités, page 44

Les scénarios verts

1
- Oh, pardon. Excusez-moi.
- Ne vous inquiétez pas. Pas de problème, hein.
- Oh, je suis désolée!
- Ça va...

2
- Excusez-moi... C'est libre?
- Oui... bien sûr...
- Merci. Je m'appelle Thierry... et vous?

3
- Salut. Tu loges ici?
- Oui, je suis avec un groupe scolaire. Et toi?
- Je suis en vacances avec des amis.
- Salut.
- Tu veux sortir avec nous?
- D'accord...

Unité 5: Face à face
A l'écoute: feuille numéro 8

Questions et réponses
- Comment tu t'appelles?
- Je m'appelle Guy. Tu es britannique?
- Oui, c'est ça... je suis de Birmingham.
- Tu es en vacances ici?
- Oui, je suis en vacances avec ma famille.
- C'est ta première visite en France?
- Oui, c'est ma première visite. Tu connais la Grande-Bretagne?
- Oui... je connais Londres un peu.
- Tu habites à Paris?
- J'habite à Poissy... tout près de Paris. Tu aimes Paris?
- Oui, j'adore Paris.
- Tu voudrais boire quelque chose?
- Merci... je veux bien.
- Tiens, comment t'appelles-tu?
- Martyn.

Unité 5: Face à face
A l'écoute: feuille numéro 8

Conversation avec Jacqueline
- Comment tu t'appelles?
  (*pause*)
- Tu es britannique?
  (*pause*)
- Tu es en vacances ici?
  (*pause*)
- C'est ta première visite en France?
  (*pause*)
- Tu voudrais boire quelque chose?
  (*pause*)

Unité 5: Face à face
A l'écoute: feuille numéro 9

On sort?

Conversation 1
- Si on allait au bowling?
- Oui, je veux bien. Quand?
- Euh... mercredi.
- A quelle heure?
- A neuf heures.
- On se retrouve où?
- Au café.
- D'accord. Alors, mercredi, à neuf heures, au café.
- Oui. A mercredi alors. Salut.

Conversation 2
- Allô?
- Allô, Pauline?
- Oui. Ah, Salut, Patrick.
- Dis, tu veux sortir cette semaine?
- Ben... oui. Quand ça?
- Mardi soir, il y a un concert de jazz. C'est Max Reinhardt. Tu veux venir?
- Ah, oui. Je veux bien. Alors mardi soir, à quelle heure?
- Mm... je ne sais pas. Ça commence à neuf heures.
- D'accord. On se retrouve à neuf heures moins le quart?
- OK. A neuf heures moins le quart au Club Rex.
- Bon. Attends, je vais noter tout ça... mardi soir... neuf heures moins le quart... concert de jazz au Club Rex.

Conversation 3
- Tiens! Jean-Jacques. Salut! Ça va?
- Ah, Sophie. Bonjour. Ça va, oui. Et toi?
- Oui. Tout va bien. J'avais l'intention de te téléphoner...
- Ah, bon?
- Oui. Tu sais, j'ai deux billets pour le théâtre – samedi soir. C'est une pièce de Shakespeare, en version originale. Ça doit être super.
- Samedi? Non, je ne peux pas. Je suis occupé.
- Ben... tant pis.
- Alors, euh... je m'en vais...
- Tiens, je vais retrouver Paul au café. Tu veux venir?
- Merci. Non. Je regrette, hein... mais je dois rentrer chez moi. Au revoir.
- Au revoir.

Des phrases utiles
- si on allait...
- tu veux sortir?
- tu veux venir?
- quand?
- où?
- à quelle heure?
- on se retrouve où?
- oui, je veux bien
- d'accord
- non, je ne peux pas
- je suis occupé
- je suis occupée

Contrôle 4
Livre de l'étudiant, page 60
Cahier d'activités, page 59

- Allez allez messieurs dames, mes pommes, là, toutes belles, toutes bonnes! 5 F 50 le kilo. Pas cher! Voilà, oui, madame, 1 kilo de pommes. Ça fait 5F 50 le kilo... Et avec ça? Oui des petites tomates bien mûres, bien rouges. Combien? 2 kilos? Voilà... 2 kilos de tomates. Ça fait 18F. 18F pour 2 kilos de tomates, c'est pas cher! C'est tout?... Vous ne voulez pas de mes pêches? Regardez, elles sont belles... et délicieuses! D'accord, allez, madame, 1 kilo de pêches! Alors, ça fait 19F 50... Tout ça, ça fait... ben... 43F. 43F tout rond.

CASSETTE 2 FACE 2

FEUILLETON
Unité 1: Le voisinage
Livre de l'étudiant, page 64

- Eh bien... un supermarché, c'est bien nécessaire? Moi, je n'en suis pas sûr.
- Mais si... écoute. Un supermarché, c'est idéal comme endroit principal. Au supermarché, on discute, on bavarde, quoi?
- D'accord. Et le marché, ça doit être au centre, non?
- Bien sûr, le marché, c'est toujours au centre. Et le café... c'est un café-tabac, non?
- Oui, un café... avec une petite terrasse? Ça pourrait être joli, n'est-ce pas?
- Oui, oui, bonne idée... un café avec une terrasse.
- Et l'église?
- Oui, à côté du café. Avec le petit hôtel en face.
- Alors, il nous reste... la boulangerie ici et des appartements au-dessus.
- Oui, c'est bien. Comme tu vois, quelques maisons et l'immeuble sont un peu à l'écart... dans un petit quartier résidentiel.
- Je vois... les maisons et l'immeuble seront des endroits très importants.

Unité 1: Le voisinage
Cahier d'activités, page 47

La musique des feuilletons

1
(feuilleton chic)
2
(feuilleton réaliste)
3
(feuilleton rural)

Unité 2: Les personnages
Livre de l'étudiant, pages 66–67

Audition 1
- Eh bien, s'il te plaît... commence.
- Maman... je peux? Ce n'est pas juste! Tu dis oui à Michel. Et à moi, c'est toujours non. Oh, maman... sois gentille. Tout le monde est au café. Je ne peux pas y aller? Juste pour une petite heure?
- Je t'ai déjà dit Nicolas. Non!
- Mais, maman, tu as dit oui à Michel!
- Nicolas... Non! Tu comprends? Non, Nicolas!
- Merci.
- Je peux continuer, monsieur?
- Non, non, merci. Allez... Le prochain!

Audition 2
- Bonjour, monsieur. Je me mets ici?
- Oui, commencez, s'il vous plaît.
- Dis donc... Tu as entendu la nouvelle? Eh, bien... notre belle Hélène, elle est partie... pour le week-end... Et sa fille, Sophie, elle est restée à la maison. Une jeune fille, toute seule pendant tout le week-end, c'est pas bien, ça! Et, euh, Monsieur Desjardins, où est-il, hein? Parti! Ben, oui... parti pour le week-end. C'est curieux, ça, non?
- Madame, vous êtes concierge. Vous comprenez? Concierge! Vous êtes bavarde. Vous êtes curieuse, hein? Alors, recommencez, s'il vous plaît...
- Dis donc... Tu as entendu la nouvelle? Eh, bien... notre belle Hélène, elle est partie... pour le week-end... Et sa fille, Sophie, elle est restée à la maison. Une jeune fille, toute seule pendant tout le week-end, c'est pas bien, ça! Et, euh, Monsieur Desjardins, où est-il, hein? Parti! Ben, oui... parti pour le week-end. C'est curieux, ça, non?
- Merci... La prochaine!

Audition 3
- Bon, alors, commencez!
- Alors, je commence ici?
- Oui, oui...
- Je ne sais pas si je veux me marier une deuxième fois, Robert. Je t'aime beaucoup, chéri, mais... le divorce m'a beaucoup affectée. Tu sais, quand on est divorcée, c'est compliqué. Il y a Sophie. Je l'aime beaucoup. Elle n'a que seize ans. C'est un âge difficile. Sophie est très importante pour moi. Mais, tu veux te marier avec une femme divorcée, toi?
- Merci.

Unité 3: En scène
Livre de l'étudiant, pages 68–69

Au café

- Tiens, tu l'as?
- Oui oui... c'est dans le sac.
- Tu as vu le journal?
- Quoi?
- Le journal. Il y a sa photo dans le journal.
- Une photo. Ben, dis donc, si on...
- Salut! Qu'est-ce que je vous sers?
- Euh, oui. Euh, un... un whisky avec de l'eau, s'il te plaît.
- Oui, d'accord. Et pour toi, Michel?
- De l'eau.
- Tu ne veux pas un sandwich?
- Non, non. Merci.
- Eh, ben, dis, la photo, c'est...
- Aurélie, tu dois te sauver. Vite. Il y a une voiture de police devant ton appartement et...
- Zut, c'est la photo.
- Elle est partie? Aah, elle a laissé son sac... Mais qu'est-ce que c'est que ça?
- Euh... donne-moi le sac. Donne moi ça.
- Un revolver! ... Et l'addition? Tu n'as pas payé!

Unité 4: L'action
Livre de l'étudiant, page 70

Le mariage de Robert et Hélène

- Elle est assez jolie, hein? Mais les fleurs... elle a choisi des fleurs oranges! Ça, c'est vraiment pas joli. De toute façon, elle est gentille... mais, lui! Alors, là!... Charmant? Huh! Et la pauvre Sophie, hein? Regarde-la. Elle n'a pas l'air heureuse. Elle n'aime pas Robert, tu sais? Son nouveau beau-père... dis donc!
- Elle est où, Sophie?
- C'est la fille, là, aux cheveux blonds, mi-longs. La petite en bleu.
- Ah, oui...
- Tiens, ils ont invité les Jonsac. Ha! Elle est gentille, Madame Jonsac. Tu la vois? La Sénégalaise... Elle est belle, hein? Et son mari, c'est lui... à gauche. Il porte des lunettes. Tu vois?
- Oui.
- Ils ont deux fils... je ne vois pas où ils sont, tiens. Ah oui... Nicolas, comme il a grandi. Treize ans, dis donc! Il ressemble à son papa. Il est malin, ce petit, oh là là! Et voilà son frère, Michel. Regarde... oh, lui, il est gentil comme tout. Il est très bien élevé.
- C'est ton petit-fils là-bas? A côté de... euh ... de Sophie. C'est bien Antoine, n'est-ce pas?
- Ah... mon petit-fils! Celui-là! Oui, c'est bien ça! Une invitation arrive et... paf! C'est pour qui!? C'est pour Monsieur et Madame Durrant? Pas du tout. Monsieur Antoine, lui, il est invité. Et en plus, il accepte. C'est bien gentil, ça, hein?
- Mais il est élégant, quand même. J'aime bien sa cravate rouge. Et comme c'est marrant, la petite fleur blanche qu'il a.

Unité 4: L'action
Livre de l'étudiant, page 71

Le drame du retour

- Je ne veux plus habiter ici. Robert... il a tout gâché... tout! ... Eh... bien, je téléphone à papa. Mais, non, je n'ose pas... s'il refuse? S'il ne veut pas de moi?
- Allô?
- Papa?
- C'est bien toi, Sophie?
- Oui... écoute, papa... euh...
- Sophie, mais qu'est-ce qu'il y a? Ça va?
- Non, ça ne va pas. Je ne peux plus rester ici. C'est impossible... avec Robert...
- Quoi? Robert... qu'est-ce qu'il a fait? Je vais...
- Non, non, papa... ce n'est pas ça.
- Oui, Hélène, Sophie est avec moi. C'est sa décision. C'est elle qui a décidé... pas moi.
- Je ne comprends pas... On doit en parler, Christophe. Elle n'a rien dit...
- Ne t'inquiète pas... ça va maintenant. Je te téléphone demain, d'accord?
- Oui, oui. Tu me téléphones demain. C'est sûr, hein?

Unité 5: Moments à suspense
Livre de l'étudiant, pages 72–73
Cahier d'activités, page 54

Scénario A

- Ecoute chérie... ce n'est pas ma faute.
- Ce n'est pas ta faute!? Ha! C'est ma faute, alors?
- Non! Ecoute...
- Non, je n'écoute pas! C'est fini... Je veux un divorce!

Scénario B

- C'est bien ce restaurant, hein?
- Oui, j'adore manger des grillades.
- On va à la discothèque?
- Non, il est minuit passé et... ahh!!

Scénario C

- ...
- Qu'est-ce qu'il y a?
- Oh... rien, rien... je...
- Et alors?
- Je... nous... je vais avoir un bébé.
- Un bébé?!

Scénario D

- Tu en veux?
- Oui. Passe-le moi.
- Tiens.
- Merci.
- C'est fort, hein?... Ça va?

Unité 5: Moments à suspense
Cahier d'activités, page 55

A suivre...

Scénario A

- Allô? Je peux parler à Vincent?... Allô? Vincent? On peut se voir ce soir?
- Oui, bien sûr. A quelle heure?
- A neuf heures... et je viendrai chez toi. D'accord?
- D'accord.
- Oh... je dois raccrocher.

Scénario B

- C'était bien vous, le conducteur de la voiture?
- Oui, oui.
- Vous veniez d'où?
- Du village.
- Qu'est-ce que vous aviez fait là-bas?
- On était dans un restaurant. Le restaurant 'Chez Gilles'.
- Et vous avez bu de l'alcool, monsieur?
- Moi... non... ben, oui... un petit verre de vin. C'est tout.
- Monsieur, le résultat de l'alcootest est positif.
- Ah... non!

Scénario C

- Il faut en parler.
- Il n'y a rien à dire!
- Ne fais pas l'imbécile! Ne dis pas de bêtises... C'est...
- Ecoute... moi, je ne veux pas ce bébé. Je suis enceinte...
  C'est mon bébé... C'est ma grossesse... C'est mon
  corps.
- Mais, non. C'est notre enfant, c'est notre bébé. Et moi, je le veux... je veux ce bébé.

Scénario D

- Ici! Venez ici ... Il est ici!
- Doucement, doucement.
- Passez-moi l'oxygène.
- Attention!... attention!
- Ça va bien, hein?
  Il va se remettre, non?
- On ne sait pas... En ce moment, ton copain est très malade.
- Attention! Attention!

Contrôle 5
Livre de l'étudiant, page 74
Cahier d'activités, page 60

Exemple

- Oui, c'est vrai. C'est bien, hein? Je sors avec Robert. Oui... Robert! Oh, il est sympa! Tu sais, je crois que je suis amoureuse de Robert.

1

- Mon grand malheur: j'aime Nicole. Mais elle ne me regarde pas! Je pense à Nicole. Je rêve de Nicole... Je dis bonjour à Nicole... Rien! Pas de réaction.

2

- Allô! Claude, salut! Je te téléphone pour dire merci pour les fleurs! Je t'aime, tu sais...

3

- Allô, mademoiselle? Georges est avec vous? Je suis la fiancée de Georges. Dites à Georges s'il vous plaît que c'est cassé. C'est fini. C'est terminé! Je ne l'aime plus.

4

- Alors on sort ce soir ma Julie? A huit heures, devant le cinéma. Je t'embrasse ma Julie, je t'adore. A ce soir.

5

- Caroline est enceinte mon vieux. Oui, c'est moi le père. C'est une catastrophe. C'est épouvantable.

A la gare

A l'écoute:
feuille numéro 1

E 1

1 Ecoute la cassette.
Ecoute les trois conversations.
Remplis la grille.

	destination	heure du train	aller simple?	aller-retour?	fumeur?	non-fumeur?	place	prix F
conversation 1								
conversation 2								
conversation 3								

2 Ecoute la conversation 1 encore une fois.
Lis les phrases de la conversation.
C'est quoi en anglais?

français	**anglais**
un aller simple	
un aller-retour	
fumeur	
non-fumeur	
Je voudrais réserver	
une place dans le train pour Paris	
qui part à dix-huit heures	
ça fait deux cents francs	

3 Ecoute les phrases utiles.
Répète les phrases et indique les symboles.

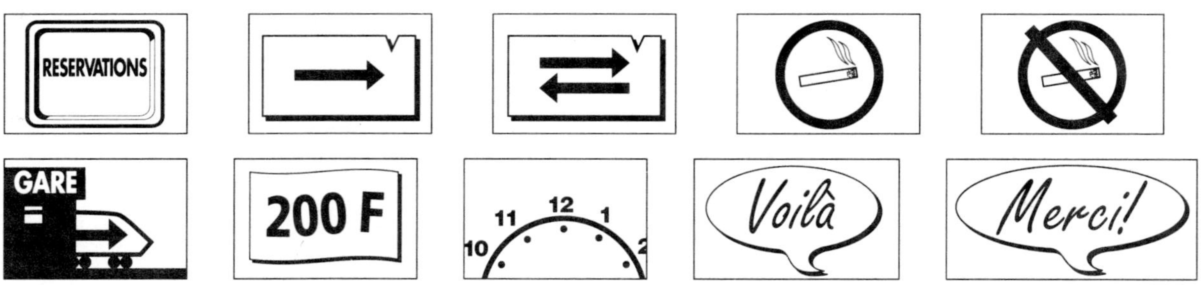

4 Travaille avec un/une partenaire.
Inventez d'autres conversations.

Au bureau de change

A l'écoute: feuille numéro 2

E2

1 Voici les monnaies de differents pays européens.
Choisis la bonne monnaie pour chaque pays.

Légende

DM = deutschmark
£ = livre sterling
L = lire
Sch = schilling
Dr = drachme
FF = franc français
Pes = peseta
FB = franc belge
FS = franc suisse
Fl = florin
Esc = escudo

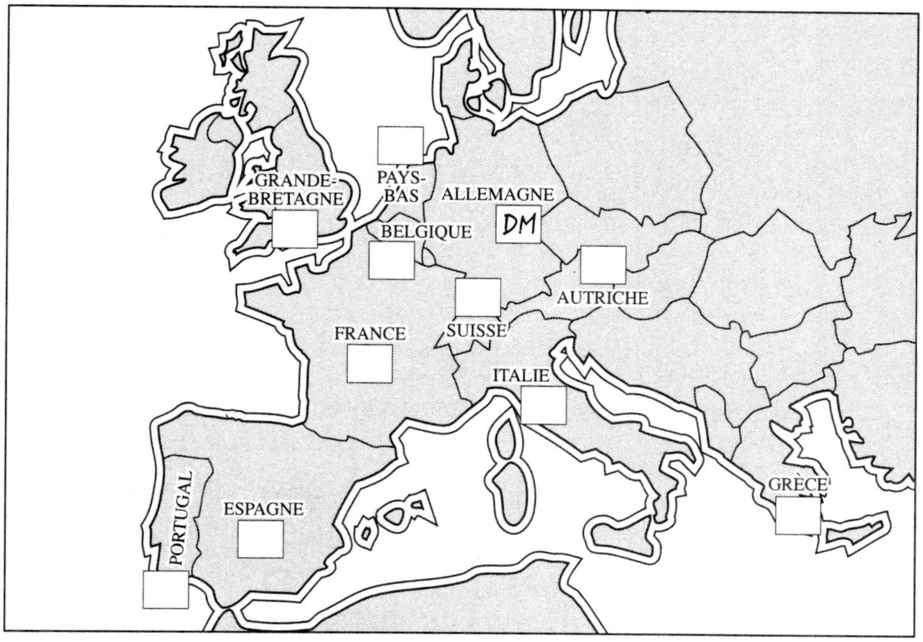

2 Ecoute la cassette.
Remplis la grille.

	monnaie	somme à changer
touriste 1		
touriste 2		
touriste 3		

3 Ecoute les phrases utiles.
C'est quoi en anglais?

français	**anglais**
Je voudrais changer	
une pièce d'identité	
voilà mon passeport	

4 Travaille avec un/une partenaire.
Inventez d'autres conversations.

Le logement

A l'écoute:
feuille numéro 3

E3

1 Ecoute la cassette.
Les quatre conversations se passent où?

	à l'hôtel	au camping	à l'auberge de jeunesse
conversation 1			
conversation 2			
conversation 3			
conversation 4			

2 Ecoute les phrases utiles.
Répète les phrases et indique les symboles.

3 Travaille avec un/une partenaire.
Inventez d'autres conversations.

4 Voici la conversation 1 en désordre. Quel est le bon ordre?

– Je voudrais une chambre pour deux personnes, s'il vous plaît.	– Avec douche, s'il vous plaît. C'est combien par nuit, s'il vous plâit?
– C'est à quel nom?	– Bonjour, madame
– Bonjour, monsieur. Vous désirez?	– Jones.
– C'est trois cents francs par nuit.	– C'est la chambre quarante-quatre. Voici votre clé.
– Très bien.	– Comment ça s'écrit?
– De rien, monsieur.	– J-O-N-E-S
– Bonjour, monsieur. Vous désirez?	– Merci.
– Trois nuits.	– C'est pour combien de nuits?
– Vous désirez une chambre avec salle de bains ou douche?	

A l'office de tourisme

A l'écoute:
feuille numéro 4

E4

1 Ecoute la cassette.
Le touriste numéro 1 voudrait une liste des hôtels.
Et les autres touristes?

2 Ecoute la cassette encore une fois.
Qu'est-ce qu'ils demandent?
Remplis les bulles.

1 J'ai besoin d'.*une*............
liste des hôtels,............
s'il vous plaît.............

2 Je voudrais ....
....
....

3 Avez-vous ....
....
....

4 Je voudrais ....
....
....

5 J'ai besoin d' ....
.... et ....
....

6 Je voudrais ....
....
....

7 Avez-vous ....
et aussi j'ai besoin d'.............
....

une liste des hôtels	un horaire des trains	une liste des monuments importants
un horaire des autobus	un plan de la ville	une liste d'excursions
une liste des musées	une liste des campings	

3 Travaille avec un/une partenaire.
Inventez d'autres conversations.

Au restaurant

A l'écoute:
feuille numéro 5

E5

1 Regarde l'addition.

2 Ecoute la cassette.
Ecoute la conversation numéro 1.
Il y a deux erreurs sur l'addition.
Corrige-les.

1

Le Mistral

2 salades de tomates
1 bifteck aux champignons
1 omelette
2 tartes maison
bouteille vin rouge
1 eau minérale
2. café

TOTAL 180 F

3 Ecoute les conversations 2 et 3.
Ecris l'addition pour chaque touriste.

2

Le Mistral

TOTAL 95 F

3

Le Mistral

TOTAL 80F

4 Travaille avec un/une partenaire.
Inventez d'autres conversations.

Les courses

A l'écoute:
feuille numéro 6

E 6

1 Ecoute la cassette.
Remplis la grille.

							autres détails
touriste 1							
touriste 2							
touriste 3							

2 Ecoute la cassette encore une fois.
Où sont les touristes?

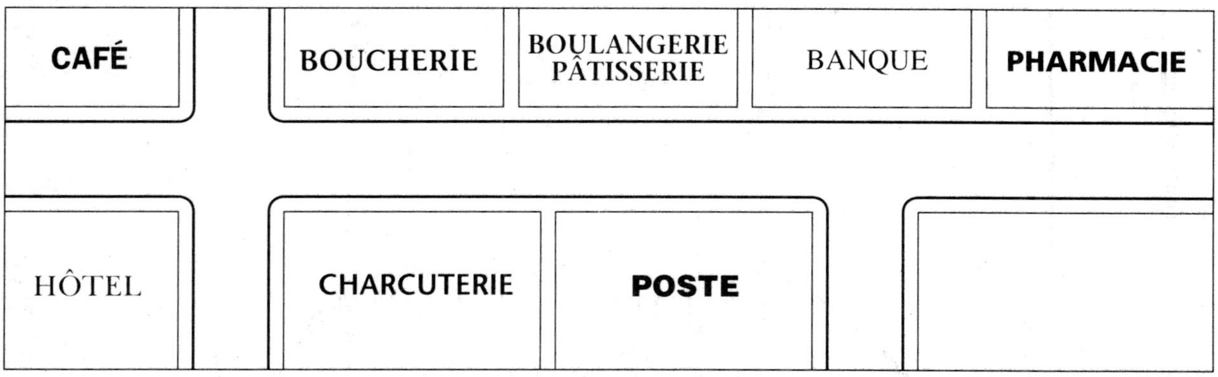

3 Ecoute les phrases utiles.
Répète les phrases et indique les symboles.

4 Travaille avec un/une partenaire
Inventez d'autres conversations.

Le shopping (1)

A l'écoute:
feuille numéro 7

E7

1 Ecoute la cassette.
Quel touriste (1–9) achète quel souvenir (A–I)?

1	2	3	4	5	6	7	8	9
C								

2 Ecoute les touristes encore une fois.
Complète les phrases.

1 "Avez-vous un .... avec la Tour Eiffel dessus?"

2 "Je .... le petit nounours, s'il vous plaît."

3 "Je prends le petit flacon de parfum, ..."

4 "Ça coûte ...., cette paire de boucles d'oreilles, s'il vous plaît?"

5 "Je .... les chocolats belges."

6 "Je voudrais .... torchons comme ça, s'il vous plaît."

7 "Avez- .... d'autres porte-clés?"

8 "Je peux voir le .... là-bas?"

9 "Je .... la petite Tour Eiffel, s'il vous plaît."

voudrais
vous
combien
stylo
deux
prends
préfère
t-shirt
s'il vous plaît

Le shopping (2)

3 Ecoute les trois conversations.
Remplis la grille.

					autres détails
touriste 1					
touriste 2					
touriste 3					

Questions et réponses

A l'écoute: feuille numéro 8

E8

1 Quelle question va avec quelle réponse?

questions		réponses	
1	Comment tu t'appelles?	A	Oui, c'est ça. Je suis de Birmingham.
2	Tu es en vacances ici?	B	Oui, je suis en vacances avec ma famille.
3	Tiens, comment tu t'appelles?	C	Je m'appelle Guy.
4	Tu voudrais boire quelque chose?	D	Oui, j'adore Paris.
5	Tu aimes Paris?	E	Merci. Je veux bien.
6	Tu es britannique?	F	Oui, c'est ma première visite.
7	C'est ta première visite en France?	G	Oui, je connais Londres un peu.
8	Tu connais la Grande-Bretagne?	H	J'habite à Poissy, tout près de Paris.
9	Tu habites à Paris?	I	Martyn.

2 Ecoute la cassette.
Vérifie ta version de la conversation: c'est correct?

Conversation avec Jacqueline

3 Imagine ta première conversation avec Jacqueline.
Ecoute ses questions et réponds-y!

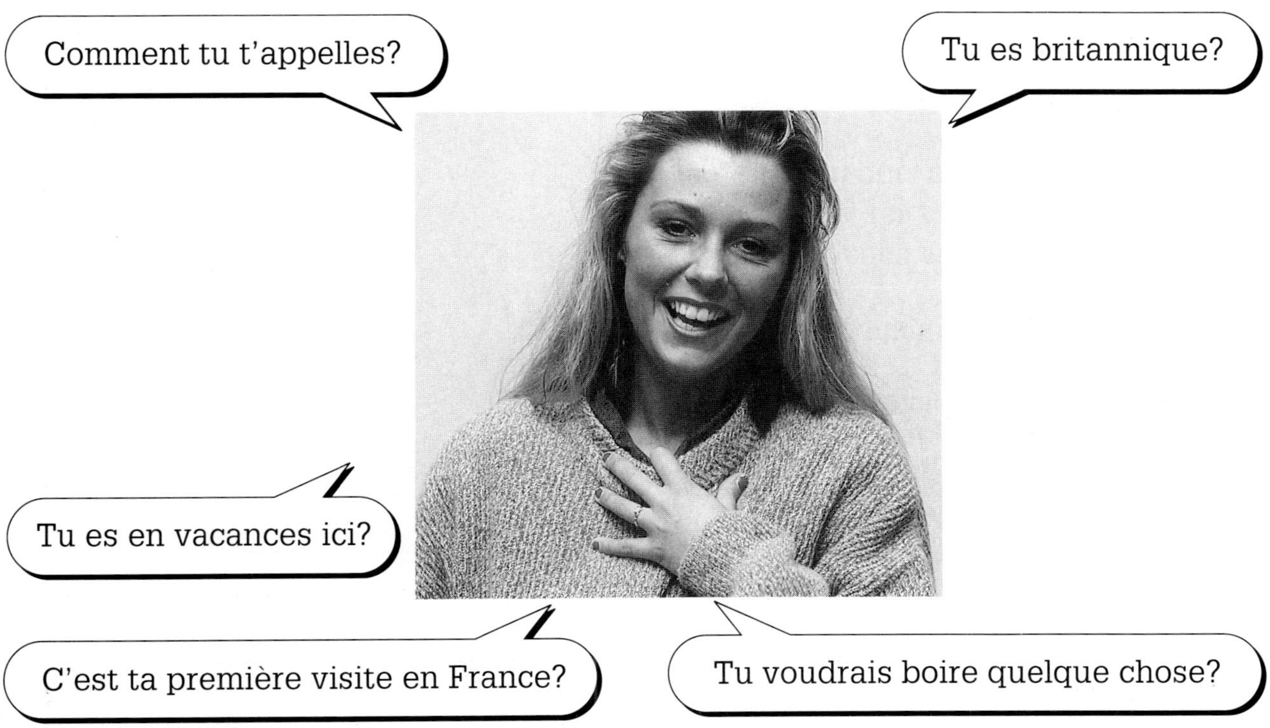

On sort?

A l'écoute:
feuille numéro 9

E9

1 Ecoute la cassette.
Ecoute les trois conversations.
Remplis la grille.

	activité	jour?	à quelle heure?	où?	on sort? oui/non
conversation 1					
conversation 2					
conversation 3					

2 Ecoute la conversation numéro 1 encore une fois.
Lis le texte.

– Si on allait *au bowling*?
– Oui, je veux bien. Quand?
– *Mercredi*.
– A quelle heure?
– A *neuf* heures.
– On se retrouve où?
– *Au café*.
– D'accord. Alors, c'est *mercredi*, à *neuf* heures, *au café*.
– Oui. A *mercredi* alors. Salut.

3 Travaille avec un/une partenaire.
Changez les mots *en italique*.
Inventez d'autres conversations.

4 C'est quoi en français?

anglais	**français**
How about going ...?	
I'd like to.	
When?	
What time?	
Where shall we meet?	

Tous les jours

R1

la pédale	**le levier**	**l'assiette**
la chaîne	**le bol**	**le verre**
la corde	**le coussin pneumatique**	

Tous les jours R 2

les courses
la cuisine
le ménage
la vaisselle
la lessive
le jardinage
le lit
le bricolage

Tous les jours

R 3

ma mère **mon père** **ma sœur**

mon frère **ma grand-mère** **mon grand-père**

Tous les jours

R 4

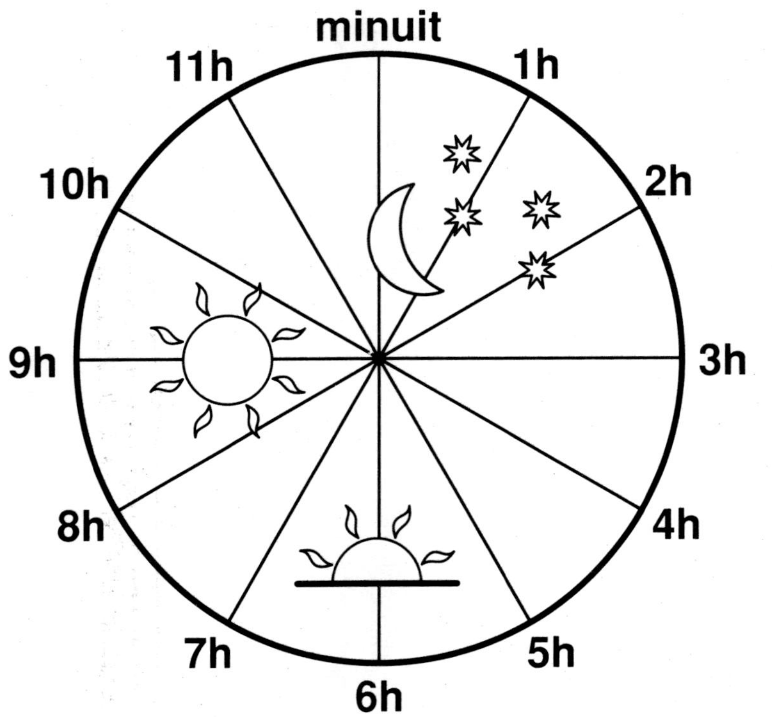

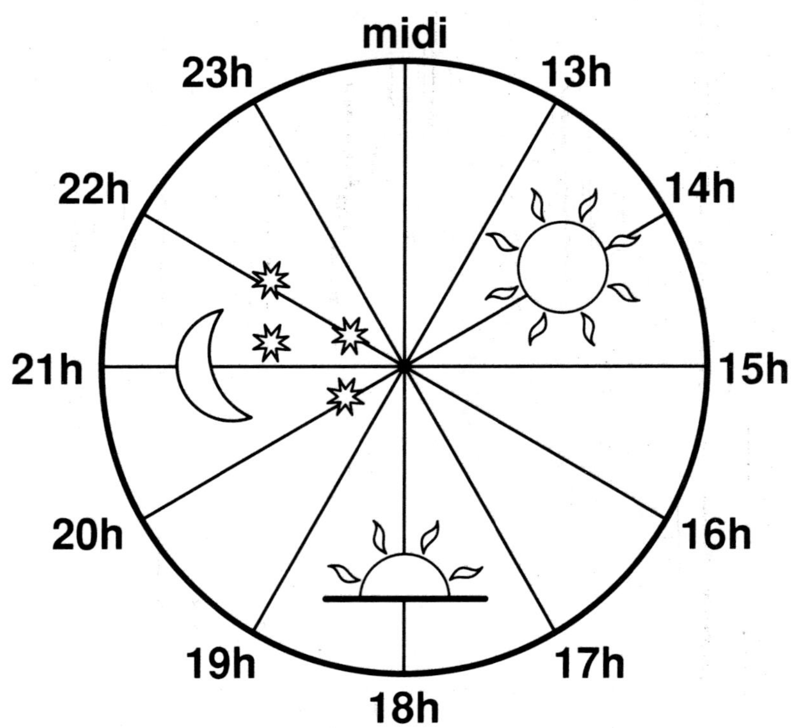

Tous les jours

R 5

Je suis toujours pressée

Je me lave les dents rapidement,
Et je me coiffe les cheveux,
Je suis toujours pressée!

Je mange mon petit déjeuner,
Et je bois une tasse de thé,
Je suis toujours pressée!

Je mets mon manteau,
E je pars prendre l'autobus,
Je suis toujours pressée!

J'arrive à mon travail,
Et je me dépêche de monter l'escalier,
Je suis toujours pressée!

Je vais à mon bureau,
Mais il n'y a personne!
ZUT! C'est dimanche!

Carolyn Scutt

I am always in a hurry

I brush my teeth quickly,
And I comb my hair,
I am always in a hurry!

I eat my breakfast,
And I drink a cup of tea,
I am always in a hurry!

I put on my coat,
And I catch the bus,
I am always in a hurry!

I arrive at work,
And I hurry up the stairs,
I am always in a hurry!

I go to my desk,
But there is nobody there!
DRAT! It's Sunday!

Tous les jours

R6

Marie pense au futur

Je vais...	oui bien sûr	non	à mon tour
m'occuper des factures			✓
faire la vaisselle	✓		
faire le ménage		✓	
m'occuper des enfants			✓
faire le jardinage		✓	
changer un fusible	✓		
réparer la voiture	✓		
faire la cuisine	✓		
faire le repassage		✓	
faire la lessive			✓
faire les courses			✓

Marc pense au futur

Je vais...	oui bien sûr	non	à mon tour
m'occuper des factures			✓
faire la vaisselle	✓		
faire le ménage		✓	
m'occuper des enfants			✓
faire le jardinage		✓	
changer un fusible	✓		
réparer la voiture	✓		
faire la cuisine	✓		
faire le repassage		✓	
faire la lessive			✓
faire les courses			✓

Tous les jours

R 7

Sexiste ou pas sexiste?

1 Les femmes sont plus affectueuses que les hommes.

2 Les hommes sont capables de soigner les enfants.

3 La vie d'une mère est plus stressante que la vie d'un père.

4 Faire le ménage, c'est la résponsabilité de la femme.

5 Faire le ménage, c'est la responsabilité de la femme et de l'homme.

6 Les femmes sont capables de comprendre les moteurs.

7 L'homme est le chef de famille.

8 Les hommes détestent faire les courses.

9 La vie d'un homme est plus difficile que la vie d'une femme.

10 Les hommes sont incapables de faire la cuisine.

L'écolo

R 8

Un poisson a besoin d'eau.
Un oiseau a besoin de vers.
Une fleur a besoin de lumière.

Une voiture a besoin d'essence.
Un moteur a besoin d'huile.
Un bébé a besoin de lait.

L'écolo

R 9

L'écocide

On dit que la forêt partout disparaît,
On dit que la Terre perd ses poumons,
On dit que la mer devient une poubelle,
Et qu'on tue les dauphins en tuant les thons.

On dit qu'il existe un trou dans l'ozone,
On dit quand il pleut, il pleut de l'acide,
On dit que le monde est tombé malade,
Et voilà comment on fait l'écocide.

Tant pis! N'oublie pas:
Nous sommes riches,
Nous sommes riches,
Et je m'en fiche,
Car nous sommes riches!

On dit qu'on fabrique trop de voitures,
On dit que les puits de pétrole s'épuisent,
On dit qu'on a faim dans un pays lointain,
On dit que la Ville des Anges est en crise.

Tant pis! N'oublie pas:
Nous sommes riches,
Nous sommes riches,
Et je m'en fiche,
Car nous sommes riches!

Tant pis! N'oublie pas:
Nous sommes riches,
Nous sommes riches,
Et je m'en fiche,
Car nous sommes riches!

Ecocide

They say that the forests will soon be all gone,
They say that the Earth is losing her lungs,
They say that the sea is becoming a tip,
And as we slaughter the tuna, the dolphins die too.

They say there's a hole in the ozone layer,
They say when it rains it rains acid,
They say that the world is looking sick,
There you go, we're committing ecocide.

Never mind, don't forget,
We're rich,
We're rich,
And I don't care a bit
Because we're rich!

They say that we're building too many cars,
They say that the oil wells are drying up,
They say someone's hungry in a far away land,
They say the City of Angels is sinking fast.

Never mind, don't forget,
We're rich,
We're rich,
And I don't care a bit
Because we're rich!

Never mind, don't forget,
We're rich,
We're rich,
And I don't care a bit
Because we're rich!

L'écolo

R 10

On est vert au collège?

Légende:

 = le terrain de sport | ☐ = ______________________

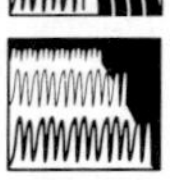 = la pelouse | ☐ = ______________________

 = les jardins | ☐ = ______________________

 = les grands pots de fleurs | ☐ = ______________________

 = le bassin | ☐ = ______________________

Les médias

R11

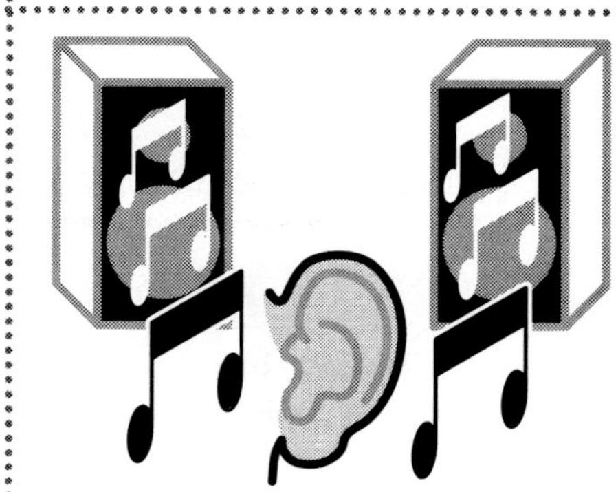

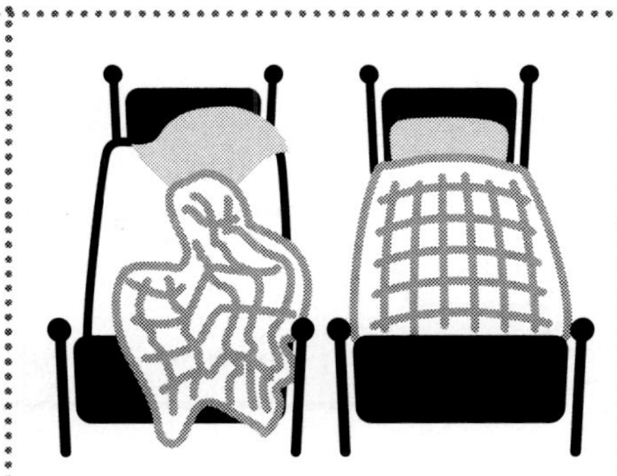

je regarde la télé
je fais du sport
je lis des livres
je lis des journaux

je fais mon lit
je lis des magazines
je fais du shopping
je fais la vaisselle

je vais à la disco
j'écoute de la musique
je fais mes devoirs
je vais au cinéma

Les médias R 12

CRIME ... STOP!

Partenaire A

Tu habites dans la rue de la Paix.
Tu as vu l'attaque du 23 septembre.
Explique tout à la police.

Voici des idées:

- il portait un jean et des baskets blanches ...
- la femme avait 18 ou 19 ans ...
- elle avait les cheveux bruns ...
- le 23 septembre, vers minuit ...
- elle portait un jean et un blouson blanc...
- il avait les cheveux noirs ...
- il a poussé la femme dans la voiture ...
- la voiture était bleue ...
- il a parlé avec la jeune femme ...
- la voiture est partie très vite ...
- un homme est descendu de sa voiture ...
- il avait environ 30 ans ...

Partenaire B

Pose des questions.
Prends des notes.

Voici des idées:

- C'est tout?
- Qu'est-ce que vous avez vu?
- C'était quand?
- C'était où?
- Il était comment?

Les médias

R 13

La voix de Mistral

Les médias

R 14

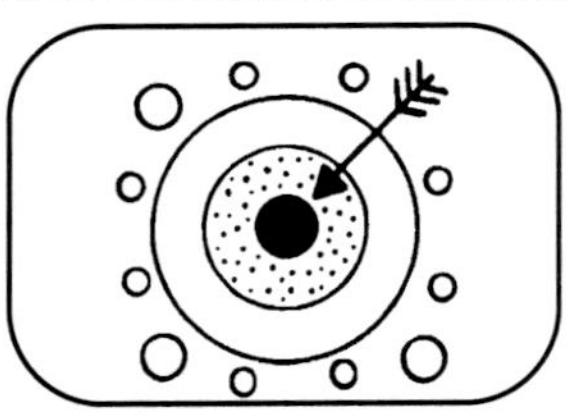

les feuilletons
un film d'épouvante
les documentaires
un western
les émissions pour les enfants

un film romantique
les informations
un film de guerre
un film d'aventure
un film à suspense
un dessin animé

les jeux
un film de science-fiction
les émissions de sciences naturelles
un film policier
une comédie

Les médias

R 15

La télé: pour ou contre?

C'est intéressant et éducatif.	It's interesting and educational.
C'est bien pour se relaxer.	It's good relaxation.
C'est amusant.	It's fun.
C'est important pour les informations.	It's important for the news.
Quand on regarde la télé, on n'est pas actif.	When you watch TV you're not active.
Quand on regarde la télé, on n'est pas sociable.	When you watch TV you're not sociable.
La conversation est impossible devant la télé.	Conversation is impossible when you're watching TV.
Beaucoup d'enfants regardent des émissions violentes.	Lots of children watch violent programmes.
Les émissions sont souvent idiotes.	Programmes are often stupid.
Il y a des émissions éducatives pour les enfants.	There are educational programmes for children.

Paris: Le Guide Mistral

R 16

Je voudrais changer cent livres sterling en francs français.	Le train pour Nantes part à 16h50.
	Ce magazine est votre guide.
En version originale, le film s'appelle Kindergarten Cop.	C'est un zoo?
Le Guide Mistral vous recommande Le Café Mistral.	Aieeee!!!!
	C'est un engin spatial?!
Autrefois c'était une gare, maintenant c'est un musée.	Bienvenue! Welcome! Wilkommen!
Le monument le plus célèbre de Paris?	On y achète un peu de tout.
	Je peux aller aux toilettes?
Le système du Métro n'est pas difficile à comprendre.	Voir Paris en vélo.
Strasbourg et Toulouse ... ce sont deux sortes de saucisson.	Voir Paris sur l'eau.
	Une balle de tennis gigantesque!
C'est moins cher qu'un hôtel et il y en a deux à Paris.	Des bureaux ou des appartements?
On dit que Quasimodo habitait dans ce bâtiment.	Les trains sont très fréquents.
	Des souvenirs du passé.
Il est un personnage très populaire dans les BD françaises.	Attention au feu!
Il y a beaucoup de jardins publics à Paris.	On peut jouer au basket ici.
	La musique, c'est l'art.
15 francs le kilo ... venez, venez ... première qualité!	Le fast food est arrivé.
Dans ce centre commercial il y a toutes sortes de magasins.	J' ❤ lire.
	On dirait du lego en grand.
C'est l'Opéra? Non! C'est un grand magasin.	C'est un monument de guerre.

Paris: Le Guide Mistral

R 17

Paris: Le Guide Mistral

R 18

Le Guide Mistral **Paris** **Bon voyage!**

Bienvenue! **Bon appétit!** **Ville vivante!**

Face à face

Infos voyage **Campings** **Hôtels**

Restaurants **Auberges de Jeunesse** **Shopping**

Phrases utiles	
français	**anglais**
....	....
....	....
....	....
....	....
....	....

Paris: Le Guide Mistral

R 19

On sort?

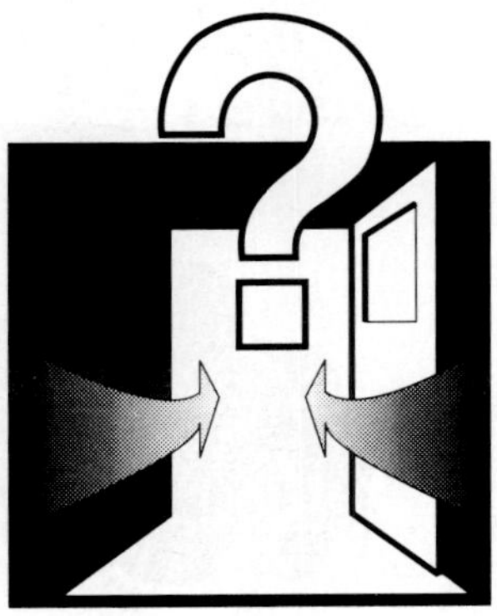

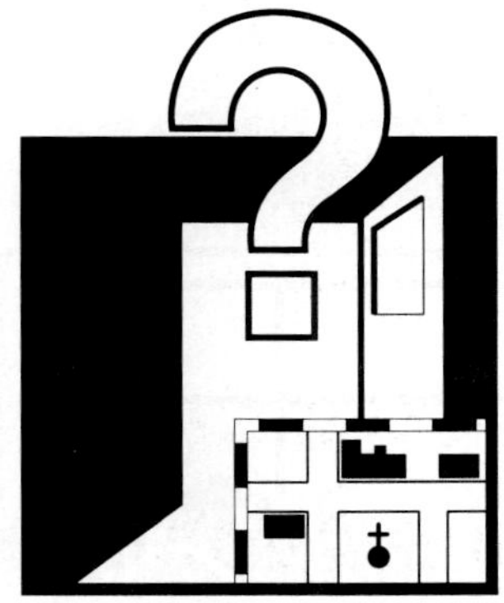

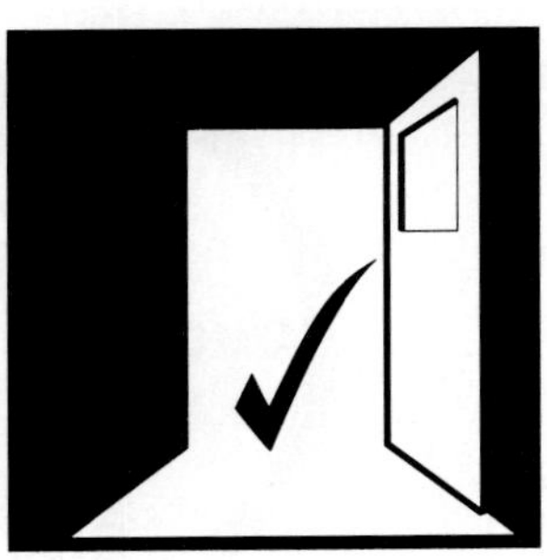

Si on allait ...?

Quand?

On se retrouve où?

Tu veux sortir?

Où?

Oui, je veux bien.

Tu veux venir?

A quelle heure?

Non, je suis occupé.

Non, je suis occupée.

Feuilleton

R 20

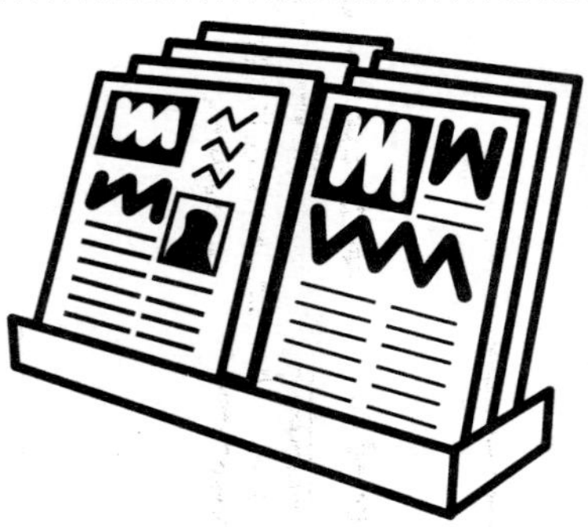

un café-tabac
une maison de la presse
des maisons
un supermarché

un pub
un immeuble
une église
un jardin public

une épicerie
un marché
une boulangerie

Feuilleton

R 21

les personnes âgées
le couple BCBG
la famille solide et stable
le groupe de jeunes
les gens de passage
la femme fatale
le personnage malhonnête
la famille mono-parentale

Page dictionnaire

R 22

French Word	How I discovered the meaning						English Word
	It looked like English	I've heard it before	I asked someone	I looked it up	I guessed	I found another way	

Lexique

R 23

A

on	a besoin	we need
	achetez	buy
ces	affiches	these posters
	aider	to help
	ajoute	add
en	anglais	in English
	approprié(e)	correct
	après	after
l'	arbitre	the referee
les	arbres généalogiques	family trees
tu	as	you have
	attention!	be careful!
ils	auditionnent	they are auditioning
vous	avez	you have

B

	bavarde	chat
les	blancs	the spaces
le	bon ordre	the correct order
une	bonne mémoire	a good memory
la	bonne phrase	the correct sentence
nous	buvons	we drink

C

	ça se passe	it happens
des	cadeaux	presents
le	Cahier d'activités	the Workbook
	calcule	work out/calculate
la	case	the box
la	cassette	the tape
	c'est	it is
	c'est à toi de jouer	it's your turn to play
	c'est la journée de qui?	whose day is it?
	changez	change
une	chanson	a song
	chaque	each
	cherche	look for
	chez eux	at their house
	chez toi/chez vous	at your house
	choisis(sez)	choose
	choix	choice(s)
	coche	tick
	colle	stick
	colorie	colour in
	combien	how many
	combien de choses?	how many things?
	comment ça marche?	how does it work?
	comment dessiner	how to draw
	comment jouer	how to play
	comment s'appellent...?	what's the name of...?
	compare(z)	compare
	complète	complete
tu	connais...?	do you know...?
on	consomme	we consume
nous	consommons	we consume
	contre	against
	correspond	goes with
	couvre	cover
le	cycle	the life cycle

D

	dans quel ordre?	in what order?
	décide de ce qui arrive	decide what happens
	découpe	cut out
	décris	describe
	défendu	forbidden
	demande	ask
le	dessin	the drawing
	dessine	draw
	dis	say
ils	discutent	they are discussing
	donne	give

E

	écoute	listen
	écris	write
tu	entends	you hear
tu	es d'accord?	do you agree?
on	est tous	we are all
	explique	explain

F

la	fable	the story
	fais	make/do
il/elle	fait	he/she does
	faites	make/do
il	faut	you have to
il	faut quinze trombones	you need fifteen paperclips
les	feuilletonistes	the soap-opera writers
cette	fiche	this sheet
en	français	in French
le	futur	the future

G

	gagne	win
ils	gagnent quel prix?	which prize do they win?
tu	gagnes	you win
la	grille	the grid

H

l'	heure	the time
	hier soir	yesterday evening

I

	ici	here
tu t'	identifies avec	you identify with
	il y a	there is/there are

Lexique

R 24

ces images ..... these pictures
imagine(z) ..... imagine

J

joue(z) ..... play
les joueurs ..... the players

L

la légende ..... the key
lis(ez) ..... read
le Livre de l'étudiant ..... the Students' Book

M

manger ..... to eat
mets ..... put
moins de ..... less

N

le nom ..... the name

O

ils ont choisi ..... they chose
ils ont reçu ..... they received
ton opinion ..... your opinion
où ..... where

P

parle(z) ..... talk
ton/ta partenaire ..... your partner
pendant ..... during
pense ..... think
plus de ..... more
le poids ..... weight
pour ..... for
pourquoi? ..... why?
pose des questions ..... ask questions
prends ..... take
prépare ..... prepare

Q

que pensez-vous? ..... what do you think?
quel/quelle/quels/quelles...? which...?
quel genre? ..... what type?
qu'est-ce que...? ..... what...?
qu'est-ce que tu as fait? ..... what did you do?
qu'est-ce que tu as vu? ..... what did you see?
qu'est-ce qu'ils crient? ..... what are they shouting?
qu'est-ce qu'on peut...? ..... what can you...?
qui? ..... who?
qui fait quoi? ..... who does what?
quoi? ..... what?

R

range ..... sorts out
rassemble ..... collect
recommandes-tu? ..... do you recommend?
tu reconnais...? ..... do you recognize...?
regarde ..... look at
relis ..... re-read
ils rentrent ..... they get home
la réponse ..... the answer
remplis ..... fill in
les résultats ..... the results
les résumés ..... the summaries

S

la scène se passe ..... the scene is happening
une scène semblable ..... a similar scene
selon ..... according to
si ..... if
un sondage ..... a survey
suggère ..... suggest

T

le titre ..... the title
tous les combien? ..... how often?
tous les objets ..... all the objects
travaille avec ..... work with
trouve ..... find

U

on utilise ..... we use
utilise un dictionnaire ..... use a dictionary

V

va avec ..... goes with
je vais ..... I will/I am going to
tu vas écrire ..... you are going to write
la vie ..... life
voici ..... here is/here are
leur voyage de noces ..... their honeymoon